Remembering the Wilderness Road

Stories from the Founders of Therapeutic Camping

Vol 1 – The Dallas Salesmanship Club Boys Camp

Stephen Ashton

Volume 1 First Printed September 2017

ISBN: 9781520864716

Cover Image is of Campbell Loughmiller and Buford MacKenzie in front of a teepee that stood outside Chief Lock's home in the early days of the Salesmanship Club Boys Camp.

CONTENTS

DEDICATION

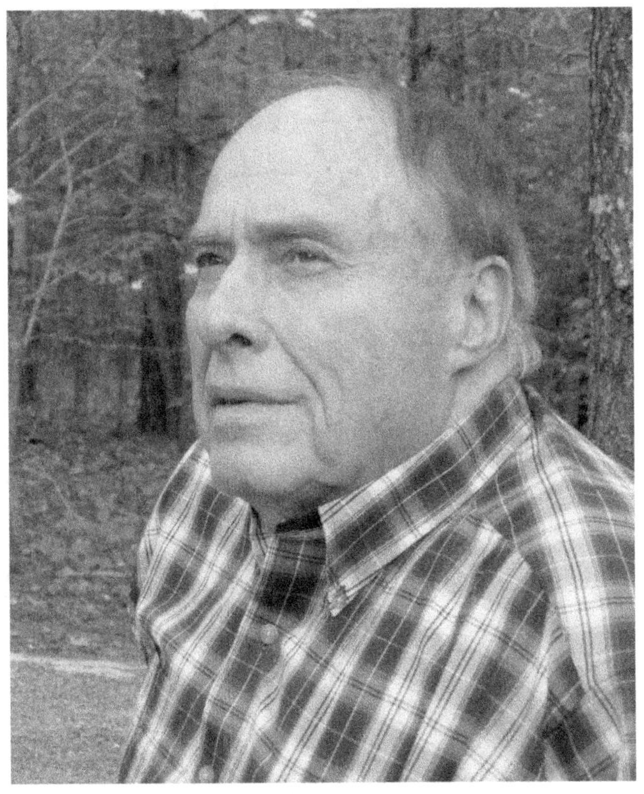

Buford "Chief Mac" McKenzie

October 12, 1919 – October 15, 2013

ACKNOWLEDGMENTS

There are many people who have made this book a possibility. I am forever indebted to Buford (Chief Mac) and Lois McKenzie who allowed me to scour the closets and corners of their home and barns for scraps of camp history, then sat for hours telling stories and helping me to make sense of what I found. Tim and Kayla Gibson, and Bill and Karen Collins additionally have been invaluable sources of information. I have greatly appreciated their partnership in the writing of this book. Ken and Flora Edgar have honored me with lengthy discussions and trading of written documents, editing of my chapters and sharing videos that have forever enriched my life. I am eternally grateful. Helen Lindstrom has shared many stories of her work with Everett at camp. I look forward to telling more of their story in the next volume. Thank you to Grover Loughmiller for reading several drafts of this work, allowing me interviews, and sharing books and videos of interviews with his father.

Julie Carlson was instrumental in helping me to understand the role of L.B. Sharp in the beginning of the Salesmanship Club Camp. She was an invaluable source of material sending me letters between Sharp and Loughmiller, and early documents to understand the evolution of the thought of L.B. Sharp and the creation of National Camp. Jim Jackson at the Salesmanship Club of Dallas was a tremendous assistance in digging up artifacts from the early days of the Salesmanship Club Camp. The video he unearthed and restored is nearly priceless. I also have Jim to thank for introductions to Tom Harrover and William Hood who both wrote memoirs about their time at the camp. Additionally Andrew Barnhart unearthed wonderful resources about Rocky Mountain Mennonite Camp that have enriched this work. Thank you to my Father-in-law Ronald Ellyson for editing and proofreading.

Finally, none of this would have been possible without the support of my wife, Abigail, and my four boys who allowed their dad to travel, read, write, and edit.

FOREWORD

My dad grew up in a large family with seven brothers and three sisters. He was born in 1906 – an age where children were a financial asset and contributed significantly to the family's survival. He spent his formative years working on the farm learning the value of hard work and the merits of creative problem solving. In the free times on weekends after knocking off work around noon, he and a friend would explore the woods and fields, play Tarzan in the sassafras thicket, swim in the lake, shoot the 12-gauge, race horses, or pick blackberries. His experiential learning on the farm was formative. He found the idea of learning being something you did only in school or a building to be a most foreign concept, one so foreign that he could barely contemplate it.

All of these and many other factors that merged into my dad being who he was, had their most fruitful confluence in his work at the camp. My dad reached back into his farm era notions of survival needs, where you cooperated and worked with Mother Nature, or she gave you a learning experience which you did not soon forget. He reached back in to the quiet principled, caring; the firmness in what's right. He knew boys needed more than a survival experience. Survival experiences prove individual mettle, but they don't require the daily, repetitive cooperation, caring, and leadership that makes for harmonious and happy social living and good character. That cannot be taught in a week or a month. It comes through the furnace of daily living and is hammered into useful form on the anvil of unrelenting daily struggles and cries. The hammer must fall repetitively, over and over before the shape takes form. That takes time.

When my dad began camp in 1946, group therapy and the theory of group therapy did not exist. As they stumbled upon its' effectiveness, he looked everywhere trying to find information on it, but nothing existed. Every step of the way was self-created in response to situations as they arose in the group. It became the major method for therapy and the vehicle for learning. Those who do not understand the group process can easily overlook its depth, particularly when watching someone who is skilled with the concept. My dad and Chief Mac worked closely together to develop these principles.

I remember after I had been a counselor a short while, but long enough to discover my ignorance in how to use the group process, I went down to Beaver's campsite when Chief Mac was there. When I walked in I beheld what to me was nothing short of a miracle. The group was in the process of planning menus and were sitting around the kitchen table. Miguel Hernandez was leading the discussion on menu planning. Chief Mac was in the background, working casually on a woodcarving, comfortably observing what was going on. The boys were calm, almost sedate, paying attention to the project at hand, but others were also carving, one writing down the menu ideas decided on, and one getting a drink for everybody. The campsite was spic and span. The trails were neatly raked. There was an air of peacefulness and serenity. At that point in my learning and training, if I had experienced something like this in my own group, I would have thought I had died and gone to heaven or was having an out of body experience.

Stephen Ashton has had the privilege of watching Chief Mac in action and learning alongside men like Ken Edgar and Paul Daley. He has done an excellent job of compiling stories from these men and including them in this volume. My dad believed that camp should not be static and unchanging. He was always searching for the best methods to help young people. He also was one to learn from mistakes and hold foundational principles. Among those were a decentralized program; the centrality of partnership and relationship; preserving a simple boy's world and keeping out adult notions of efficiency and complexity; fostering curiosity and wonder free from rigid academic accruements that hinder creativity, critical thinking and problem solving; and providing a world close to natural consequences that is ripe for experiential learning. It is my hope that this volume will help to solidify the principles my dad worked so hard to safeguard and continue to promote the foundational philosophies of camp to a new generation.

Grover Loughmiller

Psychologist and Founder of the Loughmiller Institute
Son of Founder, Campbell Loughmiller

Once, when probably six or seven years old, and before attending first grade, there was some road surface repair being done in our neighborhood. A Steam Roller, among other pieces of equipment used to finish the blacktop surface, had been left unattended during a lunch break and all the operators were nowhere to be seen. Yep, you guessed it! The keys were in the ignition, and I knew about the floor mounted starter button! Unfortunately, the machine was also left in gear, apparently to prevent it from rolling away on its own. The engine quickly roared to life, and I was off and rolling, without a clue how to steer or stop my forward motion. I turned the steering wheel, but the machine went in the opposite direction and targeted a neighbor's front door! I was so frightened that I didn't think to turn the key off! To my horror I was rolling right up the walkway to the front door of a house!...

No question about it, I was a wild child with little or no restraint at that age. With no mentoring and no appreciable guidance, I had become a true menace to the society in which I lived. It would not get better, and eventually I would come to a bad end on the present course I was maintaining.

I was definitely headed in the wrong direction, because I had no hands-on direction at home. Camp Woodland Springs changed that significantly, overnight.

-William S. (Billy) Hood

INTRODUCTION: A LIFE WORTHY OF THE GOSPEL

Eulogy by Jared Collins – Buford McKenzie's Grandson
10/18/2013

We are here today to honor Buford Lester McKenzie. To many he is known as Chief Mac, Dad, or Granddaddy. But for everyone who has ever come in contact with him, he is known as a Disciple of Jesus Christ. Granddad was a man whose life was defined by the Gospel.

He was born in southern Mississippi and as a boy he was a troublemaker to say the least. He would run around with his friends causing trouble, making bootleg whisky, and singing in the church choir while drunk. He always talked about how he was a chicken stealer. To this day I don't know if that is literal or if that was how he referred to living in sin. Nevertheless, at age 14 he was overcome with conviction and he prayed to the Lord "If you're going to take me, don't just take part of me, take all of me; from the top of my head to the tip of my toes." From then on, the Holy Spirit transformed his life.

Granddad furthered his education in his college career and went on to excel in various jobs. One thing I greatly admired about Granddaddy was how he lived by Ecclesiastes 9:10 which says "Whatsoever thy hand findeth to do, do it with thy might." In 1949 he met Campbell Loughmiller, a man with a revolutionary idea of how to impact the lives of troubled teens. The two developed the structure of therapeutic camping and put their ideas into action. Granddad committed his whole life to camp and went on to establish fourteen therapeutic camps throughout the country. Camp is what his hand found to do, and he did it with all his might.

It is arguable that none of this would have been possible without the assistance of Lois Ellen Ray, or Grandmommy, the absolute love of his life. The proposal was everything but traditional as he said to her "Lois, I want you to be my wife for the next hundred years, after that you're free to go." For whatever reason, she agreed to it and the two got married on August 11, 1951. They had six wonderful children together; the second one (my mom) was especially great. Their third child, Kent tragically passed away when he was three. As they grew up, Granddad was blessed with 19 grandkids and we will always remember those great banana and oatmeal milkshakes, and weekend cookouts, and the time spent singing around the fire.

In all, Granddad committed 64 years of his life to the ministry God called him to. In Acts 20:24 Paul writes "But I do not account my life of any value nor as precious to myself, if only I may finish my course and the ministry that I received from the Lord Jesus, to testify to the gospel of the grace of God." This verse perfectly explains Granddad's life. In talking about his life I do not mean to boast in his accomplishments; that's not what he would want. Everything he ever did was for the sake of the Gospel: it was his life, his passion. Philippians 1:22-27 says "If I am to live in the flesh, that means fruitful labor for me. Yet which I shall choose I cannot tell. I am hard pressed between the two. My desire is to depart and be with Christ, for that is far better. But to remain in the flesh is more necessary on your account. Convinced of this, I know that I will remain and continue with you all, for your progress and joy in the faith, so that in me you may have ample cause to glory in Christ Jesus, because of my coming to you again. Only let your manner of life be worthy of the gospel of Christ, so that whether I come and see you or am absent, I may hear of you that you are standing firm in one spirit, with one mind striving side by side for the faith of the gospel."

Granddad had been talking about heaven for a long time. He knew how much greater it would be to live with the Lord than to live in the flesh but he daily strove to live a life "worthy of the Gospel of Christ." His love for Christ abounded in his life. Whenever he met someone his first question was "Do you know the Lord?" This was his primary concern. He wanted everyone to experience Christ the way he had. In his last years he was preaching the Gospel to every nurse and doctor who assisted him and every visitor that came to see him. One of my favorite memories of Granddad was how he would tell everyone how special they were. I probably heard him say, "you're special" over a thousand times in my life. He did not say it out of routine or as a kind gesture: he said it because he truly wanted everyone to know how special they were to him and to the Lord.

Throughout his life he experienced many trials and he of all people knew what it means to suffer. Since he was five years old he walked with a stiff leg. This was a daily struggle for him and caused him to walk with a cane or crutches for much of his life. He tragically experienced losing a child as well as many other close family members. For nearly 13 years Grandmommy has suffered from Alzheimer's and has lost most of her ability to function. Despite her inability to communicate he continued to express his love to her and pray with her daily. He, of all people, had legitimate reasons to complain but complaining was something you would never hear him do. Some of his last words he said to me were "You know, I can't find a thing to complain about. My only wish is that I could put into words my praises and thanks to the Lord for all He's done for me." 2 Corinthians 4:16-18 says, "So we do not lose heart. Though our outer self is wasting away, our inner self is being renewed day by day. For this light momentary affliction is preparing for us an eternal weight of glory beyond all comparison, as we look not to the things that are seen but to the things that are unseen. For the things that are seen are transient, but the things that are unseen are eternal." He did not focus on his sufferings and his inner self was being renewed daily. His focus was on things that are unseen and His focus was on the Gospel. He strove to glorify God in everything he did.

So we are here to celebrate, not simply his accomplishments and life on earth, but a life lived worthy of the Gospel and the perfect, eternal life he is experiencing with the Lord.

PROLOGUE: A BRIEF HISTORY OF CAMPS FOR "NEEDY CHILDREN"

From the 1870's to the late 1920's, programs for "needy children" mainly focused on "gathering children together and sending them to the country, without giving much thought to...the program of activities."[1] "'Feed 'em well and let them breathe fresh air' was the slogan."[2] These types of programs began in New York City. A fund, called the "Fresh Air Fund," was established by the Children's Aid Society to pay for these children's vacations.[3]

> The story of that first fresh-air work reads like a modern folk-tale, for it recounts how the people as a whole were moved, not just a few far-seeing men and women here and there. New York as a city became alive to the sufferings of its children, was touched by their helplessness, and gave of themselves with their alms. Day by day the progress of the venture was recorded in the *New York Times*, and contributions were received at the *Times* office. As the ideas spread and took hold of the imaginations of men and women, the fund grew. But more than that, people came forward with emotion and offered themselves with their purses. It was this gift of the giver with his gift that made the project succeed, turned it from an experiment into an achievement. Because the city took to heart the unhappiness of little children crowded in the reeking heat of the tenements, no summer has since gone by without thousands of New York girls and boys catching their first sight of green fields or feeling the bracing wind come in from the sea.[4]

---

[1] Sharp, *Education and the Summer Camp*, 20-21.

[2] Adrienne Brant James, "Roots: The Life Space Pioneers," *Reclaiming Children and Youth* 17 no. 2 (2008): 6.
E. DeAlton Partridge, "National Camp," *Nature Magazine* 36 no. 6 (1943): 322

[3] Ibid., 7.

[4] Sharp, *Education and the Summer Camp*, 7 Quoting the seventy-second annual report of the Children's Aid Society, May 15, 1925, p. 13.

It was a grand idea – an opportunity to give a child a chance. The chief aims were "'fresh air' and increased weight."[5] As soon as a child had "regained normal weight and health (he would return home) to make room for others."[6] A headline in the *New York Herald* Tribune on November 10, 1925 read, "1,507 Children Gain Two Tons in Weight in Country Air."[7] The *Dallas Morning News* mentions children spending the morning "swimming, weighing in for the annual weight gaining contest and getting camp clothing."[8] This was the type of program run at the Salesmanship Club from the 1920 to 1943. Initially, it had been a "recreation camp for orphans, [but later] extended its services to include underprivileged children.[9] The cartoon below depicts the focus of the program.

Dallas Morning News - August 14, 1942

Programs of this nature were focused on the plight of the poor. In 1925, a *New York Times* articles praised the Children's Aid Society and the Association for Improving the Condition of the Poor by taking "to heart the unhappiness of little children crowded into the reeking heat of the tenements"[10] and implored readers to send money to help, "maintain as many heat-stricken children and mothers at camps on Staten Island and elsewhere as possible."[11] It further explained that,

---

[5] Ibid., 33
[6] Ibid., 33.
[7] Ibid., 34.
[8] June 3, 1941, Dallas Morning News clipping, Underprivileged Kids, 207 of 'Em, Go to Camp.
[9] Bert Kruger Smith, *The Worth of a Boy* (Austin: The Hogg Foundation, 1958), 4.
[10] August 10, 1925 New York Times, 12.
[11] June 8, 1925, New York Times, 14.

> There children can play by cool waters and in shaded fields, soothed by the winds from the ocean...there, under good care, given nourishing food, they and their offspring – the lucky ones whom the association's funds make it possible to receive – can forget the horrors of the sidewalks and the stifling tenements.

The living conditions in the tenements were terrible. There was no light, no heat, no toilets, no running water, no garbage removal, and owners were well known for their price gouging rent. By the late 1800's government legislation had forced such amenities, but they were still inadequate. Bathrooms and showers were communal. There was no way to cool the apartments and there were far too few windows. The need for children to have an escape was palpable.

Because the need was so dire, careful consideration had not been given to maximizing the impact of the summer programs children were attending. In 1925, the Children's Welfare Federation realized "that problems and methods of caring for children in camp (hadn't) received much careful study."[12] Agencies had been so concerned with problems of transportation and logistics in getting children out of the "slums" that not much concern had been given about what happened in the vacation places.

During the next three years, four individuals visited one hundred and twenty-eight camps representing "seventy-five percent of all the camps providing summer vacations for children."[13] The study found that: 49% had no safe method of supplying drinking water to the students, 35% had no tubs or showers, 52% had no system for preventing sharing of towels and toothbrushes, 72% had no nature lore program.

> The average number of campers to each counselor was over ten, and in many of the camps each counselor had as many as thirty children to care for. It was quite common to find them grouped in squads or companies of twenty-five each.[14]

---

[12] Sharp, *Education and the Summer Camp,* 21.
[13] Ibid., 23.
[14] Ibid., 27.

Only 33% of camps had a thought out, planned recreation program[15] and these were often subordinate to the emphasis placed upon gain in weight. The *Children's Heath Camp Manual* published by the State Committee on Tuberculosis and Public Health of State Charities Aid Association in New York advises

> there is a danger of working so hard...that normal gain of the children is hindered...Out of-door games, walking, and climbing are all legitimately a part of the camp recreation, but children often become so eager in their play that they get out of hand, and fail to make the desired weight gains.[16]

The study concluded that,

> the welfare or charity program of the 'fresh air movement' was far from desirable in its aims, activities, and methods of caring for children. Conditions existing in many of these charity camps were of such a very low standard that they should not have been permitted to continue. In short, these camps showed lack of purpose planning and leadership.[17]

The Salesmanship Club seems to have been a bit ahead of their time. According to a news article from 1939, they had a nature program, adequate tooth brushing, a recreation program (including carving and pottery facilities), and even movies shown on a bi-weekly basis.[18] However, even for the Salesmanship Club, the findings of this study would cause major change in the realm of childcare and camping.

---

15 Ibid., 25.
16 Ibid., 34.
17 Ibid., 2.
18 June 1, 1939, Dallas Morning News Clipping, Concentration Camps Exist In Dallas, but Toothbrushing, Butterfly Chasing are Routine.

CHAPTER 1: LAYING A FOUNDATION

Building Chucktent for Tejucana Group

"In the fall of 1920 Dallas stood poised at the starting line. World War I was over, young men were returning from service, others were just getting out of college and universities after finishing their war interrupted education"[1] and the pieces were beginning to fall into place to organize the Dallas Salesmanship Club.[2] The Club was created for "the chief purpose of establishing and operating a camp...[that would] serve the needy children of Dallas."[3] On July 25, 1921, the camp was officially dedicated, "To the children of Dallas who will need it...in the name of the little Child who was born in a manger."[4] Then for the next year and a half

> with hoes, pick, shovels, axes and saws the members...cleared the site of a wilderness of trees and underbrush for the building

[1] 1968 Roster of the Salesmanship Club of Dallas, December 1, 1967, 8.

[2] The club was organized in November 1920

[3] L.B. Sharp, "Report of Children's Camp Project Salesmanship Club of Dallas," Feb 2-6, 1946. Obtained from Salesmanship Club of Dallas.

[4] 1968 Roster of the Salesmanship Club of Dallas, December 1, 1967, 10.

> that was to come. While their husbands were getting sunburns and blisters at the campsite, the wives of members launched an irresistible campaign on Dallas merchants for donations of money, lumber, hardware, and everything else needed for building and equipping the camp...As a result of unselfish leadership, combined enthusiasm, hard work and generosity, the Salesmanship Club Camp for Orphans was erected at a cost between $20,000 and $25,000, and was conceived, built, paid for, dedicated and occupied within the unbelievably short space of ninety days.[5]

By 1931, over 2,000 children were being served at the camp each summer.[6] The orphan's camp, situated at Bachman's Lake, grew to contain, Ferris wheels, swings, seesaws, tennis courts, a baseball diamond, and a swimming pool.[7] Children came for two weeks at a time and twelve counselors staffed the program for a total of 150 underprivileged children to "supervise their play and their search for health."[8] The camp was still strictly recreational. There was no instruction. Everything was furnished. They children had only to come and have fun.[9] A 1939 article outlines benefits of the program that include 12 hours of sleep, tooth brushing drills, large nutritious meals, hiking, crafts, swimming, movies, and "the strictest part of the routine at camp," a two-hour nap in the afternoon, "where a pound gained is something to write down in your diary."[10]

As the program grew, they moved beyond just serving orphans to serving a wide range of "underprivileged youth." The children were chosen for the program, "through the co-operation of school nurses and teachers"[11] and social workers.[12] "By tradition, girls...[had]...priority at

---

[5] 1968 Roster of the Salesmanship Club of Dallas, 10.
[6] *Dallas Morning News,* April 19, 1931.
[7] "Salesmanship Club Children Enjoying Week at Camp," *Dallas Morning News*, June 9, 1933.
[8] Ibid.
[9] According to "Salesmanship Club Children Enjoying Week at Camp," the ratio was about 12 to 1 – 150 children to 12 counselors.
[10] "Concentration Camps Exist In Dallas, but Toothbrushing, Butterfly Chasing are Routine."
[11] Ibid.
[12] Ibid.

the Salesmanship Club Camp,"[13] and in 1932, at least one week was dedicated to "Mexican Kids...getting wholesome food and fresh air."[14] The program continued to expand, and in the summer of 1941 4,000 children were served.

This growth continued until 1943 when a polio epidemic hit Dallas and the State Health Department ordered all camps closed. The Salesmanship Club Camp was

> turned over to the use of noncommissioned officers stationed in the armed services in and near Dallas. It made an excellent club house and grounds area for them and was a contribution to Dallas'[s] war effort...the pause thus created gave opportunity for much thought to be given to future work with children.[15]

In the spring of 1945, after the war ended, the Salesmanship Club turned its attention to opening camp again. Much had changed. L.B. Sharp noted, "For some years before the last war there was realization among members who had been active in camp work that there was a need for some basic changes and reorganization."[16]

Lloyd B. Sharp

In January 1925 "Edith Shatto King came...to the School of Education at Columbia to ask if there was someone there who could help them reorganize Life's Fresh Air Farms." Mrs. King spoke with John Dewey, Boyd Bode and William Heard Kilpatrick and,

> all three recommended that she talk to L.B. Sharp. So she interviewed him, and he asked her, "What do you do?" And she said, "Well, we take the kids

[13] June 3, 1941, Dallas Morning News Clipping, Underprivileged Kids, 207 of 'Em, Go to Camp

[14] September 7, 1932, Dallas Morning News Clipping. Week of Fun for Hundred Mexican Kids in Camp.

[15] 1968 Roster of the Salesmanship Club of Dallas, 10-11.

[16] Sharp, Report of Children's Camp Project Salesmanship Club Dallas, 1.

> into the out-of-doors and to these camps."...He said, "What do you do at these camps? " And she said, "Oh we give them an experience in the fresh air. We call them Life's Fresh Air Farms." So L.B. said to her, "Well, I know you farm corn. And I know you farm beans. And I know you farm potatoes, but I've never heard of anyone farming fresh air...That's a crop I haven't heard of before." [At the time] She didn't know quite what to make of this brash young man who was asking these questions.[17]

That very month she placed him on the committee to evaluate camping programs across New York, and in April of that year she hired him as the new director of both the Fresh Air Farms.[18] L.B. had many ideas that were new and radical for his time. As a result, when he was hired, he accepted the position on the condition that he would "have free rein" to make changes. He promptly changed the name from farms to camps, changed many policies, set "the whole program upon an educational basis,"[19] set out to increase the staff to student ratio, and began recruiting.

L.B. Sharp explains that

> according to the dictionary *to camp* means: "to pitch or prepare a camp to sleep out of doors," and this is precisely what the first camps attempted to provide for youngsters. But as time went on and camps grew in size it seemed to become more and more necessary to *organize* the camping experience and to *schedule* activities. In other words, instead of taking care of greater numbers by setting up more small camps with all the inherent values therein, expansion came by developing larger and larger camps with centralized programs. This centralization of program and organization meant the need for more and more specialists to head up the various "departments" of the camp. There were water-front specialists, the craft specialist, the nature specialist, the sports specialist, the evening program specialist and even the hiking and camping specialists. Along with the specialists in many camps have come the "gadgetters" and the assembly-line

[17] Julie Carlson, *Never Finished...Just Begun: A Narrative History of L.B. Sharp and Outdoor Education* (Edina, MN: Beaver's Pond Press, 2009), 26-27.
[18] Ibid., 27.
[19] Sharp, *Education and the Summer Camp – An Experiment,* 11.

> gadgets where the child is simply the last step in a pre-fabricated construction experience...in too many cases the camp is simply an organized playground with all of the equipment and devices that are used in the city simply moved out into the woods...the youngsters have not had a chance to participate in the experience of living and planning their lives in small groups. All of these tendencies have moved camping away from the original meaning of the term and, at worst, have robbed the youngster of the very experience for which he should be going to camp...[being] placed in a situation that requires of them a disposition to solve their own problems, co-operate with others, and come to know the ways of nature.[20]

To deal with this problem, L.B. Sharp outlined eight principles for a school-camp program:

1. Avoid regimentation.
2. Involve every camper in planning the activities.
3. Emphasize self-discovery, finding a place in the group, and understanding how people live together.
4. Teach problem solving connected with basic human needs for food, clothing, shelter, group living, and spiritual values.
5. The camp should motivate its program by causing children to do for themselves and to solve their own problems. It should emphasize experience by putting the native materials into the hands of the students at the spot where such materials are naturally found.
6. Camp life should give youth the optimum chance for serving others first and making self secondary to the group.
7. Require counselors or teachers to live with the campers and share common experiences with them.
8. Whatever the learning and whatever the philosophy, camp from the point of view of the campers is for fun and it should be so conducted that both campers and staff find it so.[21]

---

[20] L.B. Sharp and E. DeAlton Partridge, "Some Historical Backgrounds of Camping," *Bulletin of the National Association of Secondary School Principals* 31 (1947), 17-18.
[21] Taken from both Sharp, "Why Outdoor and Camping Education." 316-317. and Clifford Knapp. "Learning From An Outdoor Education Hero," *Taproot* (Summer 2000): 11.

In short, *camp must be a boy's world!*

> With these ideals in mind, Sharp set out to find responsible counselors, counselors who could work well under this plan. The first counselor that he hired was a lady by the name of Rya Gelzvitz. He went to this Girl Scout camp, and he said, "I heard about a good counselor here. Her name is Rya Gelavitz. Can you tell me where I might find her?"...This woman director said, "She went...up that hill into the woods two weeks ago. We haven't seen her since." L.B. Sharp turned around and rubbed his hands together and smiled and said, "That's the counselor for me."[22]

> L.B. had high expectations for his staff. Since the program was not centralized, there were no staff specialists in nature, music, or dramatics to turn to for help. The counselors had to be generalists and learn these skills to guide the campers. L.B. did not believe that knowledge should be separated into the traditional disciplines. He thought, in solving life's problems, we usually draw from many of these subjects when needed and they are rarely separated from the others.[23]

Sharp's notion of camp became quite successful. "On September 15, 1937, the Committee on Instructional Affairs of the Board of Education, of which Johanna M. Lindlof was Chairman submitted"[24] a resolution to develop a plan for conducting "a camp for underprivileged children, under the auspices of the Board of Education of the City of New York."[25] In the summer of 1939, the committee visited Life Camp and "was deeply impressed with Dr. Sharp as an educator and as a person. He had won nation-wide recognition as the outstanding man in his field. His vitality, enthusiasm and knowledge left no member of the Committee untouched."[26]

---

[22] Carlson, *Never Finished...Just Begun: A Narrative History of L.B. Sharp and Outdoor Education*, 28.
[23] Knapp, "Learning From An Outdoor Education Hero," 9.
[24] *Adventures in Camping*. New York, NY: Johanna M. Lindlof Camp Committee for Public School Children, 1943, 9.
[25] Ibid., 9.
[26] *Adventures in Camping*. New York, NY: Johanna M. Lindlof Camp Committee for

That summer, he took "110 New York City public school children under the aegis and auspices of the Johanna M. Lindlof Camp Fund for Public School Children."[27] Sharp's notion of camp continued to gain traction. In 1940, "Mrs. Franklin Delano Roosevelt and former Governor and Mrs. Herbert H. Lehman...accepted membership on the drive committee"[28] to provide funds to send these underprivileged school children to Life Camp. Soon demand was growing for leaders in these new camping education techniques.

In June of 1940, National Camp was opened to fill those needs. National Camp's primary function was to train "teachers in...'decentralized camping' and 'camping education'...based upon a new and different type of camping administration evolved at the three Life Camps."[29] The central idea was that *"youngsters...learn best and grow most in the outdoors when they must solve their own basic problems of food, shelter, daily living, and self-occupation."*[30] A six-week session at National Camp carried "six points of graduate credit with New York University. Students [came] with ...specific problem[s] [in establishing] camping education in their own communities, and [for advice on] develop[ing] [these] program[s] in consultation with camp faculty."[31] L.B. Sharp's influence grew until "At one point, every major outdoor education leader in the country came through L.B.'s National Camp."[32]

The Salesmanship Club

By the spring of 1945, after World War II, when interest was rekindled in opening the Salesmanship Club program again,[33] these revolutionary ideas were sweeping across the nation. The Salesmanship Club sold "the old property...and a new site was purchased on August 6,

---

Public School Children, 1943, 11, and *Extending Education through Camping,* New York, NY: Life Camps, Inc, 1948, 15.

[27] *Adventures in Camping*, 11.

[28] Ibid., 11.

[29] E. DeAlton Partridge, "National Camp," *Nature Magazine* 36 no. 6 (1943): 322

[30] Ibid., 321.

[31] Partridge, 323.

[32] Carlson, *Never Finished...Just Begun: A Narrative History of L.B. Sharp and Outdoor Education*, 42.

[33] L.B. Sharp, "Report of Childrens Camp Project Salesmanship Club of Dallas." 1.

1945." [34] The beautiful wooded, hilly property consisted of 200 acres located on "Jim Miller Road off the Seagoville Highway seven and one-half miles from Dallas."[35]

When it came time to develop a program The Salesmanship Club sought out the best mind in the country, a man who would became known as the father of experiential education, L.B. Sharp. It was requested that Sharp

> make a preliminary study of the entire camp program, and also of the new property, so that the whole project could be evaluated and a new procedure outlined, with the hope that it would be an outstanding project not only for Dallas but throughout the section of the country.[36]

Sharp sent a twenty-six page report to the Salesmanship Club dated February 2-6, 1946 that outlined a rudimentary decentralized outdoor education program.[37] In it, he wrote:

> To carry out the program envisioned will require adequate leadership. The management of this camp project is a full-time, year-round position requiring the highest professional and educational qualifications, and certainly a knowledge and skill in camping...This person should have the responsibility of selecting the staff. The directorate position is comparable to the principalship of a school. The working season and hours are longer and the responsibilities are heavier. He and his staff are responsible for everyone in camp for twenty-four hours a day. The most effective way to prepare the administrative leadership needed would be to send at least two people to National Camp this summer. They should take as their specific project a through-going study of the camp program you propose to carry out. At National Camp they would have opportunity to visit and study various kinds of camps along with their work.[38]

---

[34] Ibid., 1.
[35] Ibid., 1.
[36] Ibid., 2.
[37] Ibid., 1.
[38] Ibid., 12.

Campbell (Chief Lock) and Lynn Loughmiller

On May 1, 1946 the Salesmanship Club hired Campbell Loughmiller to begin the camping program Sharp had outlined in Texas.[39] In his autobiography, Campbell writes at that time "I didn't know beans about organized camping."[40] Chief Lock had

> earned a degree in philosophy and English from the university of California at Berkley in 1935, and afterwards a one year certificate in social work (a new degree program) from the same institution. He has worked as director of Welfare Services in Del Norte County in southern California, as the 8-state regional Assistant Director for the War Food Administration, and several other government jobs, mostly related to the war effort.[41]

He had a long history in social work and had "camped extensively as an individual, and with [the] family...[but he] had never attended (any) camp."[42] At first glance, this does not appear to be a good resume for a camp director. It definitely does not fit with L.B. Sharp's recommendations, but Mr. Ira McCollister[43] was the Chairman of the Salesmanship Club Camp Board at the time[44] and he knew what Mr. Loughmiller was made of.

---

[39] Manual of Policies and Procedures of Camp Woodland Springs, (n.d.), 1.

[40] Campbell Loughmiller, *These Fish Had Wings*, vol. 1 (unpublished autobiography, 1980), 291.

[41] Grover Loughmiller, "Origins and Directions of Therapeutic Camping," copy of keynote address delivered April 15, 1996, at the annual Conference of the National Association of Therapeutic Wilderness Camps, 8.

[42] Ibid., 291.

[43] Owned a Chevrolet Dealership as Mac recalls.

If Chief Lock had a defining characteristic, it was his "insatiable curiosity"[45] coupled with a belief in the good of people. His son, Grover, recalls:

> Everything interested him...As children, he almost drove my sister and me to distraction at times. We would be driving down the road as a family, and his ever-alert eyes would light upon a flower (at 60 miles per hour) that he never remembered seeing before. He would immediately stop the car, back up, get his camera out, set the tripod up, get out his light meter and check the light, adjust the range finder, then check the light again to make sure it hadn't changed while he was checking something else, and then he would take his picture. Then the whole process was reversed and we were back on the road. It might take 15 or 20 minutes for this process. At times we almost groaned when he saw another flower. Other times were more interesting even to us. I remember once in West Texas when we had stopped by the roadside to take care of the necessaries, he spotted a dung beetle, and motioned us to come watch...We watched this dung beetle for an hour, and seeing it through his eyes, it was better than watching a Hitchcock thriller. As I said, nothing escaped his attention, and he absolutely had to know about it...His curiosity carried over to people as well (or more so). He loved to learn from them, and assumed every single person on the face of the earth was a "mother lode" waiting to be tapped...People sensed that his curiosity was genuine and not a "gimmick" and sensed his

[44] Loughmiller, Origins and Directions of Therapeutic Camping, 8.
[45] Grover Loughmiller, "Talk at funeral – December 8, 1993" 3.

> excitement about learning. They became excited, too. They began to realize how valuable <u>they</u> were to him out of his curiosity about what they had to offer him.[46]

This leads to a second characteristic, Lock's belief in the good of people. This was not a naïve belief; Grover describes it as a "determination to like all people."[47] One day, during Chief Lock's years as a merchant marine, he went to the ship's library and found a book by Jules Payot. In the book, the author challenges the reader to, "Select the person in all the world whom you dislike most and treat him as though you liked him for 30 days, and by that time you <u>will</u> like him."[48] Lock immediately put this philosophy to the test trying it "on a universally disliked man on the ship, and made him a trusted friend and learned of the man's sad history."[49]

Buford McKenzie recalls an experience of a similar nature with Chief Lock when Mac was a young Chief. Mac was seated with his group on logs and "an eight year old boy walked up to Lock. 'Chiieeeeff, I need to talk to you.' Lock turned 100% of his attention to that kid, took him off on a log and sat down."[50] Mac said to himself, "that kid does not need that kind of attention. [But gradually] I learned how to stick in there with and love a kid in that manner." Now Mac frequently said, in the spirit of Lock, that "everyone who comes to camp is loaded and we can't let them leave here without putting a word on what they've seen."

Ira McCollister knew these characteristics well. He had hired Lock, as the first Director of the Dallas city-wide welfare department. [51] Later, when looking for a director for the camp program, Lock sprang to mind. His son Grover recalls, "He liked my dad and what he did at the agency."[52] He also knew Lock hated working in the city.[53] "So he approached him about being the Director of the Club's new venture."[54]

---

[46] Ibid., 3-4.
[47] Loughmiller, "Talk at funeral – December 8, 1993," 5.
[48] Ibid.
[49] Ibid.
[50] Buford McKenzie in interview with the author, August 25, 2010..
[51] Grover Loughmiller, Origins and Directions of Therapeutic Camping,., 8.
[52] Ibid.,8.
[53] Campbell Loughmiller, Speech at Dedication of Loughmiller Monument, Salesmanship Club Youth Camp, September 10, 1994.
[54] Grover Loughmiller, Origins and Directions of Therapeutic Camping,., 8.

When Ira first contacted him, Lock had a terrible cold and turned him down flat; he did not desire to go anywhere. But Ira persisted, Lock says, "He had the oldest Chevrolet dealership in Dallas and I guess that's how he got it...persistence. I saw the woods and was sold immediately. I had looked for four years for a place with three oak trees in the front yard and here was 200 acres of beautiful virgin woods."[55]

The board put Lock in charge and supported him. A board member, Ed Rose, once said, "'If this is not the best program in the country, you need to let me know so we can go get it.' They were production people and they wanted to spend their time and money effectively."[56] History confirms Mr. McCollister's decision. That summer the Salesmanship Club decided to follow L.B.'s recommendation to send at least two staff to National Camp. Lock, his wife Lynn, and his children headed to National Camp to attend "a six-weeks adult training camp in New Jersey, operated by Dr. L. B. Sharp." [57] Campbell Loughmiller's "insatiable curiosity" and belief in the ability of people to change, combined with his experiences at National Camp, would uniquely qualify him for the pioneering work in therapeutic camping to come.

The Influence of L.B. Sharp

Lock's first impression of camping education at National Camp was not favorable. In the beginning he said, "If this is education, I don't want any part of it."[58] L.B. Sharp instructed Lock to hang in there and try it a while longer. Given time, Lock not only caught on, but fell in love with it.

That summer they "lived in a 'hogan' (a tent structure), did some outdoor cooking, learned how to use nature in craft projects, how to teach in an outdoor setting and a little about groupwork – at least the importance of

---

[55] Campbell Loughmiller, Speech at Dedication of Loughmiller Monument, Salesmanship Club Youth Camp, September 10, 1994.
[56] Buford McKenzie in interview with the author, August 12, 2009.
[57] Campbell Loughmiller, *These Fish Had Wings Vol 1*, 291.
[58] Buford McKenzie in interview with the author, April 21, 2009.

getting along in a small group."[59] Campbell's son Grover recalls:

> There were hikes hip deep in the bog picking blueberries, there were all day cross-country compass hikes in the Catskill Mountains to see how close you could end up at the established destination (or alternately have to be rescued.) There were swimming, canoeing, and other water skills in Lake Mashiplakong. There was the peeling of bark off logs to get the raffia from the under layer of the bark, from which ropes were made. There was the soaking and pounding of Ash tree annual rings that were later woven into pack baskets. There were nature hikes with those who quoted from their own books, those who had a deep knowledge and appreciation of nature. There was primitive baking of breads, desserts, and buffalo steaks cooked on live coals. There were campfires, rich in singing, folklore, stories, fun. And there were processing sessions around potbellied stoves. Though my dad was raised in a time where primitive skills were part of daily living, I'm sure the experiences he had added deeply to the camp he developed and its programs. Also friendships established there persisted the rest of his life, one group of which led to the National Council of Churches to write a set of two books for church camps to use across the country as a training guide and reference manual, which they did. Armed with these types of additional experiences, my dad and mom returned to their own camp.[60]

Campbell's wife Lynn adds, "The whole experience was educational, helpful for our own planning, and fun."[61] The influence of National Camp and L.B. Sharp is undeniable. It was here that many camp principles came into being. Special meanings for terms like Chief, Mom, Chuck Wagon, Pow-wow, and Hoya-hoya originated with L.B. Sharp. Other foundational concepts like using groups of 8-10 boys; putting those boys in charge of their program; having them build their own shelters; and plan their own meals and trips originated at National Camp. Even the annual "turkey in the hole" celebration began in that

---

[59] Lynn Loughmiller, *Camp Life* (unpublished memoir), 2.

[60] Grover Loughmiller, Origins and Directions of Therapeutic Camping, 9.

[61] Lynn Loughmiller, *Camp Life,*2.

venue. Lock writes, "[it was] there I got on to the idea of camping in small semi-autonomous groups with two leaders. L.B. was a great person and our friendship deepened over the years. He came to camp for consultation many times"[62] and the club sponsored a yearly scholarship for one staff member a year to attend National Camp for training.

In 1950,[63] when Buford McKenzie (Chief Mac), who "helped initiate many of the procedures...employed"[64] at the Salesmanship Club Camp, became the first group work supervisor, Lock and the Salesmanship Club felt it was necessary to send him and John Spencer[65] for a six-week session at National Camp as well, from July 6 through August 17.[66] Later, in 1951, Chief Lock and Lynn returned to National Camp with their children, Grover and Camelia, four years after their first visit,[67] to work part of the summer on the staff at National Camp. Lock writes that he needed "a little purification of thought that comes from swapping shop with others in the same business."[68]

Dr. Sharp's great contribution to summer camping was *experiential education*. In his doctoral dissertation he writes that "Camp is more than a place to keep children while they are not in the city; it furnishes a positive, purposeful, carefully planned program of enjoyable living, the outcomes of which are educational."[69] Adding education to the summer camp was the pioneering work of L.B. Sharp. Due to his influence, Camp Woodland Springs began as an education-based "summer recreation program."[70]

---

[62] Campbell Loughmiller, *These Fish Had Wings Vol 1*, 291.
[63] Date on Mac's National Camp Paper.
[64] Campbell Loughmiller, *Wilderness Road*, Austin, TX: Hogg Foundation, 1965, ix.
[65] National Camp Roster, July 6 – August 17, 1950.
[66] Buford McKenzie in interview with the author, April 21, 2009.
[67] Loughmiller, *These Fish Had Wings,* 292.
[68] Campbell Loughmiller, letter to L.B. Sharp, dated October-November 1948.
[69] Sharp, *Education and the Summer Camp – An Experiment*, 2.
[70] Bert Kruger Smith, *The Worth of a Boy* (Austin: The Hogg Foundation, 1970), 7.

CHAPTER 2:
GETTING CAMP OFF THE GROUND

Boys Traveling After Parent Drop-off

After returning to Dallas from National Camp, much work was to be done. Upon their return, Campbell found the caretaker, Mr. Bryant, clearing an area and "stopped his axe in mid-air" until they could contact the Camp Board Chairman, Mr. McCallister.[1]

> Mr. Mac came out and they went to the area and he said to Campbell, "Now don't you think this (where he had cleared out the underbrush) looks a whole lot better than that?" (where he had not cleared.) Campbell said, "I'll tell you what we'll do, Mr. Mac, we'll bring some boys out here and if they head for the open area, we'll clear it, but if they head for the area with the undergrowth, we'll leave it." Mr. Mac said, "I see what you mean and we're going to have just one Director, and you're it."[2]

This was the beginning of the conservationist mentality that pervades camp to this day.

---

[1] Loughmiller, *Camp Life* 2.
[2] Ibid., 2.

Conservation took on a different meaning to the Loughmillers than it does to most. The Loughmillers' first house at camp was an architecturally beautiful log house. It had an eight-foot wrap-around porch on three sides and was set deep in the woods. While beautiful, it was also problematic. Because it was in the woods and had such a deep porch, it was "so dark that a light was needed on the brightest days."[3] The builder had sealed the logs with concrete. As the logs dried the concrete pulled. This might have had the benefit of allowing light to enter, except that the porch on three sides still kept light out, and allowed drafts and woodland creatures in. Lynn writes, "We kept company with rats and mice, a wren, and a copperhead snake in the broom closet. Also spiders, and once a swarm of honey bees."[4] "It was normal to catch five or six scorpions a day in the house."[5] To make things worse, the living and dining rooms had no ceilings, and as a result were very pretty, but "impossible to heat or cool."[6] A large fireplace added to beauty and helped when you stood in front of it, but did not compensate for the cracks in the walls or the lack of ceilings.

> The house was just too hot to eat supper in the summer. The ceiling fan just didn't get the job done, so we ate in the front yard. The Screech Owls were so tame they scooted up and down on the railings, not 15 inches from us, bending at the "ankles" and turning their heads to scrutinize us. A faucet at the corner of the house dripped. They would hang upside down to drink from it. We had a bird feeding shelf on a post in the front yard. Swamp rabbits as large as jack rabbits would chase each other round and round it. The raucous barn owls would wake us, telling us "I cook at our house, who cooks at you alls?"[7]

Despite its drawbacks, the new home was a welcome step up from the "one room storage room attached to the car shed"[8] they moved into until they could head to National Camp to live in a hogan-style tent.

---

[3] Ibid., 1.
[4] Ibid., 1.
[5] Loughmiller, "Origins and Directions of Therapeutic Camping," 10.
[6] Loughmiller, *Camp Life*, 1.
[7] Ibid., 5-6
[8] Ibid., 2.

That first summer after they returned, they dove straight into to starting up camp. Grover recalls, "My dad (Chief Lock) hired two well-educated Latin Americans, Oswea and Alejandro, students from Perkins School of Theology at SMU [Southern Methodist University], and others, to help with campsite construction."[9] Later, "Campbell Loughmiller hired John Spencer and one other Theology student from S.M.U."[10] to help get things started. They had three-day[11] weekends free to go to "a community of their choice and minister to them."[12] John was "an outdoor person, with skin tanned and tough."[13] Lynn recalls that she once attempted to give him a typhoid shot, but when she "hit the needle into his arm, it just bounced and John laughed at her being upset."[14]

They spent those days purchasing basic camp equipment, locating sites, laying out the trails, building teepees, and making preparations for camping on weekends in the fall.[15] There were "no buildings, none whatever, and [we] didn't want any, because we didn't have the faintest notion whether we would go full time or not. That wasn't in the thinking of the club at the time."[16]

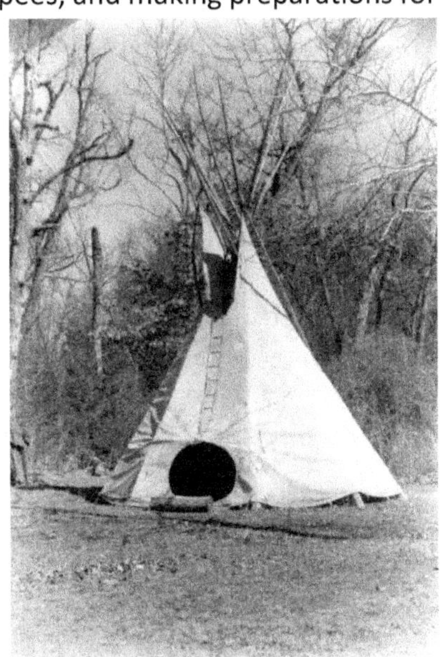

The lack of buildings was not a problem in itself, but Campbell recalls, "I had never put up a teepee, and there was more to it than I imagined. Lynn read the instructions and John and I followed them. It took us two days to erect two teepees and a cooking tent"[17]

---

[9] Loughmiller, "Origins and Directions of Therapeutic Camping," 9.
[10] Loughmiller, *Camp Life,* 2.
[11] Loughmiller, *These Fish Had Wings*, 293.
[12] Loughmiller, *Camp Life*, *3.*
[13] Ibid., 3.
[14] Ibid., 3.
[15] Loughmiller, *These Fish Had Wings*, 293, and Manual of Policies and Procedures of Camp Woodland Springs, 2.
[16] Loughmiller, *These Fish Had Wings,* 293.
[17] Ibid., 293.

as part of a "neat little mini-campsite there that reflected the spirit we hoped to develop. It was attractive and sparked the imagination of kids and counselors."[18] It would later become the place where most of the original counselor training took place.

The First Group Arrives

On November 12, 1946 – the day Walt Disney released "Song of the South"[19] and the Exchange National Bank of Chicago, Illinois, opened the first drive-in banking service in America[20] – the first group of eight boys inaugurated weekend winter camping at Camp Woodland Springs.[21] By June, "after camping through the winter on weekends, we had four camps of eight boys."[22] The facilities were nothing fancy. Lock used his farmhouse for the kitchen and they ate under a "20 x 50 foot naval hospital tent."[23] Water was piped into the campsites to allow groups of campers to take care of most of their needs in the campsite. There was no bathhouse initially.

Trips were popular and the groups went out frequently in the early days. A letter dated July 29, 1947 details a "five day canoe trip down the Trinity River, [with] 8 boys and 2 counselors making the trip in two canoes."[24] Lock continues in the letter saying that,

> others have gone to a small 1600 acre ranch about 40 miles from Dallas where there are several lakes, several cownags to ride and lots of good fishing. Still others have gone to Lake Dallas, one of the largest Texas lakes, and camp(ed) for a week or so on an island which we have taken over as the '19th hole'.[25]

---

[18] Ibid., 293.
[19] http://www.songofthesouth.net/movie/campaigns/1946.html. Accessed April 7, 2009.
[20] http://www.history.com/this-day-in-history.do?action=Article&id=7788. Accessed April 7, 2009.
[21] Loughmiller, *These Fish Had Wings*, 293. and Letter written to L.B. Sharp by Campbell Loughmiller dated July 29, 1947.
[22] Loughmiller, *These Fish Had Wings*, 293.
[23] Campbell Loughmiller, letter to L.B. Sharp, May 16, 1947
[24] Campbell Loughmiller, letter to L. B. Sharp , July 29, 1947.
[25] Ibid.

"The following summer, there were fifty-six campers in seven different groups, ranging in age from eight to fifteen inclusive."[26]

Chief Lock writes that, in the early days of camp "[we had] no intention of doing 'therapy,' we were just having a good time."[27] "There was no thought of working with emotionally disturbed boys, but some were accepted for one reason or another."[28]

The boys served at camp were "primarily under-privileged financially, which included many West Dallas Boys. Some of them were rough customers, pretty fouled up." In some cases, the boys' family situations deteriorated while they were at camp for the summer. [29] In other cases "we thought they made some visible improvement during the month at camp."[30] We wanted "to help them as much as possible before the next school year began,"[31] so we decided to invite some of the "most troublesome" [32] to stay for the second session, or even for the entire summer. We began to seek out psychiatrists and psychologists to help us work with the boys. But a peculiar thing happened. While we were out looking for consultants to help, the boys were getting better."[33] We made the decision to put these boys who were staying on together into one group.

> John Spencer said if we couldn't get anyone else to take that group, he and his co-counselor (Sam Inman)[34] would, so I quit looking. John was as good as we ever had. Things went fairly well and at the end of the second month even their mothers started talking about the improvement. [35]

---

[26] Manual of Policies and Procedures of Camp Woodland Springs, 2 and the Salesmanship Club Boys Camp Woodland Springs Brochure.
[27] This comes from a conference with Chief Lock in Southern Pines North Carolina that is outlined in the Cameron Boys Camp *Camp Management Manual* p. 84.
[28] Grover Loughmiller, "Origins and Directions of Therapeutic Camping," *Camp Management Manual* p. 61.
[29] Loughmiller, "Origins and Directions of Therapeutic Camping," 61.
[30] Loughmiller, *These Fish Had Wings*, 294
[31] Wilber Clarence Breining, Jr., *A Follow Up Study of Seventy-nine Maladjusted Boys Who Received Treatment at Camp Woodland Springs, Dallas, Texas* (Denton, Texas: North Texas State College), 1956, 2.
[32] Ibid., 294.
[33] McKenzie in interview with the author, April 21, 2009.
[34] Ibid.
[35] Loughmiller, *These Fish Had Wings*, 294.

No one was certain exactly what to attribute the success to, but efforts began to be made to explain it. While this was going on, this new group was re-evaluated and it was decided to keep the experiment going for a third month. "The thing that compelled all of us to look at it seriously was the fact that we had three stutterers in the course of the summer. One of them, [Paul], the worst I ever saw." [36] Campbell relates that at times, when he saw the boy coming, he would hide behind a tree, because he simply did not have time to listen to him attempt to say good morning. Each day the boy would endeavor to say good morning and, no matter how long it took, wouldn't quit until he got it out.[37] To deny him the opportunity would be disastrous as well. Lock recalls, that Paul "made up for what he couldn't say with his fists."[38] When he

> lost his temper, he had a phrase he unloaded on the object of his wrath without respect of persons whatsoever. In order to deliver the phrase with the correct enunciation and appropriate force, Paul would rotate at the waist in a back and forth wind-milling fashion, with both arms straight out from his body, building momentum. At just the right moment, he would spin completely around very quickly in a perfect 360-degree spin. While spinning around, he would shout without a trace of a stutter, 'You jackass [s___]-bomb!'[39]

Once this occurred, Lock and the group as well would be caught in a problem solving session. It seemed to Lock that his best alternative was to hide behind a tree and let the group pass in peace. Of course Paul was not always the victim. Grover Loughmiller recalls that Paul had a way of pouring gas on the fire of any boy's anger in the group. It seems when a boy would get agitated, Paul would come really close, wriggle his fingers in the boy's face and chant "mad ball, fire ball, puffed up, wooo!"[40]

A basic tenet of camp philosophy was - and is - that problems are to be solved. No matter how big or small, a problem cannot not cease to

---

[36] Ibid., 294.
[37] Campbell Loughmiller, conference held in Southern Pines, NC, June 1988.
[38] Loughmiller, *These Fish Had Wings*, 294.
[39] William S. Hood, *1950's Camp Experience*, (unpublished memoir), 22.
[40] Grover Loughmiller in interview with the author, September 3, 2010.

be dealt with until it had been resolved and all parties felt at ease. As a result, Campbell Loughmiller and the counselors were not content to allow these types of problems to continue.

The Influence of Fritz Redl

One of the psychologists Chief Lock worked closely with was Fritz Redl. Redl was the Director of the University of Michigan Fresh Air Camp from 1941 to 1945 where he "began converting the program to a therapeutic orientation in 1941."[41]

It was natural for Chief Lock to seek out this international expert who was running a therapeutic camp to explain the progress at Woodland Springs and further develop the program. Redl's practical psychology fit Lock's pragmatist approach and his ideas further enhanced and clarified what was already being experienced at Woodland Springs.

Redl came to camp several times to share ideas with Chiefs. He had a unique ability to describe what a disturbed boy was like and help Chiefs clarify and set boundaries for their experimentation.[42] Redl's ideas of democratic education were similar to those of Sharp and his notions of using relationships and communication instead of coercion, rewards, or punishments to manipulate behavior fit with Lock's own beliefs. The ideas of using the same techniques with parents that were used with the boys also spawned from work with Fritz Redl. His ability to use a life space interview to maximize a teachable moment became a primary tool Chiefs used with their group to help a boy grow. "Problem, Solution, Prevention" (PSP) is used at camp to this day:

1. ***Problem – State the Problem***
   Accept responsibility and partner with the group in discussing what the problem was and where it began. It is important to distinguish the root problem from the symptoms and to identify the beginning to develop a prevention at the end.
2. ***Solution – Take steps to resolve the hurt and/or anger the problem caused***

---

[41] James, "Roots: The Life Space Pioneers," 8.
[42] Buford McKenzie in interview with the author, September 17, 2010.

Involve everyone in the group in discussing what needs to happen to solve the problem. Everyone's feelings matter. Several people may need to apologize to the group. Identify together any steps necessary to make restitution, develop a plan to make restitution, and, as necessary, group members should ask for forgiveness.

3. ***Prevention – Decide on a plan to prevent the problem in the future.***
   Since everyone understands the origin of the problem, see if others in the group relate. This help the boy realize he is not alone in the problem. Develop 2 or 3 preventions and choose one.[43]

If the program in Texas was anything, it was a grand experiment. Counselors and staff at Woodland Springs would

> present a problem, determine what the central ingredients of the problem are, and decide what interventions might affect the outcome. You try out your small theory, and if it works, you draw deductive conclusions. Inch by inch, the process began. Experiment on experiment led to better ways, as well as discarded ideas, beginning to generate a lore of more and less effective strategies for dealing with behavior...All steps were taken on a day-to-day experimental basis, incorporating into tomorrow's actions the things learned today. And thus, the store of useful knowledge began to become additive and to increase in volume. Boys responded. Groups instead of being disabled by one or two boys or incidents, dealt with issues and moved on. So, dealing with problem behaviors began to become an integral part of the whole outdoor experience.[44]

This type of creative, collaborative spirit emanated from Lock to all of the counselors and staff. In daily tasks, boys and their Chiefs worked together to plan and execute their program. If a problem or a question came up – whether it was educational, relational, or simply just about meeting daily needs – it was the job of the Chief to work with his group

---

[43] Taken from Cameron Boys Camp Philosophy Manual written by Buford McKenzie and edited by the author

[44] Loughmiller, conference held in Southern Pines, NC.

to discover the answer. As this occurred, trust was built. As trust was built and this relational group work process occurred, the boys were getting better.

It was Paul Grimes' mother who was the first to make comment on the significant progress being made. Lock recalls thinking, "you must have a good imagination."[45] But in time, Paul (the boy who had the stuttering problem) "became a regular blabber mouth"[46] and "a good little musician."[47] He had been at the Parker Foundation for three and a half years and they had discharged him as being too dull to help, but in 60 days at camp, he was understandable.[48] As a matter of fact, there were three boys with speech problem and all three

> improved until anyone could understand them. If it had been some change in behavior I might have thought they would return to their old ways when they got out of camp. I assumed when they came they needed a speech therapist, but we had nothing like that. Most of these disturbed and maladjusted boys made considerable progress that first summer. It was noticed that the amount of improvement gained by any boy was cumulative, and disproportionate to the few weeks longer spent in camp by that particular boy. It was theorized, for example, that a two-month session produced more than twice as much improvement as a one-month session.[49]

"By the end of the summer, it was obvious we had something pretty powerful, but none of us in his wildest dreams had any thought of going into fulltime camping."[50]

Two facts inspired the thought of attempting a year-round group. One, the results thus far had been very encouraging; [51] and two, many (8 to 10) of the boys had no other place to go.[52] "On the evidence gained during that summer, the camp sponsors decided to begin a pilot

---

[45] Loughmiller, conference held in Southern Pines, NC.

[46] Ibid.

[47] Hood, *1950's Camp Experience*, 23.

[48] Conference held at Marriot hotel in Southern Pines, NC on June 1988.

[49] Breining, 2.

[50] *These Fish Had Wings*, 294.

[51] Ibid.

[52] Interview with Chief Mac, 4/21/2009.

program for maladjusted boys on a continuous, year-round basis."[53] They asked "the Dallas School District for permission to keep them at camp during the semester"[54] and permission was granted.

It came about that in September 1948[55] that Tehuacana (Pronounced Teh-wá-ká-knee), the first year-round group of 7-11 year old boys began.[56] Six months later, in March,[57] Tejas, a second group of older boys age 12-15, was added.[58] In June of 1949 a third group, the Beavers, was added and the camp population reached 30 boys. A report from 1950 shows a year- round population of 30 and a summer population of 60.[59] The summer program utilized three additional counselors and lasted ten or eleven weeks. One counselor was responsible for a group of eight boys in the summer, while in the year-round program, two counselors served ten boys.[60] The summer program closely resembled the year-round program. The details of the summer program have been outlined in Lynn and Campbell Loughmiller's book, *Camping and Christian Growth*.

---

[53] Breining, 2.
[54] *These Fish Had Wings*, 294.
[55] Loughmiller, letter to L.B. Sharp, October-November 1948. Pinpoints the date as September 1948. This date is also handwritten into the history of camp portion of a Camp Woodland Springs Manual.
[56] Buford McKenzie in interview with the author, August 17, 2010.
[57] Brochures and Woodland Springs Manual.
[58] McKenzie in interview with the author, August 17, 2010.
[59] Salesmanship Club of Dallas, "A Report on the Present Operation and Future Need of Camp Woodland Springs by A Special Committee," September 11, 1950, 2.
[60] Ibid., 4.

Buford McKenzie (Chief Mac)

On May 27, 1949, Chief Mac was hired as the summer swimming pool manager at Camp Woodland Springs.[61] Two months later he became a group counselor and began the third group. Billy Hood was at camp during the same period as Paul and he writes:

> I remember one specific event when [Paul] applied this [wind milling] reaction to Chief Buford McKenzie. Apparently, Paul did not like a decision the Chief had made regarding a disciplinary action. This time it was not the least bit funny! We all believed that Chief Mac could call down lightning from the heavens. He didn't, as it turned out, and we were all relieved.[62]
>
> Buford McKenzie, known as "Chief Mac," was largely responsible for weeding out the riffraff. Chief Mac was our in-house trouble-shooter. He was the Chief of Chiefs and answered to the Director, Campbell Loughmiller. When it was necessary for Chief Mac to come help solve a problem, everybody knew there was going be hard times!
>
> Buford McKenzie was a huge man with a golden singing voice and a no nonsense approach to living agreeably with others. His word was law in the camp. There were times I feared his presence, and times I was really glad to see him coming up the trail, with little dust clouds puffing from beneath his huge shoes with every step. Chief Mac had a stiff leg and walked faster than any man I ever knew. To us kids, with our short little legs, he was at a dead run pace most of the time. You could spot him from a mile away, approaching in his quick lumbering gait.

---

[61] *Club and Camp News*, Salesmanship Club Boys Camp, Sam Adams Jr. (Ed.), vol. 40, no.1, (September 29, 1966) and Tribute to Buford McKenzie Adopted by the Board of Directors and the Camp Board, June 1, 1961.
[62] Hood, *1950's Camp Experience*, 23

Looking back 50 years, Billy Hood recalls:

> I don't know how he was injured, but I like to think he was a decorated combat wounded veteran of the Second World War with Germany and Japan. As I look back, it would fit him well. He was a hero in real life, a dedicated man, not at all like the fanciful crafted stories of Hollywood writers. His legacy still lives among us today, in the productive lives of once wayward baby boomers. As I think of him now, and his devotion to his work, which was each and every boy in the camp, it was evident in everything he did. [63]

A Crushed Leg...A New Life

Buford McKenzie was born October 12, 1919, two years after the conclusion of World War 1. He was the fourth of six children born to a family of poor share croppers who lived in a log cabin shack on a farm on lower Mississippi. The "battle injury" Mac carried with him his entire life was not from World War 2. As a pertinacious five-year-old boy, Mac became determined to climb atop the family mule in the pasture. After a great deal of effort, he managed a short ride that morning before the irritated mule hurled the small boy into a fence post shattering his left thigh. Mac lay on the ground for several hours before he was found and taken to the doctor. There, it was discovered his left leg was broken in three to four places between the knee and the hip.

A country doctor provided the best care available, but the injury compounded when infection set in and the leg was nearly lost. The next five months were spent in the hospital fighting gangrene. In the end, the leg was spared amputation, but a full-leg cast prevented normal bone growth and caused a permanently stiff knee and bowed femur.[64] To even walk again would be nearly miraculous. There were no physical therapists or specialists to help this young boy take his next steps. However, the "easy road" was seldom an option for this tenacious young man. Mac was soon fitted with a special shoe and spent months learning to walk again. Not only did he learn to walk, he worked alongside his family on the farm and would become known as the fastest runner in his elementary school class. From a young age Mac

---

[63] Ibid.,. 8-9.

[64] Buford McKenzie in interview with the author, June 16, 2011.

became known for his grit and determination. He never let anything slow him down.

A few years after the leg injury had healed, the McKenzie family was rocked by a second crisis. On October 29, 1929 the stock market begin a decline that resulted in a loss of 30 billion dollars in two days – touching off the Great Depression. From the age of 10 until he left home, Mac knew the realities of living off powdered milk, dried beans, and potatoes. He worked evenings and weekends on the farm to grow the produce needed to feed his family. He could remember a time when a day of work bought a can of syrup and recalled Christmases when an orange in a stocking was his only Christmas present.

In the free time available to him, Mac spent hours in the woods. He loved exploring, trapping, hunting, building forts, and playing cowboys and indians. There, like Chief Lock, Mac learned the value of hard work and the merits of creative problem solving.

As he got older his fun became less innocent. Hard experiences made Mac quite industrious. He used to tell a story about sneaking into a neighbor's chicken coop, stealing his chickens, then returning to his neighbor's front door the next day to sell the farmer's own chickens back to him. Mac also learned to make "home-made refreshments." He recalls,

> we had corn beer and berry wine in burned out stumps on every possum and coon trail for miles around. On hunting trips, we enjoyed pausing and partaking. But for me this kind of fun began to lose its thrill."
>
> One evening, I was a bit 'high' while singing lustily in the choir at our country revival. After the service, with glowing self-confidence, I told the preacher how much I had enjoyed his sermon. He ignored the compliment.
>
> 'Are you a Christian?' he asked.
>
> Having joined the church as a youngster and spent years singing in the choir I replied, 'Yes sir, I think so.'
>
> 'You think so!' he responded and he went on shaking hands.

> But I had been shaken to the core of my being. A little later at home I was tinkering with our Model T truck when the burden of sin overwhelmed me...I was so overtaken I had to quit working. I prayed, 'Lord, if you're going to take me, don't just take part of me, take all of me; from the top of my head to the tip of my toes.' I followed my Savior in really meaningful baptism. My life had been transformed. I had new purpose.[65]

Whatever came next – Mac had found purpose. His life came to personify Col 3:23 and Ecc 9:10 – "Whatever you hand finds to do, do it will all your might – working as unto the Lord, not unto man – Knowing from the Lord you will receive the inheritance as your reward."

Finding a Mission

Growing up, Mac developed a love for singing in church choirs. After surrendering his life to Christ, that love was further cultivated by the noted musician and music teacher J.B Coats. Coats wrote many well-known gospel songs including, "Where Could I Go (But to the Lord)?", "I'm Winging My Way Back Home," and "My Soul Shall Live On." He was a lifetime writer for the Stamps-Baxter Music Company, and was inducted into the Gospel Music Hall of Fame in 1992. He also was the choral director at Northeast Jones High School in Laurel, Mississippi. Mac and J.B's son Edsel became good friends.

Upon finishing high school, Mac was determined to enter college. He approached the school president at Jones County Junior College in Ellisville, Mississippi and said, "I don't have any money but I have to go to school. When do I start?" The president disregarded him off at first, but Mac's persistence managed to win him over.

Three months after beginning college another a third crisis occurred that would leave an indelible mark on the life of Chief Mac and his generation. December 7, 1941 the Japanese bombed Pearl Harbor. Unable to fight in World War II because of his stiff leg, Mac continued his studies. His senior year of college he served as principal of a grade school in Purvis, Mississippi.

---

[65] Unpublished Autobiography – Buford McKenzie

Groupwork and Fresh Air

[66]In 1945, upon graduating with a degree in History and Social Studies, Mac moved to Chicago to pursue music opportunities. There he participated in re-opening a Chicago settlement camp for underprivileged youth as the Assistant Director of Camp Farr[67] (A fresh-air children's camp where children from Chicago spent 2 week sessions raising vegetables, caring for animals, and participating in sports, games, and swimming in the camp's pool).[68] In 1946, Mac opened a division of the YMCA in Chicago that had been shut down during World War II.

He pursued work at the YMCA and in the settlement houses for three years and did graduate study in group work at George Williams College. George Williams College was named after the founder of the YMCA and was, "a national center for the development of group work as a profession."[69] There he encountered the work of Lyman Hudson, Harrison Elliott[70], Hedley Dimock, Louis Blumenthal, John Dewey, and

---

[66] https://www.lib.uchicago.edu/projects/centcat/city/city_img35.html

[67] https://www.geocaching.com/geocache/GC5Z35W_camp-farr-history?guid=5e96526a-c43b-4186-a320-3823d77e210d

[68] https://www.geocaching.com/geocache/GC5Z35W_camp-farr-history?guid=5e96526a-c43b-4186-a320-3823d77e210d

[69] "George Williams College: An Inventory of Its Records". University of Minnesota. Archived from the original on April 17, 2015. https://web.archive.org/web/20150417013829/http://special.lib.umn.edu/findaid/html/ymca/ygwc0001.phtml

[70] In the How and Why of Group Discussion written in 1923, Harrison Elliot writes, "Persons in the long run do successfully only what they figure out for themselves. Likewise enthusiasm for any course of action is in proportion to the amount of thought and effort a person has put into planning and deciding upon it."

"In discussion, the group members seek to share with each other the most serious problems and deepest convictions of their lives. There is no thought of trying to restrain persons with convictions from presenting them. If persons withhold their views for the sake of harmony, the conclusions will be unreliable compromises. Indeed the trustworthiness of group conclusion lies in the fact that no opinion can fully be relied on that has not been considered in the presence of those with contrary opinions…Group

others.

The ideals of groupwork resonated deeply with Mac. In these processes he saw synergy with the world we knew growing up on the farm and with his love for music. For Mac groupwork, problem solving, faith, the natural world, and music were linked!!

Mac would often say, "If my group can sing together, we can do anything together!" Singing required listening to those around you, submitting to a leader, agreeing on a tone, harmony and rhythm. Leading singing was far more than standing in front of a group and starting a song. While working for the YMCA, Mac attended a workshop on song leadership. A workbook from that conference he often referred reflects his ideals about leading music well:

> Leading in song is a skillful blending of many acts and the harmonizing of many attitudes. It is like driving an automobile and calls for the same awareness and coordination. The driver's feet are responsible for the clutch pedal, the brake, the accelerator, the starter. His hands must care for the wheel, the horn, the lights, the windshield wiper, the windows, the gear shift, the parking brake, the ignition, the radio, the heater, the sun visor, the cowl ventilator, and many other details. His eyes must also be busy with traffic, pedestrians, signs, lights, and visibility, and his ears also have important function. SO IT IS WITH THE SONG LEADER. Eyes, ears, mouth, hands, feet, and body, all have their definite functions to perform. The blending of all of these functions into a smooth-flowing, well-coordinated succession of clear, harmonious, understanding directive

---

discussion must go forward not in the spirit of bickering and petty jealousy and argument, but in that fellowship which recognizes that others hold contrary viewpoints with equal conviction and the progress demands that those in the discussion instead of compromising, attempt to integrate their experience and their conviction in a newer and better group will - which may be for these persons really the will of God. As Professor Sheffield has well said: 'Any solution of a controversy which is really to prevail in a practical sense must get from the group something more than a majority assent. It must take up into itself most of the emotional forces that have centered in the differing ideas represented in the group. A decision will be carried out far more satisfactorily if the minority against it have been brought into some adjustments toward it, instead of merely beaten as a faction. Such an adjustment is possible only if the decision embodies something contributed by the minority.'"

gestures – this is interpretative song leadership.[71]

This experience at the YMCA prepared Mac uniquely for his future work with Chief Lock and the Dallas Salesmanship Club Boys Camp.

In 1948, Mac returned to Mississippi for a year of work with the State Health Department as Assistant Coordinator for the Tuberculosis Control Unit. While there, Mac "traveled the state doing community organization and education."[72] Then, in 1949, "feeling the Lord's leadership,"[73] Mac went to Dallas, Texas, with his friend Edsel Coats where he "attended Music School while seeking new employment."[74]

After school, Edsel returned to Mississippi and lived in Gitano, wrote music and played piano for a number of gospel music groups including the Blackwood Brothers. He became the choral director at Northeast Jones High School in Laurel, Mississippi. There he put together a quartet made up of a few basketball players he drafted from a local park and a young man in his the choir named Ronnie Cottingham. The quartet began to sing together at District and State Festivals and, under Edsel's tutelage and accompaniment, later had radio success under the names the Troubadours and the Trailsmen.[75] Ronnie went on to become a successful evangelist and gospel musician.

Camping on Purpose

Mac dreamed of singing in a gospel quartet[76] but writes that "through the ministry of closed doors"[77] he finally wound up visiting the welfare department in Dallas where he was informed about Campbell Loughmiller's efforts to begin a camp for troubled boys. Intrigued, on May 27, 1949, he went for a visit.[78] Lock told him he may like it and he may not. Well, Mac liked it. He recalls, "I stayed 12 years on that visit,"[79]

---

[71] R. Clare Heald, "Good Song Leadership A YMCA Asset," Conference Handout for YMCA Midwest Conference Held at Lake Geneva Wisconsin, July 7-12, 1941.
[72] Ibid., 3.
[73] Ibid.
[74] Ibid.
[75] Ronnie Cunningham in interview with the author, April 3, 2017.
[76] Collins, "Tribute to Chief Mac and Lois."
[77] McKenzie, *Autobiography*, 3.
[78] *Club and Camp News: Salesmanship Club Boys Camp.* Vol 40, Thursday Sept 29, 1966. Insert in publication.
[79] McKenzie in interview with the author, August 17, 2010.

dropping out of music school and beginning to work at camp immediately.

Mac had found his mission. He often recalled, "The Lord said to me, 'Mac do camp!'"[80] The Lord showed him how to do it and never let him quit. He spent the rest of his life developing and perfecting the program. Mac would move quickly from summer pool manager to group counselor – beginning the third group, Beavers – in July 1949, less than two months after being employed at camp.[81] As early as 1950, Chief Mac was leading discussions in Chief orientation on groupwork[82] and late in 1954, Mac became the first Groupwork Supervisor.[83]

While at the pool, Mac made an important discovery. The camp had hired a champion swimmer to teach swimming to the boys, but the boys would not go near him. Mac recalls that "that professional swimmer was the loneliest person in camp. There was counselor in the Tehuacana group who could not swim. That was who the boys in the group wanted to teach them to swim."[84] "They would follow that Chief into the pool like an old hen with her chicks."[85] The ability did not matter. It was the relationship that made the boy feel secure to trust the counselor to teach him to swim. Chief Mac often says that, "the only thing worth a grain of salt at camp is the relationship between a boy and his Chief."[86]

Mac excelled at building relationships with at-risk youth and group work partly because of his leg injury as a child. He says

> I realize that all handicaps, be they mental, physical, or emotional, are related at a deeper level...Through the years my crippled leg has often given me an inroad to identifying with problems of others. It has provided unspoken communication to

---

[80] Ibid.
[81] Brochures and Woodland Springs Manual.
[82] A 1950 Chief Orientation manual reads, "The basic unit which we have to work with is the group. In the discussion by Chief Mac on groupwork, many problems will arise as to what to do. Use this sheet to make notes of the specific problems."
[83] Buford McKenzie in interview with the author, August 18, 2010. (Said he was a chief for 41/2 years before he became a supervisor.)
[84] Buford McKenzie in interview with the author, July 4, 2005.
[85] McKenzie in interview with the author, August 18, 2010.
[86] McKenzie in interview with the author, September 27, 2008.

> campers and their families that we don't have to let a problem stop us.[87]

Through these experiences and those throughout the rest of his career, he realized there were some things he could not do and that he needed his group's help. Throughout his career in working with troubled youth, Mac genuinely needed their help. The boys appreciated that, and Mac learned to use a group, not as a tool to manipulate, but because of what they had to offer. These ideas would become foundational to the development of the Loughmiller model.

The fruit of these relationships could be evidenced throughout the camp program, but the Chuck Wagon[88] program was a unique time when groups could share and build spirit. It is here Paul would share his accordion abilities, or Chief Mac would lead a song with his "golden singing voice"[89] or a Chief would play a guitar or piano. Sometimes sharing would be at the expense of good-hearted supervisors or other staff members. Billy Hood recalls one particular incidence where all of those present at Chuck Wagon shared a good laugh at Chief Mac's expense.

> Every once in a while we had an opportunity to perform planned skits, for the whole body of campers, after evening meals in the Chuck Wagon. We would sit around the campfire in our evening powwow in our campsite, and plan what we would do the next night. Our counselors would offer helpful suggestions and advice on the presentations. One time, on the prompting of our own Chiefs, we did an echo skit for the benefit of Chief Mac. Three campers positioned themselves at intervals of about one hundred feet apart, trailing away from the Chuck Wagon front door. One camper stood in the doorway, and would shout something for the other campers to repeat as echoes, falling away into the night. The last echo sequence of the skit was to be "Chief Mac is a good Chief!" Unbeknownst to the camper in the doorway, when he shouted "Chief Mac is a

---

[87] "Buford McKenzie Retires from Cameron," *Charity and Children* 102, no. 1 (January 1989), 7.

[88] The name for the dining hall at the camp. After meals it was common for groups to share with each other and sing during "Chuckwagon Program."

[89] Hood, *1950's Camp Experience*, 8.

> good Chief!"; the echo battalion was to respond "Ba-loney!"... "Ba-loney!"... "Ba-loney!" All went as advertised until that final echo sequence. The look, which contorted the face of the camper in the doorway, brought the house down with laughter from everyone, including Chief Mac.[90]

While Mac did have a unique knack for building relationships with troubled boys, in Chief Mac's style of groupwork it was not always the counselor who was able to get through to a boy. There was a boy who had been at camp for months and no one had ever been able to get through to him. After lunch one day, the 75-year-old dishwasher affectionately named Pa-Paw asked the boy, "Johnny, do you have a pocket knife?" That conversation was the breakthrough that boy needed. Mac learned it was important to work as a team. Everyone – the cook, the office worker, the maintenance man, the family worker, the Chief – has to, be saying the same things. When we are all working together, singing the same tune, we can move a boy forward.[91]

A key difference between the work of Redl and the work at Woodland Springs centered around the use of the group. Chief Lock's genius was combining treatment and groupwork.[92] Lock and Mac found that camp worked best with only two Chiefs in the group. A third added too much Chief power. "The counselor should not dominate the discussion, but...guide it in a way that elicits the honest feelings of all members."[93] Any one Chief, including Mac, often required the help of the group. From cooking, to rambling, to tent building, to talking through feelings, to problem solving, to restraining an angry camper, the group was always involved in the entire process and together the group learned from the problem. If a boy was angry, the group helped him calm down. In the early days, if he was out of control, the group helped the Chief restrain the boy. "It is in the repeated use of this [group] process that a boy develops the greatest insight into his own

---

[90] Ibid., 23.

[91] Nearly every conversation the author has had with Mac somehow includes these principles.

[92] McKenzie in interview with the author, September 17, 2010.

[93] Campbell Loughmiller, *Kids in Trouble: An Adventure in Education* ([city], TX: Wildwood Books, 1979), 69.

behavior."[94] Mac often described what love is to a camper using the illustration of a three-legged milking stool. Each leg – tender touch, personal responsibility, and firm limits – must be of equal length. If any one leg is too short or too long, the stool falls over. All three components must be working together equally for stability. Campbell Loughmiller said it this way:

> Although we cannot *make* a boy do anything, we do not let his negative behavior go unnoticed. He cannot just walk away when he is finished. He has to take responsibility for his behavior, face the reaction of his buddies and the counselors; but all of them are his friends. He is not coerced. His dignity is not affronted. He is not mistreated...his peers face him squarely and forcefully. He is not shielded from *anything*, but he is supported by *everything.* I have not seen a boy who could withstand the consistent effort of the group to help him when it was done firmly and realistically.[95]

At the Salesmanship Club Boys Camp all of Mac's experience found its culmination and application – his years growing up on the farm and exploring the woods, his love for music, his time working as a school principal, his degree in history and social studies, his fresh-air work, his YMCA work with at-risk youth, his groupwork training, and his faith.

---

[94] Ibid., 26.
[95] Ibid., 68-69.

CHAPTER 3: TRIAL AND ERROR

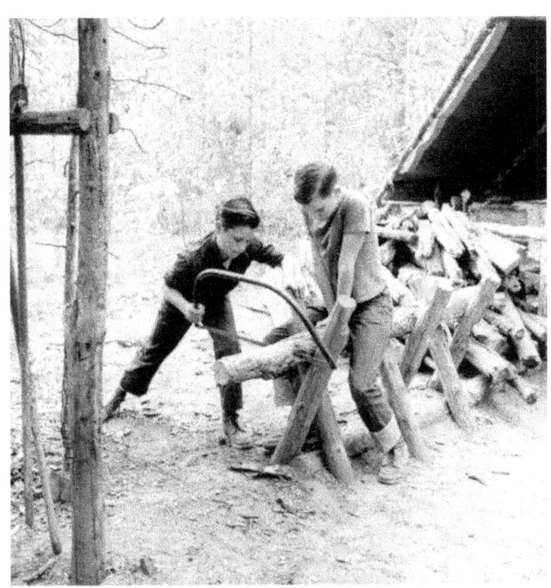

Camp Program

Camp Woodland Springs continued to grow and Lock recalls, "We made every mistake in the book!"[1] The third year brought a fourth and fifth group (Frontier and Trailblazers).[2] Yet camp remained simple. Chief Lock's home, for the first few years, served not only as a family dwelling, but was the office, commissary, hospital, first aid station, laundry, storage room, and whatever else was necessary.[3] The first cook was hired so the boys could

invest more of their time in something besides cooking. A dietician was also hired, but she had just graduated and asked if

[1] Loughmiller, conference held in Southern Pines, NC.
[2] Buford McKenzie, "Experience Curriculum in Camping and Outdoor Education at Camp Woodland Springs, Dallas Texas," paper developed at National Camp Aug 17, 1950, 1.
[3] Loughmiller, *Camp Life,* 3.

> she could have her friend join her and split the salary. They shared a tent and our house was where they did their washing and ironing and "primping."[4]

Lynn recalls:

> Once the camp board met at camp – where else? at our house. I wasn't home and the phone kept ringing. Mr. Mac said, "who answers the phone when you aren't here?" "My wife," Campbell said. "You need a secretary," he said. So a desk was installed in one corner of the 20' x 30' living room, and we had our office and a part-time secretary.[5]

Eventually the Chuck Wagon, store room, an office, a warehouse, and a swimming pool were built. Even when these other buildings were established, the Loughmiller home was often the hub of activity. For example, very late one night a counselor,

> John Spencer...came into our house, pulled up a chair beside our bed, and proceeded to expound his latest problem. There was a sort of rapport between us all—and we learned...about bed-wetters, liars, thieves, those with low self-esteem, speech defects, hate, poverty, fear – the whole gamut of human disorders...In the final analysis, it was as Campbell often said, "You just love the hell out of them."[6]

These types of late night discussions were not uncommon. Not all took place by the director's bed, but it was through these types of discussions that camp philosophy was hammered out. Mac recalls many late nights sitting out on the porch with Lock talking through camp processes and ironing out the program.

---

[4] Ibid., 3.
[5] Ibid., 3.
[6] Ibid., 4.

Cows, Rifles, and Power Tools

There was much to iron out in those early days. One time, inspired by L.B. Sharp, a Covered Wagon Group was attempted.[7] The boys lived in campsite in covered wagons and the board purchased a pair of mules to pull the wagons when the boys wanted to go on a trip. All types of boys were brought into camp. On one occasion a boy got angry and "disemboweled a horse,"[8] and on another, a boy tried to pluck out an animal's eye. "About 30 per cent of boys are seriously introverted, the others are the 'acting out' type whose 'acts' may include anything from...gouging out the eyes of rabbits and squirrels, ripping canvas shelters, setting fires in [the] camp's wooded areas...or stealing and wrecking cars."[9] With these types of boys, covered wagons and animals were not a good idea.

However, animals were attempted once more when a board member suggested having the boys care for cattle. The board then purchased 40 head of cattle. The cows provided at least one lesson in group work. Mac recalls gathering the boys around and saying, "Watch this group work!" Mac walked over and started talking to the head cow, and after a couple minutes the cow went in the gate and the rest followed. The problem was, over time, the Chiefs ended up taking care of cows while "the boys raised Cain and went fishing."[10] Chief Lock said that "in less than one year, we unanimously agreed that cows were not camp material."[11] It was decided that Woodland Springs would be a boys camp not a cow ranch.

A similar fate came to a gardening attempt. Tom Harrover, a camper at the time recalls that

> probably of some significance regarding the operation of a 'therapeutic camp' was the decision that we boys should have the experience of raising our own food. Don't know where this inspired idea came from, but I'm fairly sure that it came to us

---

[7] Lock had attended National Camp where they had Covered Wagon groups and the article "Catch Up! Catch Up!" written about Covered Wagon Camping, published in 1935 and 1943, was found in Mac's files with Lock's name on it.

[8] Smith, *The Worth of a Boy*, 3.

[9] Ibid.

[10] Buford McKenzie in interview with the author, August 18, 2010.

[11] Loughmiller, conference held in Southern Pines, NC.

> from above. The camp's ranger had a tractor and plow and he did the basic preparation for a huge garden, in the large open field on the property that had been lying fallow for many years. Using hoes and rakes, we were shown how to do the final preparation for planting. We then set out corn, green beans, yellow squash, potatoes, spinach, lettuce and tomatoes and probably more. From that point forward, our daily routine included at least an hour or more in the field, learning to tend a growing garden...The entire enterprise was a losing proposition from the get-go. Between voracious insects, drought and hours of tedious work in the Texas heat, our efforts resulted in significant disappointment. Inadequate thought had been given to the fact that every boy in camp was there because of difficulty in toeing up to responsibilities and this effort turned out to be overwhelming responsibility in spades. We eventually began going out of our way to avoid even seeing the field. If we produced enough of any single item to make a meal in the dining hall, I am unaware of that.[12]

Mac adds that extended trips also made gardening an impossibility.[13]

Other suggestions were made as well. One board member thought there should be a craft shop complete with every power tool a boy could need. Campbell was not in favor of the idea, he said, "Our boys can't focus that long...a disturbed kid would cut his finger off...a boy has everything he needs to whittle or paint in campsite."[14] But he was persuaded to allow the board to try it. After a short time, they locked up the shop and didn't use it, without any protest from the boys or the board. Another time, a board member thought it would be good if the boys learned to shoot rifles, so rifles were purchased and kept locked in the Trading Post. All went well until a boy broke into the Trading Post, stole a rifle, and took it out into a field, where he leveled it at Mac when Mac came looking. Promptly it was decided to collect all the rifles and the range ceased to be a part of camp life. Other ideas too ridiculous to consider were proposed. Among them were electric lights and flush toilets. The boys took pride in being able to meet their own

---

[12] Tom Harrover Memoir, p. 6.

[13] McKenzie in interview with the author, August 18, 2010.

[14] Loughmiller, conference held in Southern Pines, NC.

needs and "could do so without the help of the electric company."[15] Lock points out that if pit toilets were installed, "you need a road to empty the toilets and that would mar the environment that we prized greatly."[16] Boys took such pride in their pit toilets they often wanted to show them off. No one could see a reason to deprive a kid of such an accomplishment.

Not all accruements of this nature, added to the program. "They were all in the same basket and abandoned for the same reasons:"[17] the advantages of a de-centralized program and the enjoyment and therapeutic value of routine camp living. Gradually it was realized that most of the growth at camp occurred in campsites – in routine living. The boys enjoyed the experience of coordinating their own program. Additions like caring for livestock, gardening, a rifle range, archery, and horseback riding required coordination of schedules and limited group autonomy. Second, camper exit interviews showed that boys' favorite experiences in camp revolved around building and maintaining their campsites.[18] Other program additions became distractions and took away from the therapeutic process in campsite instead of aiding in a boy's progress. It is in this simple setting that "a disturbed boy faces basic realities. Here he is able to acquire self-sufficiency and to learn how to get along with other people in order to function better in the larger society to which he will return."[19]

Democracy in Action

This leads to another important principle. Camp was democracy in action (or at least a republic in action). It was not, and is not, a place where kids are told what to do. Boys planned their own program, and as a group they chose what they wanted to do. They were responsible. A counselor would not often tell his group to do this or to do that; rather, camp was a program where the boys were responsible for their own programming and welfare. The boys got to (or had to) decide what to do and how to handle situations. L.B. Sharp writes:

---

[15] Ibid.

[16] Ibid.

[17] Grover Loughmiller in interview with the author, September 5, 2010.

[18] Ken Edgar and Grover Loughmiller in interview with the author, September 5, 2010.

[19] Bert Kruger Smith, *The Worth of a Boy* (Austin: The Hogg Foundation, 1958), 6.

> A study of the struggles and living conditions of our early settlers gives us a basis for our camping program. They lived a life of daring and adventure. They were on their own as individuals and families. Out of their pattern of living was created our concept and form of democracy. A careful study of their progress will show that shelter, food, self-occupation, spiritual influence, group living, and community effort were basic elements in the development of our country.[20]

These were core elements at Camp Woodland Springs. Boys were held responsible and were free to set their own agendas to pursue whatever adventures they put their minds to. "There is no need for regimentation, regularity, and conformity to the general camp program. There are no departments or activities. Theirs is a life unto themselves, bringing successes, pleasures and adventures – *camping*."[21]

For boys who were failing in the public school system, it provided a remarkable opportunity for them to be caught up in learning, being successful without realizing they were learning at all. When a boy is outside,

> the sociology of the classroom disappears. The marshalling of children in uniform rows no longer has any point or purpose. The rule of silence simply falls away. The children swarm all around the object of study; they *ask* to be allowed to see; they *ask* to know. They make their own questions, and under a wise teacher, they will be teased into making their own answers. Teacher and pupil almost exchange places. The answers are *found*; they are not *given*. And every phenomenon that is observed, is seen in its proper relationship with everything else with which it has any affinity.[22]

---

[20] L.B. Sharp, "Camping and Democracy." *1939 Year Book*. (Washington DC: National Park Service, United States Department of the Interior) 7.
[21] L.B. Sharp, "The Role of Camping and Our American Heritage," *The Camping Magazine* 14 (February 1942): 36.
[22] Lawrence H. Conrad, Sr., "Lloyd B. Sharp's Philosophy of Education," in *Perspectives on Outdoor Education...Readings*, eds. George W. Donaldson and Oswald Goering (Dubuque: Wm C Brown Company Publishers, 1972), 17

In the book, *Camping and Character*, Dr. Hedley S. Dimock writes,

> We have nothing but admiration for the boy who positively objects to attending *classes* in camp in which persons attempt to make *subjects* interesting to him. Formalized academic procedure of that kind decidedly is in competition with wholehearted group purposes. It does not even indoctrinate. It does worse than that. It vaccinates the camper against purposeful enterprises. Learning goes on best when the need for it is seen and felt. [23]

Dr. William Heard Kilpatrick, a professor of Education at Columbia University continues,

> What is learned separately and apart from its' felt meaning connections is likely not to be integrated either into life or into character. From these considerations it follows that learning and life situations are neither to be separated from the other without hurt.[24]

At camp a boy is always dealing in one way or another with the impersonal realities of nature – the July sun or a blue norther in January, a fire in the woods or the sting of a nettle. These elements impinge from all sides"[25] and the implications of these "difficulties and problems are settled by group discussion." [26] The group must decide how to construct its shelters, plan its menus, cook some of its meals, cut its wood, repair its equipment, arrange its own recreation, provide sanitary facilities, maintain the trails and do all things necessary for safe and responsible living. These tasks provide objective discipline and play a major part in developing the camper's sense of social responsibility.[27]

It is the job of the Chief to monitor and guide, but ultimately the group must be free to decide. However, this freedom cannot exist as long as one member is afraid of another. There must be boundaries. As a result it is important that the

---

[23]H.S. Dimock and C.E. Hendry, *Camping and Character* (New York: Association Press, 1929), 85.
[24] Ibid., ix.
[25] Loughmiller, *Wilderness Road,* 78.
[26] Sharp, "The Role of Camping and Our American Heritage."
[27] Taken from the Salesmanship Club Boys Camp Woodland Springs Brochure.

> counselors are able to utilize the group in the interest of each member. This requires that all members be involved in decision affecting them...and they must share responsibility for the success or failure of anything they undertake...without this freedom – even the freedom to fail – there is little opportunity for personal growth.[28]

It is here that a group learned a major tenet of democracy: "Discipline cannot exist in a group unless each member is free to voice his opinions with confidence that they will be considered."[29] It is the counselor's job to ask, "What is the best way to do this or that?" If every boy in a group were not free to express his thoughts and opinions without fear of ridicule, rejection, or retaliation, he was not free. When a boy came, and comes, to realize this truth and feels free to speak up, he will be quick to point out when any other boy, or the counselor, squelches this freedom. However, just as is true for this principle to work in our country, it must occur continually. In a group "if this [democratic] process is not used *all* of the time, it will not work *any* of the time."[30] It is in this context that a group truly learns what it means to be free. Campbell Loughmiller writes, "[group work]...is not something employed for an hour or two a day. It is a method consistently used from the time a boy gets to camp until he leaves. It is the most effective tool we have found."[31]

Therapy

Occasionally, for some boys, "several private psychiatrists in Dallas or...the Dallas Child Guidance Clinic"[32] partnered with the program to provide formal psychiatric treatment. However, the main treatment occurred in the woods with the boys and the counselors. Lock writes:

> The delinquent boys were usually easier to work with than the emotionally handicapped and took less time to regain their footing. They had a lot of power, a lot of steam, but no sense of direction. They were serving the wrong ends, but they were capable. If one of them wanted to rob a store, he could do it as

[28] Loughmiller, *Kids in Trouble*, 61.
[29] Ibid., 65.
[30] Ibid., 65.
[31] Loughmiller, *Wilderness Road*, 72.
[32] Smith, 1958, 6.

> intelligently as anyone. So the job was to help them change their outlook, their sens..e of values, and help them move toward constructive purposes.[33]

As they experimented, they came to realize that a boy wasn't a problem that needed fixed.[34] The boy didn't need to be a patient. Lock writes that the boy was "not sick and we are not therapists...we are friends and partners in the enterprise of meeting life requirements."[35] In most cases "we undertook the full care of a boy including his educational needs, and we did it without anything resembling a school, without text books, and without psychiatrists, psychologists, or specialists."[36]

> The use of specialists...underscores the assumption that the boy is the problem...it lessen(s) the confidence of a counselor...It is what it says to the boy that matters most – [it communicates that] we see him as the problem, that we must do something to him to make him more normal when, as a matter of fact, we should be changing the things outside of the boy. *We need to remove the roadblocks and let the boy's own resources carry him forward (emphasis added).*[37]

The personality changes that took place at camp, "are not so much the result of something that is taught as they are of a relationship that is established."[38] *What the boy needs is to feel secure in a caring relationship with at least one adult he can trust implicitly.*[39]

> We tried to emphasize the positive things about each boy, to use his strengths and help him expand his area of competence. The biggest change any boy had to make was to gain respect for himself, to see himself as worthwhile, to improve his self-image. This in all cases, I believe, was the biggest single thing he had to accomplish; and they had to learn to trust adults. Almost no kid had any confidence in adults when he came to camp. We were the "enemy" and it was the biggest test a counselor had – to

---

[33] Loughmiller, *These Fish had Wings*. 297.
[34] Buford McKenzie in interview with the author, August 26, 2008.
[35] Loughmiller, *Kids in Trouble*, 22-23.
[36] Loughmiller, *These Fish had Wings*, 297.
[37] Loughmiller, *Kids in Trouble*. 42-43.
[38] Loughmiller, *Kids in Trouble*. 37.
[39] Ibid., 29.

> live through this period of distrust. Our saving grace was the group culture that developed out of their own experience after a group was constituted, and after they had lived together a few months. One boy would go home and another one would take his place, but we never had a totally new group.[40]

Grover Loughmiller cites a study done by Weisz in 1995 that found that

> in a review of 150 studies of child psychotherapy...paraprofessionals, defined as individuals without graduate training in mental health, but trained to implement a therapeutic regime, tended to generate larger effect sizes therapeutically with children than did professionals or graduate students.[41]

This harnessing of curiosity and empowerment of a boy to use the resources available to him to propel himself forward is the educational process that occurs naturally at camp. Tom Harrover, a former camper, recalls:

> if pressed to cite a single thing that accounts for the success of the therapeutic program, it would be the device of lifting a boy entirely from the environment in which he was failing, and then immersing him entirely into that of camp – a protected cocoon where the immediate concerns are life's basics and where solutions come mainly by cooperative action. I have no doubt that the brilliant success lies solely in the purity of this essence.[42]

At camp, a boy was immediately successful. He was living outside, chopping his own wood, cooking his own food, living together with nine other boys and two counselors, and making his way. He can be recognized for strengths ignored in school: a keen eye for spotting birds and wildlife, his ability to make his bed quickly, or clean a lantern. It may be his "physical strength for cutting wood, skill in handling a canoe, [the] ability to tell a good story, a good singing voice, [or] countless other ways [that help]...a boy gain the respect of his peers as well as self-respect."

---

[40] Loughmiller, *These Fish Had Wings*. 297.
[41] Grover Loughmiller, "Origins and Directions of Therapeutic Camping," 72.
[42] Harrover, unpublished memoir, 7.

Big Move

By 1953, Dallas was continuing to grow and the property 7 miles outside of Dallas was being crowded out until part of camp was inside the city limits, so Chief Lock, Chief Mac, and the Salesmanship Club board began looking for a new property.[43] After two years of intensive search, an 833-acre site was located 90 miles east of the present property in Hawkins, Texas. The property was purchased at an average cost of $65.00 per acre[44] and all of camp was "active in the site development."[45]

The first step was to determine the site for the 17-acre lake. Once this was done, "one group began cutting the timber from the lake bed, and upon the dam's completion [in October 1956], another group got it sodded and sowed winter rye to prevent washing by the fall rains." "By Easter morning, 1957, the spillway overflowed from the drought-breaking rains that spring."[46]

Groups made field trips to the new site, removing "remains of old fences[;]... some boundary fencing was done, old abandoned wells were

---

[43] Buford McKenzie in interview with the author, August 19, 2010.
[44] "How We Came to Be: The History of Therapeutic Wilderness Camping As Practiced by Jack and Ruth Eckerd Foundation" (unpublished document found in Chief Mac's files), 7.
[45] Loughmiller, *Wilderness Road.* 58.
[46] "How We Came to Be," 7.

filled in,"[47] groups aided in "clearing road ways...planting several thousand pine seedlings, [and] building check dams and diversion terraces to stop serious soil erosion."[48] "All groups participated. One boy brought to our attention the fact that we were spending more time at the new site than at the old, and suggested we declare officially that we were moved – and so we did."[49] On March 15, 1957 ,[50] the official move took place and the name of the program was changed from Camp Woodland Springs to The Salesmanship Club Boys Camp.

Since the buildings from the old campsite were to be moved to the new, it was eight months before we had any permanent facilities other than the water supply and the warehouse. Everything else was under canvas, but we did not lose a day's camping.[51]

Hospital tents were used for the Chuckwagon and gas and water lines were run into the tent to cook until the building arrived.[52] The boys lived in pup tents[53] "at sites marked for camp buildings so they would not have to do unnecessary cutting."[54] Even Chief Lock and his family moved into a tent on the property for about a year[55] while the transition was being made.[56] Lock recalls that "some of our best programming came about during this time."[57]

"Each group was given a map of the camp, a compass, and 30 days"[58] to decide where their permanent campsite would be. No group explored for less than three weeks before they made a final decision. A bathhouse and a deep well for water supply were the first amenities provided.[59] "Trails were laid out and developed" and the outdoor outdoor chapel was selected and constructed. Everyone aided in cutting down the trees, cutting them into seven-foot sections, and sawing them down the middle to complete the benches. They then "built a small

---

[47] Loughmiller, *Wilderness Road*, 58.
[48] "How We Came to Be." 7.
[49] Loughmiller, *Wilderness Road.* 58.
[50] "How We Came to Be." 7.
[51] Loughmiller, *Wilderness Road.* 58.
[52] McKenzie in interview with the author, August 18, 2010.
[53] Ibid.
[54] Loughmiller, *Wilderness Road.* 58.
[55] Buford McKenzie in interview with the author, August 25, 2010.
[56] McKenzie in interview with the author, August 18, 2010..
[57] Loughmiller, *Wilderness Road.* 58.
[58] Ibid., 58.
[59] Ibid., 58.

speaker's stand, put a sign at the entrance, and the chapel was ready."[60] "Other than the buildings themselves, most of the site development was accomplished by the boys."[61] The oldest group even mapped out the plan for the water line.

After a little instruction in the use of the transit, [they] determined the elevations from the water supply to each point where water was to be delivered; and with the use of friction-loss tables, they figured the pipe size needed in order to have enough pressure at the end of each line.[62] All of camp then pitched in to "lay the water lines from the supply to their campsite. Through roots, rock, sand, and clay, each group dug the lines for a third to half a mile, then jointed, laid, and covered them."[63] When the effort was finished, each group of boys

> moved a hundred miles to a tract of land without so much as a trail on it and, except for canvas, built themselves a new home out of native materials they found there. This called for creative imagination in materials, design, and workmanship. It elicited the best efforts of everyone...they worked like Trojans and never realized they were working...A dollar an hour, or any other wage, would not have produced half the motivation, the spark, the enthusiasm, or the results.[64]

Legally the Salesmanship Club held the title to the property, but there was no question who the boys felt it belonged to. Lock recalls:

> The point was brought to me vividly one time at the Dallas campsite, when the contractor needed to get a water line from a newly constructed building through a hundred yards of dense woods. Because he could not use the ditcher without cutting a wide swath, he told the older boys that he would pay them to dig the ditch by hand. They agreed on the price and went to work. They were nearing completion when a bright ten-year-old came along a nearby trail on his way to get food for dinner. "Whatcha doing?" he asked. "Digging a ditch for the water line," they replied. "We've done made $27.00." "Who's it for?" the youngster asked. "It's for all of us," they replied. "Whatcha getting

[60] Loughmiller, *Wilderness Road*, 59.
[61] Ibid., 59.
[62] Ibid., 58.
[63] Loughmiller, *Wilderness Road*, 59.
[64] Ibid., 60.

paid for then?" he asked. This put the boys to thinking. They had made a deal with the contractor, but the Club was paying the contractor to build a water line for their use. They had not quite thought of it in this way until the ten-year-old brought it to their attention. They began to mull it over, and finally decided to give the money to the camp. This was not a counselor-inspired decision. We compromised by accepting the money to buy something that would benefit all the boys at camp, not the one group.[65]

Problems are to be Solved

How Stealing a Cadillac led to a Graduate Degree

One of the most important aspects of camp was, and is, in dealing with problems effectively. When attitude problems arise, punishment is not doled out. And at times it can mark a significant step in a boy's maturation. Some of the most fun stories seem to revolve around the runaway. One of the greatest occurred in 1955 at the Cotton Bowl. Each year the Salesmanship Club sponsored an exhibition pre-season game and 1955 was no exception. Earlier that year Doak Walker, the standout Southern Methodist University athlete who, "led the Mustangs to back-to-back Southwest Conference championships in 1947 and 1948, while winning every individual honor college football had to offer"[66] – the man responsible for the upper deck that was added to the Cotton Bowl to handle the record crowds he attracted – announced 1955 would be his final season in the National Football League. His final game in Texas would be held at the Cotton Bowl where the Detroit Lions would face the Philadelphia Eagles in a preseason game. Forty thousand fans turned out, "not about to miss Walker's final appearance in the Cotton Bowl. In a halftime ceremony, Number 37's many admirers showered him with praise and present. The state fair gave him a solid gold, lifetime pass to the stadium he 'built' and, not to be outdone, Matty Bell, his former coach, handed him a solid gold membership card in the Mustang Club. [But it] was hard to top the showroom-new Cadillac from a group of anonymous donors."[67] It was this Cadillac that caught the eye

---

[65] Ibid., 59-60.
[66] Bartee Haile, "Doak Walker's Last Football Season." *The Cameron Herald*, July 29, 2010 Online
[67] Ibid.

of a particular camper who was helping to usher that game. When he had come to camp, the police had told Campbell: "You don't need this boy, yes you don't want him...we want to talk to him about two robberies in West Dallas." When the police approached the boy he told them, "I robbed the one on the 29th, but I am not sure about the other one. I think I did, but I can't remember." When this boy saw the Cadillac, he couldn't help himself. He told his Chief he needed to go to the bathroom. A few minutes later they went looking for him and could not find him. It turns out he snuck down, stole Doak Walker's brand new Cadillac, and was driving around the stadium. Later that boy graduated from high school as the Salutatorian and earned a master's degree from North Texas State University.

Running Away...to the Juvenile Detention Center?

Billy Hood recalls in his memoir one particular occasion he thought it prudent to leave camp property unannounced.

> Running away was not an uncommon goal among us campers. Several boys, myself included, ran away from the camp more than once...maybe it was home sickness, perhaps rebellion against being sent to the camp, the temporary "celebrity" status gained among other campers in having been a fugitive or some other peer influence. For whatever reason, some of us thought "running away" was the thing to do...We were not tied to a post, or chained to a railing, nor confined under lock and key. We were given the freedom to make poor decisions and exercise our free will. Running away did not get you out of the camp, nor did it get you locked up as a delinquent. No problems were solved, to the contrary, more were created. We learned individually, and collectively, problems do not disappear when you refuse to face them. Often they tend to fester and grow in their enormity. "Running away" adds another unpleasant dimension, which requires resolution...To learn a lesson well, sometimes it had to be learned firsthand.[68]
>
> There were two of us plotting this daring foray. I recall the other boy was Danny Hill. We were around fourteen years old when we launched our bona fide criminal careers. At the time we actually

[68] Hood, *1950's Camp Experience*, 14.

did the deed, we weren't even thinking about the gravity of the act we were committing. At about three hours into our caper, we had changed our minds about being real criminals.

Danny and I were in the Tejas tribe. Our campsite was located within a half-mile or so from the Community Building on the new camp property in east Texas. This building also had a special name, but I do not recall what that name was now. I had just recently been returned to the camp, and was still angry about being taken away from my friends in Dallas, though they were in reality part of the reason I had been sent back. The camp's central parking lot was an area in front of the Community Building. I don't recall if we actually planned which vehicle we were going to take, but the plan was to steal a vehicle and drive to Dallas, some one hundred miles west. We waited until the camp had settled down and we were satisfied everyone was fast asleep, then crept out of the campsite and made our way quietly to the parking area.

Once among the cars and one older pick-up truck, we chose the truck. It was a 1950 or 1951 Chevrolet as I remember. Perhaps the keys had been left in the ignition before and we had noticed it. I surely do not recall trying to start the truck without keys, and neither of us had developed the skills, which that would have required! As quietly as we could, we inched our way out of camp and down to highway 80 for the trip west. Just getting to the highway was a scary proposition. Between us, we had no real experience behind the wheel on open roadways. I scared myself silly more than once, and I think Danny was equally frightened on more than one occasion during our journey. None-the-less, we were on our way and in the process of "escaping" the confines of the camp. As I recall, I was driving when we entered Dallas.

The reality of what we had done began to sink in as we approached the city. I had come to the starkly clear conclusion that I did not want to be a criminal. Danny and I discussed it at length, and he also had misgivings about our crime spree. I also reached another eye opening conclusion at this particular moment. Those friends, the ones I had run away to rejoin, were not important enough for me to ruin my life over. When we reached the city, I drove directly to the Juvenile Detention Center on Harry Hines Boulevard and knocked on the door. When the

> attending officer opened the door, I explained who we were and what we had done, handing him the keys to the truck. All of those times I had been allowed to fail and recover, over the years I had spent in the camp, had come back in a rush. I recognized the failure, and pursued the recovery on my own.
>
> For me, as for others who continued to observe my progress or lack thereof, this was a long-awaited turning point in my development as a person. There must have been some that thought I would never reach this juncture of my own volition. The resulting changes, which took place in my life, would be applauded as major steps in my maturing process. Those who really cared about me had witnessed my passage from delinquency to responsibility. Now, as I look back, it was indeed a fond moment![69]

Handled appropriately, problems are not problems. They are opportunities for growth and self-reflection. Thomas Edison famously said, "I have never failed, I've just found 10,000 ways that won't work." When we listen, seek to understand, and help a boy explore his feelings instead of punishing him for having overwhelming feelings, we earn the right to glimpse inside at the real problems plaguing the young person and work together toward meaningful solutions. As boys are increasingly able to self-regulate and find their own solutions, they are ready for larger challenges.

The Importance of Adventure (Trips)

Trips have always been an integral part of the camp program. In the early days of camp, when someone spoke of a trip, they

> The Trip to Lake Texoma is one that really stands out, for having now become almost mystical in my memory. It was a summer trip and for the ride up there we were packed into the back of an old pickup and the camp's ¾-ton stake-bed truck. The canoes were secured to racks overhead and they provided welcome shade for us. I don't think that I can capture with words the experience of laying there on top of the gear in the back of the truck as we went along the two-lane highway, the hot dry air rushing by, and looking out at the passing summer fields. It is an image that is burned into my mind and it remains as haunting to me as the howl of a wolf at full moon must have been to Jack London.
>
> -Tom Harrover (former camper)

[69] Hood, *1950's Camp Experience*, 24-25.

were thinking of a day trip off camp property in a couple of the Chief's personal vehicles. The group likely got curious about a subject and decided to leave camp to study further. Trips were taken to businesses and factories like the Proctor and Gamble facility in Dallas, the Dr. Pepper Bottling Plant, Mrs. Bairds Bakery, a jelly canning plant south of Dallas, a pottery manufacturing plant and a fishing lure production facility,[70] a meat packing plant, the airport (Love Field), a dairy, an ice plant and a TV station. [71] Other trips went to natural facilities like Elm Creek, which flowed through the property, Eagle Mountain Lake, Lake Whitney,[72] or the Trinity River. [73] The first long trip[74] however, was not a canoe trip, but "a caravan of two counselors' cars and two U-Haul trailers taking Chief Lock and the Tejas group and their Chiefs into the Big Bend National park area" [75] "to explore Southwest Texas."[76] After this, trips lasting 30 to 40 days at a time were taken as far east as the Cypress Swamp of Cadoo Lake on the Border of Louisiana and as far west as the Carlsbad Caverns of New Mexico.[77]

The First Long Canoe Trip: The Trinity River

The first long canoe trip was a trip on the Trinity River. The river was close enough to camp, that groups typically hiked there. Tom Harrover recalls:

> Trips to the Trinity River were always day trips and never involved overnights. We took the canoes over there only once and about the only things I can remember from that were the extensive shallows that required exhausting portages. We were very impressed to learn that the shallows were an old and historic river ford used by Indians and then settlers after them. We must have trucked the canoes over there, because the camp was close enough to the river that we normally always hiked over – but way too far to lug the canoes on foot. Regardless, on at least one occasion we and the canoes got there somehow. In

---

[70] Billy Hood Memoir, 24.
[71] Tom Harrover Memoir, 6.
[72] Billy Hood Memoir, 9.
[73] Tom Harrover Memoir, 5.
[74] Ibid.
[75] "How We Came to Be," 7.
[76] Ibid., 7.
[77] Video, "A Boy's World: The Story of Camp Woodland Springs," approximately 1954.

> the chalky cliffs where we always made a point of hiking to, it was sometimes possible to find fool's gold and that was highly prized stuff! Fossils were also sometimes turned up and that was always fun! A number of arrowheads were also found but I was never that lucky. [78]

In December 1951 the Tejas group, after numerous day trips to the Trinity River, became curious about where the river went. The group spent several months researching the river. The Health Department said it could not be done.[79] The shallows and portages (carrying a boat on land), combined with the flooding problems, made it impossible. This however did not deter the group. When it finally came down to making a decision about going, Chief Lock told them to make up their mind whether they would do it or not. Mac recalls looking at his co-Chief Bob Walker and asking, "Are you a coward?" Bob retorted, "When are we leaving?" The next morning the first long river trip began. The Tejas group canoed 500 miles down the Trinity River from Dallas to the Gulf of Mexico. When they began, Texas was in the midst of a long drought. Mac recalls, "The water in the river was mainly sewage from Dallas and Fort Worth. In the first 15 days, we did 15 miles per day. In some places, there was just enough water for canoes to get through."[80] One time, when they ran out of drinking water, they flagged down a boater and yelled over to ask him where they could get some water. He yelled back, "It's right under you!" That night they boiled the water and made cocoa.

> Then the rains came. We had heard about the rains in Dallas and it took two to three days for it to catch up to us. Then we made 30 miles per day. At one point, the river was so crooked we ended up one day in the campsite from the night before.[81]

When they reached the end of the river, they overshot it by five miles. When they realized their mistake, there was nothing they could do because gravel had been thrown up on both banks to make a channel for boats. In addition, the tide was going out. The only thing to do was paddle back against the tide. They reached Anahuac exhausted, but the entire town had been waiting for them and gave them a grand

---

[78] Tom Harrover Memoir, 5.

[79] McKenzie in interview with the author, August 25, 2010.

[80] Ibid.

[81] Ibid.

welcome. A reporter took them to a café and fed them and put them up in a gym. A family invited them out for dinner and they ate until they were stuffed. After dinner, the family took them out in the bay to teach them to tong for oysters. The boys were so stuffed they could barely eat the oysters. Senator Lyndon Johnson from Texas even met them there. They were the first group in history, other than perhaps the Native Americans, to canoe the entire Trinity River.[82] Since then, long canoe trips have been customary at wilderness camps.

The First Turkey in the Hole

It was another long canoe trip on the Trinity River that began a tradition at camp that continues to this day. On November 11, 1967, the Tejas group left for a trip on the Trinity River. The group had been having a hard time on the trip so instead of going home for the Thanksgiving Homesday, they stayed on to complete their river trip. On November 21, 1967, they found a campsite around 3:00. After a two hour problem, they climbed up on a levee. From there they could see a ranch in the distance. The group set up camp and Chief Everett Lindstrom hiked out to check on a resupply point. It took two hours to walk from the river to Creslenn Ranch near Gallimo Lake to call camp. When he arrived, he discovered they could not get food where they were, so plans were made with Mr. Johnson and Mr. Wheeler, an old time friend of camp, for a food and supply pickup further down the river.

The next morning, the group was on the river by 8:15 to beat Chief Mac to their meeting place. Shortly thereafter, the group hit a log jam and were able to dig their way through in about a half an hour without a portage. Thirty minutes later, they passed Cedar Creek and were getting a little anxious about finding the landing where they would meet. Finally, a boy spotted it on the left side of the river. They nearly missed it! Shortly after their arrival, Chief Mac and Mr. Johnson drove up. Much to the surprise of the group, Chief Mac showed up with a turkey in his hand and a box of aluminum foil. The group unloaded the bus and while Mac was telling them

> to be sure to keep their canoes tied up, one of our loaded ones was floating down the stream. The group responded quite well,

[82] Ibid.

> and in a matter of seconds we had Chief Dale and Joe going after it. The campsite was not at all ideal, but we managed to get it set up...and sent [Mac and Mr. Johnson] on their way.[83]

It was there, just beyond the confluence of the Trinity River and Cedar Creek, that the first Turkey in the Hole at the Salesmanship Club Boys Camp occurred[84]. Everett writes,

> Thanksgiving Day and a good one indeed. We began about midnight by putting the 22-pound turkey on to cook. This we did by wrapping five layers of foil around it, putting a good sized pan of butter in, all the water we had left in a canteen, a fourth of a box of salt, a good bit of pepper in it. Then we buried it in a deep bed of coals [right there on the riverbank] covered by sand. Right after breakfast part of the group went for water and the rest of us started dinner. We fixed a big pot of dressing, a pan full of gravy, some English peas, plenty of tea and a gallon of fruit cocktail. When we put it all on the table we made, it really looked like Thanksgiving. The turkey---! It was golden brown on the outside and tender and juicy all the way through. The white meat was even juicy. We ate until we could eat no more. There was very little of anything at all left. Not even enough leftovers for supper. During the most important game of the year, we took a much-needed siesta and started packing our new food supply. By the time the aggies beat T.U. 10-7, we had most of the food ready to go. Right after supper we gathered for a Thanksgiving Service. The spirit seemed very good and we ended by singing Christmas Carols.[85]

The group continued their trip, and on December 18, 1967, they reached Anahuac, Texas, having canoed 710 miles in 37 days.

Tragedy Strikes

Another innovation during the early years at Camp Woodland Springs was the camper-built raft trip. "High on the list of adventure was this eight to nine-week journey from Lake Texoma down the Red River

---

[83] Everett Lindstrom, "Tejas Trinity River Trip Log."
[84] Coordinates are 32.073628, -96.085347
[85] Everett Lindstrom, "Tejas Trinity River Trip Log."

into the Mississippi and on to New Orleans."[86] Oil barrels were used for flotation and a close-knit group worked together to navigate and explore the river while living in tight quarters on the raft. Raft trips are often among the fondest memories of campers. However, one particular raft trip resulted in one of the darkest moments in camp history. On November 26, 1964, a headline in the Chicago Tribune read,[87]

RAFT CARRYING 11 CAPSIZES; 2 ARE MISSING

Natchitoches, La., Nov. 25 (AP) --A raft carrying nine youths and two adults on the Red river here smashed into a bridge tonight, spilling all eleven into the river. Two boys, Danny Tedford, 11, and Joe Warren, 14, are missing.

One of the adult counselors on the excursion, Ken Edgar, 26, was fished out of the river 45 minutes after the raft rammed the Grand Ecorse bridge.

The nine boys, aged 12 to 16, and the two adult counselors were floating down the river from Plain Dealing, La., to New Orleans.

Chief Lock recalls, "Every known safety measure was being followed, and every boy was wearing a life jacket."[88] There was "one pier with a whole bunch of debris on it and the water pushed the raft on top trapping two kids and a counselor underneath."[89] The counselor, Ken Edgar (who will become a prominent figure in our story) was picked up down the river, but unfortunately, two boys drowned. "A careful investigation of the accident, including that by the Coast Guard, suggested no additional safeguards that could have been employed."[90] However this was little comfort to the parents, the group, the Chiefs, and the camp staff. Ken remembers one of the boys who died in that accident had run away the night before. Ken "found him on the back

---

[86] "How We Came to Be.", 7.

[87] Chicago Tribune; Nov 26, 1964; p. 3.

[88] Loughmiller, *Wilderness Road.* 45.

[89] Campbell Loughmiller, conference held June 1988 in Southern Pines, NC.

[90] Loughmiller, Wilderness Road, 45.

side of the levee. He was crying, and said he was thinking about home. He had been at camp for two years, and as far as camp was concerned, he was doing very well and was ready to go home. But home did not want him, and he knew it."[91] He knew that his mother, who had no husband and no family, could not handle him. He also didn't know of any other place to go. The pair talked for several hours that night and the boy reminded Ken that he had accepted Christ several months ago. Ken recalls ending the talk that night with the thought that God would take care of him.[92] The other boy who drown had only been in the group for two weeks and they were just getting to know him.[93] The parents of the boys and camp as a whole struggled through their despair. As time went on, both parents were very gracious, and thanked Chief Lock and the camp for the help they offered their boys. The camp board remained supportive and there was no change in policy. Lock states, "We didn't change the policy, we just learned how to deal with the problem."[94]

How Boys Met Arnold Palmer and President Ford in One Day

Many successful trips (including a half dozen raft trips[95]) were taken and enjoyed by campers and Chiefs alike since this fateful day.[96] In the spring of 1977 a similar raft that had floated down the Mississippi River was shown off at the Byron Nelson Golf Classic in Dallas, Texas.

> Thousands of people came to the golf tournament that day, and many of them came up to the raft...Arnold Palmer sat on the corner of the raft and talked a while...Everything was going well when suddenly a number of men wearing black suits and sunglasses walked through the crowd of people. They came two by two, forming two columns carrying two yellow ropes down by their sides. When they got to the edge of the raft, they spread apart about three feet and formed a sort of walk way that extended about twenty feet back. Who came down the path was none other than the President of the Unites States of

---

[91] Kenneth and Flora Edgar with Amber Bateman, *Reflections Along the Trail* (Amazon Createspace, 2016), 84.
[92] Edgar, 84.
[93] Ibid., 84.
[94] Loughmiller, conference held June 1988 in Southern Pines, NC.
[95] Ibid.
[96] Ibid.

> America!...President Gerald Ford walked right up to the raft. The deck of the raft was about three feet high, so I reached down to take his hand and said, 'Welcome aboard, Mr. President' and pulled him up onto the raft. President Ford sat down and began talking with the boys and staff about their trip.[97]

Experience through the years has shown that while tripping of all sorts certainly enriches the program, it must be kept in balance with all the other aspects of camp. Otherwise its effectiveness soon deteriorates. Over time, fewer trips were taken. It seems two to three long trips per year is about the right number. [98]

It was through this trial-and-error process that these discoveries were made and the camp philosophy was hammered out. Chief Lock was the philosopher and Mac the practitioner.[99] In each step along the way the goal was to discover the best way to help a boy grow and solve problems. As this occurred, theories and ideas became tried and true principles. Gradually camp spirit developed and the program was molded and solidified.

---

[97] Edgar, 39-40.
[98] Loughmiller, conference held in Southern Pines, NC.
[99] Interview with Chief Mac 8/17/2010.

CHAPTER 4:
NEW PARTNERSHIPS

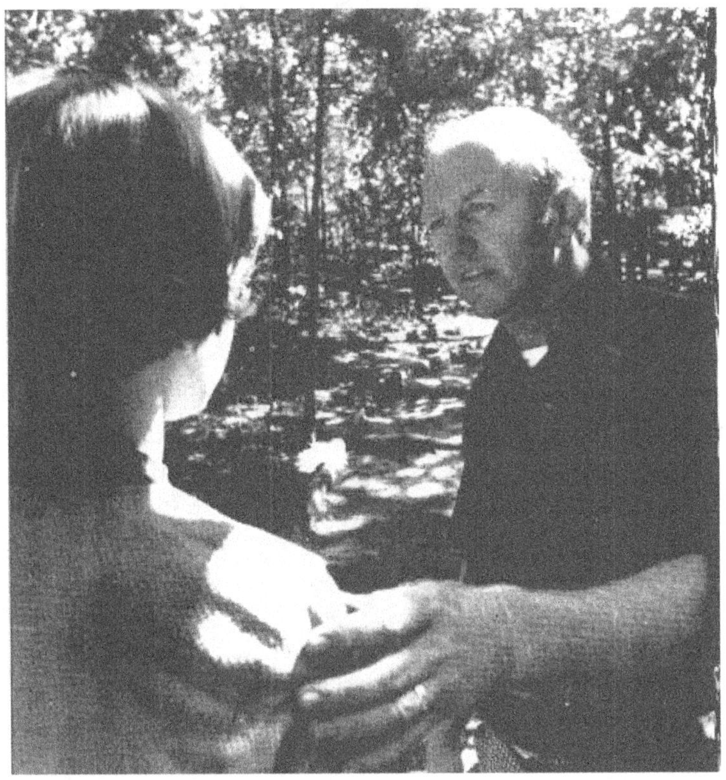

Chief Ken Edgar

As the fathers of the Wilderness Road Therapeutic Camping Model, Campbell Loughmiller and Buford McKenzie worked together to hone the principles and practices of therapeutic residential camping. Working with consultants, social workers, Chiefs, and support staff, together they developed an effective tool for equipping groups of young men to live together, take responsibility for problems, and take an active role in shaping their future. As these men labored together, the Lord brought other leaders into their lives who persevered, proved their grit, demonstrated their determination, and played an integral role in the success and growth of the camping program

Ken and Flora Edgar

Like other pillars of camp history, Chief Ken Edgar learned lessons about hard work, determination, teamwork, and problem solving on the farm. Ken spent his formative years on a turkey ranch, until his family leased a large dairy farm with 200 head of cattle. During his High School years, Ken helped his father with the family egg and poultry business.

Born September 28, 1938, in Dallas, Texas to Harold and Elizabeth Edgar, he was the youngest of 3 children. Ken had two older sisters, Barbara and Rebecca, 4 years and 2 years his senior. His mother was enormously creative and capable. She helped provide for the family by quilting, making clothes, and serving the community. Ken tells a story about a time he was in a school Christmas play and his mother made elf shoes for each child in his class. Both of his parents were stalwart Christians who modeled character and faith. Ken learned compassion, creativity, and the importance of serving others from his mother; and frugality, bold faith, and the value of hard work from his father. He recalls making butter from rich cream, drinking fresh milk, and working the fields with a horse and plow. Reflecting on his younger years, Ken quips, "I cannot recall a time when I didn't know the Lord." Faith, family, service, and a dash of adventure were a part of his life for as far back as he can recall.

One childhood story seems to particularly characterize the free time Ken spent on the farm and became a formative experience in his life. One afternoon, while working in the fields, a parachute with a radio from a sort of weather test landed in the family field. Excited and curious, Ken stashed the parachute away and told his sisters about his plan to jump off the roof of the barn and sail to the ground. His older sisters suggested perhaps he should test the chute before he jumped off the roof. Considering their idea, Ken attached a bag of feed to the parachute, threw it off the roof, and watched with anticipation as the parachute collapsed on itself and the bag of feed burst on the ground. The experiment had failed, but a passion was lit. After graduating High School in 1957, Ken would join the Air Force Reserves.

Five years later, Ken found himself on a plane fully loaded with paratroopers with the engines running and ready to take off at the President's order. On October 15th 1962, a US U-2 reconnaissance aircraft detected several SS-4 nuclear missiles in Cuba touching off the Cuban Missile Crisis. Tensions continued to escalate until October 27th when U.S. spy plane was shot down over Cuba. Nikita Khrushchev demanded the U.S. promise not to invade Cuba and that it remove missiles from Turkey. The American military forces were instructed to set DEFCON-2 – the highest ever in U.S. history. Almost daily, throughout the crises, Ken loaded on to the plane with parachute packed, prepared to take action. The next day, Khrushchev relented and the crisis ended. Ken would never parachute into Cuba, and with the missile crisis dying down, Ken landed back at camp.

Two years before that fateful day on the tarmac in 1962, Ken was attending Howard Payne College - a Baptist school in Brownwood, TX. While working at home in Tyler, Texas on summer break, he was serving in a Baptist scouting ministry at his church called the Royal Ambassadors. One evening, after the meeting, a friend shared with Ken about a chance meeting he had at a hospital while his infant daughter was recovering from an illness. Ken recalls,

> While passing time in the waiting room, my friend struck up a conversation with another father whose little girl had broken her arm. The man shared that he worked at a therapeutic wilderness camping program for at-risk youth nearby in Hawkins, Texas. When the man mentioned they were looking for counselors, my friend's ears perked up. After talking about the program for quite some time, the man mentioned the position required living in the woods five days a week. My friend realized, because he was married with a newborn baby, that was not the right position for him. However, before leaving, he wrote down the man's name and phone number. At our next RA meeting, he shared with me about his conversation and handed me a card with the name Buford McKenzie written on it.
>
> From my teenage days I had had a desire to help troubled

> young people, though I never knew specifically how to do it...The camp was only eighteen miles from my home, so I called the phone number on the card and made a plan to go check it out.[1]

When Ken arrived at the camp, Buford McKenzie, known as Chief Mac, was down in the woods filling in for a counselor who had had an accident and was out on leave. Another staff member met Ken at the office and the two of them walked down to the group. The young man took over the group and Mac began a tour by walking Ken down the trail to Chapel. As they took time to get to know each other, they talked about a number of things. Most significantly, Ken remembers Mac asking what church he attended and what Christianity meant to him. Ken responded, "Well, I am a Christian first and a Baptist second."[2] The interview that day set the direction for the rest of his life. Ken committed to work at the camp for one year and then see where the Lord led.

In his first year at camp, Ken lived in a group at the campsite, cut firewood, built tents, and did a number of small trips and bus trips. The two trips that stand out most were a 400-mile trip on the Naches River and a 600-mile trip on the Sabine River. "In those two trips alone, he paddled over 1,000 miles!" he recalls. After a year at camp, Ken visited Chief Lock and naively said, "I've been here a year now and done everything there is to do, so I guess I'll be going."[3]

Ken returned home to attend college. He worked for his father delivering poultry, served in the Air Force Reserves one weekend a month, and talked about camp constantly. He had a set of slides and he shared them so often he wore out two projectors. After a presentation, one lady asked him a question that stuck with him the rest of his life, "Why did you leave that program and why aren't there more camps?" Shortly after that conversation, Ken sat down to talk with Chief Lock again and said, "I have four goals:

1. Work at camp
2. Get married
3. Go to college
4. Be in the Air Force."

---

[1] Edgar, 11 and interviews with Ken and Flora.

[2] Ibid., 12

[3] Ken and Flora Edgar in interview with the author, March 27, 2017.

Lock responded, "I've never heard four more impossible goals to do at the same time...I'm not sure you can do all four." That day Ken returned to camp with a mission to accomplish the impossible...and...in time, he would.

Finding the Right Girl: The Flora Aten Story

Ken had known Flora Aten since High School. Together, they had attended Fellowship Baptist Church in Tyler, Texas. In fact, Ken began attending that church because a friend told him about a pair of cute twins named Flora and Sara. Soon after visiting the church, Ken and Sara began dating, but after High School, Ken and the twins parted ways as life took them different directions.

Flora made the decision to go to East Texas Baptist College in Marshall, Texas, to pursue a career in helping children and Ken went to Brownwood. Neither Ken nor Flora grew up with an abundance of wealth and both worked their way through college. Flora's mother had passed away from Leukemia when she was seven-years old; and ten years later, her father lost his battle with lung cancer. Flora's Uncle Ont and Aunt Anabelle became like parents to her, and their son Jimmy became a brother. "Being genuine Christians, they lived in such a way that we could tell there was something different about them,"[4] Flora recalls.

> They lived their faith in front of us and took us to church several times a week. I saw the difference Christ made in their lives and I wanted that kind of faith too. I remember praying to accept Christ with my Uncle Ont in our living room. I am so glad the Lord placed me with such a loving family. They taught me so much about the love of Christ and about hope and forgiveness. They are a large part of the reason I chose East Texas Baptist College and a career in teaching"[5]

While in college, Flora went on a retreat with the Baptist Student Union where a missionary spoke about places around the world and the need for people to help. After the missionary was done, they sang

---

[4] Ken and Flora Edgar in interview with the author, August 29, 2021.

[5] Flora tells the story of her parents death, moving in with her aunt and uncle, and coming to faith on p. 80-83 of the book she and Ken co-wrote with Amber Bateman entitled, "Reflections along the Trail." It a wonderful story and well worth the read.

"When I Survey the Wonderous Cross." The last lines gripped Flora's heart.

Were the whole realm of nature mine,
That were an offering far too small;
Love so amazing, so divine,
Demands my soul, my life, my all.

Flora felt compelled to go. Being a missionary to Africa sounded like one of the hardest things, and she decided she was willing.

College graduation found Flora working to pay off school loans and working to gain experience as a school teacher in Duncanville. At this time, Ken was 100-miles away in Hawkins. They saw each other now and then in their hometown of Tyler.

Each summer Flora and her roommates served at Glorietta Baptist Assembly below Santa Fe, New Mexico. Flora was in charge of setting up exhibits each week. Occasionally she would get to sit in on a session with one of the keynote speakers. During that summer, one keynote address stands out in her memory. The speaker said, "Marry your best friend." Flora immediately thought of Ken Edgar, but quickly tuned the idea out. She was determined to go on the mission field and serve in Africa, not settle down and get married.

Between sessions, at Glorietta there were weekly parties for the staff. The summer was was coming to an end and Flora had secured a date for the final party, but Flora decided to invite her friends Kay and Ken who came for the last session, and make an introduction. During their work to set up the party, Flora was struck by Ken's work ethic and confidence. After the final session of the assembly, a group of five cars caravanned to Carlsbad Caverns. At the bottom of the Cavern, the leader of the tour turned out the lights and played *Rock of Ages*. It was quite a moment. During the song, Ken reached over and took Flora's hand. Her heart began to race, but again she restrained her impulses, and dutifully went back to Texas where Kay asked Flora to set her up for a date with Ken.

For the first time, Flora felt jealous. She reluctantly made arrangements and the pair went on several dates, but could not find common ground. After a final date, Ken drove Flora back to Tyler because her car was in the shop. On the road, they talked at length about a month-long raft trip Ken was planning with the group.

On Thanksgiving Day in 1964, Flora got a call from her old friend Nancy, who once had dated Ken. "Did you hear about the raft accident," she asked? Flora felt her pulse begin to race as she admitted she had not. Nancy added, "Two of the boys didn't make it. They have found everyone but Ken."

Flora hung up the phone and immediately called Ken's mother and sister. No one seemed to know anything. As fear rose in her heart, Flora began to realize how much she cared about Ken. Days passed without any news. Flora finally found Ken in the hospital with pneumonia. She wrote him a letter and told him he was the finest Christian person she knew and she wanted to give him flowers while he was still alive.

New Beginnings

The raft accident was a formative event in Ken's life. He shared with Flora in the hospital that the water was bitterly cold and the current was so strong he did not think he would be able to reach the bank. As he fought the current, he could feel his body becoming numb and he became so exhausted he didn't think he could make it to shore. Ken says, "it was in that moment I put my life completely in God's hands. I knew I could not save myself. The moment I had that realization and turned my life completely over to God, my feet touched the river bottom. I crawled out onto the bank and passed out from hypothermia. An hour or so later, I was discovered by two men in a boat. It was a God thing. That is the only way I can explain it. God had his hand on me and had a purpose for me."[6]

> *Do you remember how Jesus called Peter? He took him on the fishing trip of a lifetime: fishing, boating, hiking, cooking, eating, arguing, going to parties, telling stories, sitting around campfires, praying, witnessing miracles. These were the tools Jesus used to make men. – Chief Ken*

Flora shares, "That November day in Texas, when I was visiting Ken in the hospital, and I recently thought I had lost him - something stirred deep in my heart. I realized how much I truly loved him. God was weaving our lives together."[7]

---

[6] Edgar, 83.

[7] Ibid., 84.

Shortly after that discussion, the pair went on a date to Tyler State Park where Ken asked Flora in his typically straightforward and understated manner, "do you want to go together?"[8] "A few months after that," Flora continues, "I was in a Bible study with my pastor's wife. I was talking about my budding relationship with Ken and my desire to be a missionary to Africa. I knew my heart was for Ken, but I felt a need to sacrifice and follow God on mission to Africa. At that moment, the pastor's wife looked me in the eye and asked poignantly, 'Flora, what makes you think God doesn't want you happy?' It was a life altering moment. I wrestled with God for several days after that but realized God gave me a love for Ken for a reason. It was part of his plan that I should go on mission with Kenneth and help him do what God has put on his heart."

Soon they were engaged and making preparations for a small wedding ceremony on August 7th, 1965. Ken was to be a supervisor and the two of them would move into a log cabin on the camp property. As the day grew closer, camp leadership realized that the counselor who was training to take Ken's place was not able to handle the job. Ken knew he could not leave his position as Chief and let the boys down. A change would have to be made. Instead postponing the wedding to be with the group, the couple decided to invite the group to attend their wedding. Ken and Flora enjoyed a one-week honeymoon, and then Ken returned to the group with the agreement that he could go home after the boys were in bed on cook-out days to spend time with his new wife.

One boy in the group, however had other plans. He was afraid of being abandoned and nightly would cause a problem that kept Chief Ken in the woods. It took weeks for the young man to settle down. Ken would come home and share the problem with Flora. They would talk about what was happening. Flora recalls, "It was helpful to talk through those things together. Knowing what was happening allowed me to offer perspective and to pray for the situation. Instead of being mad Kenneth was not coming home, I could pray for the young man who struggled so much every evening with feeling abandoned."[9]

During one of those conversations with Flora, Ken got the idea to take charge at bedtime and ask the young man to stay up and talk. They

---

[8] Most of this content comes from an Interview with Ken and Flora 3/27/2017

[9] Interview with Ken and Flora 8/29/2021

would stay up together and Ken would give him special attention. When the boy asked to go to bed, Ken would reply, "no, not just yet," and continue the conversation until the boys asked several times. Only then would Ken walk over to the tent with him and tuck him into bed. Gradually the boy became an advocate for Ken and told the group to go to bed so Chief Ken could get back to his wife. A few months after they were married, Ken was finally able to work as a supervisor and they moved into a larger house at the camp.

Buford and Lois McKenzie

The next chapter of this story simply could not be told without making a trip back to 1950 to understand the missionary spirit of Mac's wife, Lois Rae McKenzie. The pair met when Mac made a trip to Baylor University to "meet girls." Mac recalls,

> Chief Wes and I were co-Chiefs in Tejas at the time and we were heading to San Antonio for a training Session. He had graduated from Baylor University, and on the way back, we went by and stopped at the girls' dorm. When we walked in, Lois was walking down the hall with theater clothes in her arms. Wes talked to her and said, "Go find some girls and let's go to the coffee shop."[10]

Over the next few months, Lois tried to fix Mac up with her roommates and Mac always ended up with her. One day, Mac asked Wes about the missionary girl who grew up in China. Mac wrote her a note and their relationship began. The problem was that Lois was all set to go back to China as a missionary. She had grown up there, and her parents had been missionaries there for 40 years. Gradually it seemed their relationship was ending. Mac left her saying, "You do whatever the Lord leads." As he drove away, the Lord convicted him about leaving her

[10] McKenzie in interview with the author, August 18, 2010.

to make a decision like that and he drove back and said, "Lois, the Lord and I want to talk to you about another mission." Mac recalls, "The Lord and I won. We married August 11, 1951. Since then, we've had 6 kids [and] 19 grandkids, and been married 59 years."[11]

This mission mindset was part of who Lois was. "Camp would not be here today if it weren't for Lois...she trained camp wives...I'd give her a thought and she'd put it onto paper...she had a good feeling of administrative process."[12] After a Bible study discussing Abraham leaving everything and going to a land the Lord would show him, followed by a challenge about participants' willingness to follow and step out in faith, Mac woke Lois and said, "Lois, we're leaving camp." Later she woke up again and responded, "Well, why not!" Mac recalls deciding to leave the Salesmanship Club Boys Camp because he "hoped to find an area of service in which there would be even greater freedom to offer spiritual counseling as well as group work therapy to disturbed youth. I had hoped to inspire Southern Baptists to take up this sort of service, but our Home Mission Board was still too conservative."[13] On August 31, 1960, Mac told Lock that he planned to leave the Salesmanship Club effective May 31, 1961. Lock did not know what to say at the time. Later he said he was floored by Mac's request, but Mac recalls him saying, "Oh, well."[14] For the next 9 months, Mac looked for an opportunity. With two weeks to go, the Mennonites called the Salesmanship Club asking if someone could help them with counselor training in Woodland Park Colorado for a summer church camp called the Young Citizens (formerly "Welfare") Camp. Soon Mac's young family was packed up and heading further west. His daughter Karen remembers asking "Dad, where are we going?" He responded, "Wherever the Lord leads." To this day Karen is not sure he had actually been offered the job at the time.[15]

---

[11] Ibid.

[12] Buford McKenzie in interview with the author, August 5, 2008.

[13] Buford McKenzie, letter to Rev. Marcus Bishop, March 22, 1962.

[14] McKenzie in interview with the author, August 25, 2010.

[15] Bill Collins, "Tribute to Chief Mac and Lois," Wilderness Road Therapeutic Camping Association (WRTCA) Conference, August 30, 2014.

CHAPTER 5:
ROCKY HORIZONS: THERE AND BACK AGAIN

Rocky Mountain Mennonite Camp

In early June 1961, the McKenzie family was in Woodland Park, Colorado, a beautiful location on the west slope of Pike's Peak where Mac was to consult for the summer program of Rocky Mountain Mennonite Camp. The camp had successfully run many programs, including a program for "juvenile delinquents since 1956"[1] when

> the Juvenile Court of Denver arranged for 30 boys and 4 girls to spend a week at camp at the invitation of Jess Kauffman, the founder. Each summer the camp has grown...in the number of campers served, the number of days scheduled, the agencies sponsoring campers, etc. The program has also shifted from co-ed to separate camps for boys and girls. The Camp has established side-camp facilities at Rocky Ridge for boys and at

[1] Rocky Mountain Mennonite Camp, *Trail Call* 8 no. 1 (February 1962): 5.

Park Ridge for girls. These camps are serviced by the Main Camp though both operate independently of the regular camp program. They live in tent shelters that have a wooden floor and frame over which canvas is placed.[2]

The two auxiliary camps were composed of groups of ten campers each. Both camps held a pre-camp orientation week, then four two week sessions.[3] The program ran from late June through late August.[4] The Metropolitan Area Youth Campership Fund provided the basic fee of $59 per period with $2 of spending money for a child's stay at camp.[5] Helen Slaubaugh had worked at Park Ridge Camp for Girls the summer before Chief Mac came. She recalls a tremendous difference in the orientation week that Mac led in 1962. He taught a great deal about group work and how to quickly develop relationships with troubled youth.[6] At the end of the orientation week, Mac was asked to run camp for the summer.[7] Mac extended the program from a two week to a three week program to allow opportunity for relationships that were cultivated to bear fruit and became available to consult with groups and direct care staff. He also made it possible for campers to remain in the program if they were making progress. One camper attended all three sessions in the summer of 1962.[8] Helen remembers feeling relieved and encouraged in knowing Chief Mac was there to back up the staff when they encountered problems.[9]

After the summer ended, Jess Kaufmann urged Chief Mac to join the staff of Frontier Boys Camp,[10] a year-round program beginning at Rocky Mountain Mennonite Camp.[11] Mac continues, "Actually, an offer elsewhere was more appealing to me personally – and financially – but so urgent was his request that I felt this to be the Lord's will."[12] "After

---

[2] Young Citizens Camps Brochure, 1962. (Girls group at Rocky Mountain camp)
[3] Helen Lindstrom edit of manuscript, 5/22/2017.
[4] Trail Call, Vol. 8 February 1962, No. 1. Published by the Rocky Mountain Mennonite Camp, 5.
[5] Campership Manual for Participating Agencies, Metropolitan Council for Community Service, Inc., April, 1962, 15.
[6] Helen Lindstrom in interview with the author, April 3, 2017.
[7] Buford McKenzie in interview with the author, August 5, 2008.
[8] Helen Lindstrom edit of manuscript, May 22, 2017.
[9] Lindstrom in interview with the author, April 3, 2017.
[10] Buford McKenzie, letter to the Barnabas Club Board, mid-1962, 2.
[11] McKenzie in interview with the author, August 5, 2008.
[12] Letter written to Barnabus Club Board mid 1962, 2.

considerable prayer and deliberation, I accepted the offer and moved to the nearby town of Woodland Park, Colorado, in September 1961."[13] Mac says he was ready for a new challenge and he wanted to prove camp could be done anywhere. They built primarily teepees or tents with a high peak so the snow could slide off and camped at 30º below zero. The camp grew and developed. By May 1962, a third group (Frontiersmen, Trailblazers and the Rangers) was running, bringing the total number of boys at camp to 24.[14] Newsletters were published, Family Day's occurred, and the boys wrote articles for the camp newspaper. One of the favorite stories was the discovery of an underground spring that provided water to the campsites and even made refrigeration possible. It was discovered that "water flowing through a submerged container keeps foods at an even 34º."[15] They set up a travois (a rig hooked to a mule with supplies on the back), and went up 10,000 feet and camped for a week at a time. Not once did a boy get frostbite. On one occasion, a group decided they wanted to climb Pike's Peak. Four miles from the top, they reached Devil's Playground, an area above tree line where a latrine built. A storm blew in and sleet was blowing parallel to the ground. Mac recalls the boys would run into the latrine to get out of the weather, then run outside to get away from the smell. Eventually they decided the smell was not as bad as the cold. Chief Ivan put a poncho over the toilet seat, then cooked the food. Then he slid down the mountain to the ranger station and got a ranger to help retrieve the group. Mac recalls that it was good to see they could do camp anywhere.[16] By the summer of 1962, the Mennonite Colleges – Bethel, Eastern Mennonite, Goshen, Hesston and Tabor – had set up a course as part of their summer program in juvenile delinquency for college credit in conjunction with the work at Frontier Boys Camp.

In May of 1962, Chief Mac encountered a personal tragedy. Mac recalls:

> We were in the process of moving to a cottage on the campsite when our lively son Kent, three-and-a-half, succumbed to acute encephalitis from the adeno virus. Four days later on Mothers Day,

[13] Buford McKenzie, *Autobiography* (unpublished document), September 1962, 5.
[14] *Frontier Boys Camp Newsletter* 1, no. 2 (May 1962), 1.
[15] *Frontier Boys Camp Newsletter* 1, no. 4 (July 1962), 2.
[16] Buford McKenzie in interview with the author, August 25, 2010.

May 13, he left us to find new adventures farther up the trail, among the peaks of Heaven. Heartbroken though we were in our human loss, my wife and I tried to see even in this experience the opportunity to witness for our Lord. Accordingly, He gave us the strength to speak at Kent's funeral and to sing a duet of Christian assurance and joyful comfort:

"There's within my heart a melody;
Jesus whispers sweet and low,
Fear not. I am with thee. Peace, be still
In all of life's ebb and flow."[17]

Mac continues, writing "Whatever experiences the future may hold for us, we feel confident in knowing who holds the future. Indeed, we now have quite an investment in the 'Bank of Heaven.' We believe that our work with troubled youth is a definite calling and to the Lord we consecrate our efforts and our lives."[18]

Methodist Camps for Troubled Youth

Despite the success, in 1962 Mac's and Jess Kaufmann's methods "differed too sharply for amicable agreement"[19] and as a result Mr. Kaufmann chose to resign, against Mac's wishes.[20] Later, in the fall of that year Mr. Johnson, the President of the Methodist Children's Homes in Waco, Texas, and a social worker came to Colorado to visit with Mac about beginning a camp for them. Mac wrote of his experience at Frontier Boys Camp in 1962 that he had "never worked under such strain, nor can I think of a more difficult way to begin a new assignment. Only the needs of the campers and the welfare of Frontier Boys Camp as a whole, as expressed by your Board, have persuaded me to stay."[21] Eventually the conflict over program philosophy, the feeling that he was "something of an outsider, a Baptist in a staff predominantly Mennonite,"[22] and the opportunity at the Methodist Children's Home inspired Mac to take on this new opportunity in September or October

---

[17] Buford McKenzie, *Autobiography*, 5.
[18] Buford McKenzie, *Autobiography*, September 1962, 5.
[19] McKenzie, letter to the Barnabas Club Board, 2.
[20] Mac had suggested to him three different times that he should resign (letter to Barnabas Club Board, p. 2).
[21] McKenzie, letter to the Barnabas Club Board, 3.
[22] McKenzie, letter to the Barnabas Club Board, 2.

1962.[23]

Mac packed up the family and returned to Texas. Upon his arrival at the Methodist Children's Homes, it was apparent something was not right. His U-Haul stood in front of the office for two weeks. The family stayed in a hotel while they waited for the Children's Homes to find them a place to stay.[24] The Children's Homes never did find a place for them, so the family borrowed his mother's Silverstream camper and placed it on a nearby ranch while they waited.[25] Mac then spent the next three months trying to see Mr. Johnson about beginning the camp program. Mac wrote a nine-page statement of purpose outlining the program and went nearly every day dressed in a shirt and tie to see Mr. Johnson. His secretary would just smile and say he is out to this or that. Undaunted, Mac continued working. During those three months, Mac and Lois worked to compose the camp manuals which are the backbone of many of our camp manuals today.[26] Finally, the Children's Homes gave Mac a pink slip without his ever having the opportunity to begin anything.

After that occurred, the chairman of the Methodist organization requested a meeting with Mac. He told Mac the organization had wanted to get rid of Mr. Johnson for 20 years, but people were afraid of him. He asked Mac if he would write a report and testify about what was going on in the organization. Mac wrote a 16-page report and the chairman called all the big shots together. Across the table from Mac sat Mr. Johnson and his lawyer. Mac opened saying, "Mr. Johnson, it sure is good to see you! I've been trying to see you for the past three months and I have a few things I need to say."[27] After a few minutes, his lawyer interrupted saying, "What Mac is saying needs to be said in court."[28] The chairman told him to sit down and that they were going to discuss this right there. Mac went on for 3 or 4 more pages when the chairman said, "That is enough."[29] Mac recalls, "I wasn't able to start a camp, but I was able to get 500 kids social work help and I got six months of

---

[23] Mac's Autobiography written in September 1962 was sent to the Methodist Children's Homes as part of an application process.
[24] Interview with Karen and Bill Collins 3/28/2017.
[25] Ibid.
[26] Bill Collins, "Tribute to Chief Mac and Lois". WRTCA Conference, August 30, 2014.
[27] McKenzie in interview with the author, August 25, 2010.
[28] Ibid.
[29] Ibid.

severance pay from the Children's Home in appreciation of my efforts" [30] That was a scary experience, he adds. "It would scare the pants off me to do that again. The Lord gave me strength and courage."[31] Unfortunately, neither of these opportunities resulted in a sustainable camp program. However, these difficult experiences prepared Mac for future opportunities.

Mac's Return to The Salesmanship Club Camp

On May 16, 1963, [32] after the finishing his responsibilities with the Methodist Homes, Mac returned to Hawkins to visit with Chief Lock, and Lock requested he stay around for a while to help "tune up" camp. In Mac's absence, Lock had hired a supervisor who had never been a Chief. He had given each kid an axe to carry around and the kids were running Chiefs off left and right. One day, Mac walked down to Tejas, the oldest group, to find a Chief hiding under a table while the kid was threatening him with his axe. Mac said, "If any of you pick up an axe, you'll eat it!"[33] Mac took the axes away and left just those necessary for chopping wood in the tool tent. In three weeks, Mac felt he had finished his consulting work and was ready to move on. Lock, however, requested he stay on and run camp, so Mac returned to Hawkins on June 1, 1963[34] and the man who had been group work supervisor in his absence moved on.

---

[30] Ibid.

[31] Interview with Chief Mac, 8/25/2010 and 8/5/2008.

[32] *Club and Camp News*, Salesmanship Club Boys Camp. Sam Adams Jr. (Ed.), , vol. 40, no.1 (September 29, 1966).

[33] McKenzie in interview with the author, August 25, 2010.

[34] "Salesmanship Club Boys Camp Loses McKenzies," *Reporter-Journal and Tri-Area News*, September 12, 1968, 4.

CHAPTER 6:
FURTHER EXPERIMENTATION

The First Female Chiefs: Helen Slaubaugh and Ruby Horst

In March of 1967, Helen Slaubaugh was working in student personnel at Goshen College in northern Indiana. She had been there five years and was ready for a change. She was thinking about moving on to a new job or going to grad school at the end of the school year. That same year, Ruby Horst was teaching second grade in the Newton KS School System. The Salesmanship Club was pressing Lock and Mac to experiment with women counselors as Chiefs in an attempt to improve the program, help boys improve relationships with their mothers, and shorten camper stay. Neither Mac nor Lock loved the idea, but if Mac was going to hire female staff, he knew just the two. Mac recalled Helen and Ruby's work at Rocky Mountain Mennonite Camp and contacted them both to see if they would be interested in joining the staff. Both Helen and Ruby agreed to interview and have the opportunity to meet the staff at camp. Helen's interview started at the main camp office in Dallas before going to camp to meet staff and see the camp setting. Because of Ruby's work schedule, she went to the camp on a weekend and was interviewed there. In those days, there were no groupwork supervisors, only two senior counselors each in charge of two groups. Gary Johns and Everett Lindstrom were the senior counselors. The group had dinner that night at Chief Mac's house and Helen returned to Indiana. Later both she and Ruby agreed to join the program and became Chiefs in fall of 1967.

The experiment with female direct care staff lasted about 18 months, and no more women were hired as Chiefs. Helen and Ruby were a tremendous asset, but the dynamic was difficult because of the openness of camp sleeping shelters. A female staff member could not supervise boys as closely in mornings, at night. At shower time a senior counselor was needed to be with the group. Additionally, controlling boys physically when situations became unsafe was more challenging. Supervisory staff had to be available consistently. Chief Ken recalls that when he moved to Florida to begin the first Eckerd Program, Chief Lock said to him, "Ken, duplicate everything in the program except for the skirts."[1] Though the experiment with female direct care staff was not seen as beneficial in the Salesmanship Club Program, the hiring of Helen Slaubaugh was a tremendous benefit to therapeutic camping. She would play significant roles later in the development of Eckerd Youth Alternatives.

The Adventure Trails Program

On June 4, 1965, prior to his formal retirement, Chief Lock inaugurated a new type of program "in an effort to serve greater numbers...The camp experimented with a short-term camping program of a month to six weeks for boys with incipient problems."[2] The first trip lasted six weeks and left from "Pleasant Oaks Recreation Center at 2 PM, less than an hour after [Edward Titche Elementary School, in southeast Dallas] let out."[3] The group of 4th, 5th, and 6th graders 10 – 12

[1] Ken and Flora Edgar in interview with the author, March 27, 2017.
[2] Loughmiller, *Kids in Trouble.* 56.
[3] Evaluation of the Adventure School – Report from Summer of 1965, 1.

years of age left for "Metzger's Lake, seventy miles east in Van Zandt County."[4] After five days, the group had learned enough camping and relational skills the counselors felt they could take the group on a bus trip. "Three days before the end of the trip, the group stopped at Lake Whitney State Park, a half-day out of Dallas to wash the bus...wash all dirty clothes...clean equipment...[and] evaluate the trip."[5] At the conclusion of the trip, two days were spent evaluating with individual boys. The second trip got under way five days after the first one ended. This type of program continued, and a girls' program was added in 1969.[6] By 1971, girls were being taken "out of school for four weeks. In groups of 10 they [were] taken on hiking or canoe trips, away from home and school, teacher[s] and parents. The girls plan[ned] their own itinerary, perform[ed] their own chores, [and] learn[ed] self-reliance and the give-and-take of group living."[7]

The trips involved considerable travel, as groups usually went to Colorado or New Mexico. They were designed to serve limited goals because the boys, obviously, could not come together as a group and establish serious purposes in the short time they had before leaving. They were unaccustomed to having as much influence on what they did and how they did it as the boys who lived at camp, so adult decisions came to guide them more than was anticipated. [8]

Chief Ken Returns to the Salesmanship Club

In May of 1974,[9] Ken Edgar returned to the Salesmanship Club Camp as camp director. Ken had worked as a Chief there from 1960 to 1964, then became a groupwork supervisor staying at camp until 1969 when he left to begin the first Eckerd Program.[10] Upon his return, he felt the program had drifted quite a bit and hoped to get it back on track.[11]

---

[4] Ibid., 1.
[5] Ibid.,. 1-2.
[6] Chronological Highlights of Development of Girls' Adventure Trails Program printed near August 1971.
[7] "Failure Cycle Broken by Wilderness Adventure," *Criminal Justice Highlights* 3, no. 9 (September 1971) 1.
[8] Loughmiller, *Kids in Trouble.* 56.
[9] Dudley Lynch, "Investing in Children of Despair," *Dallas [name of publication]*, November 19, 1975, 50. States Ken has been Chief [Mac?]'s chief for about year and a half.
[10] Ken Edgar in interview with the author, January 29, 2009.
[11] Ibid.

The camp had hired a well-known social worker from Dallas to run the program. He was very knowledgeable of social work and had good intentions, but had no knowledge of camp. He was also facing pressures to modify the program, and did not have an experiential basis with camp to know how to do this. They had changed the group names hoping for a fresh start, but by the time Ken returned, camp culture was so negative they were eating in campsites until they could function in the Chuckwagon. One of the first changes Ken made was to end the Adventure Trails program. It involved too much trip taking and not enough emphasis on group, and was utilizing all of his best staff and requiring tremendous effort. He then worked to rebuild camp culture, reopen the Chuckwagon, balance the groups, and create healthy group and camp culture.

Ken notes that throughout camp history there were cycles of trial and error. Groups moved from "no trips" to "all trips," and then found a happy medium. Groups went from "no cookout" to "always doing cookouts," but again there was a happy medium. Time together in Chuckwagon programs and homesdays are important. When a correct balance is struck, a gang becomes a group, and a group becomes a family.[12]

Once camp was in a healthy place, Ken experimented with a short-term camping at fixed sites. "The groups were taken directly to an isolated tract of woods available to them."[13] Moving to a fixed site was a major step in becoming more effective. The boys lived in campsite, maintained the campsite and planned trips just as a typical group. When groups worked well enough for a trip they would plan one. "The 'tripping' program stabilized into a pattern that allowed for one week of orientation and preparation, four weeks on the road and one week for evaluations and winding up."[14] A second important step was the decision to send no more than "two boys home at a time and replace them with new ones [each week] so as to gradually develop a group culture."[15] In the long run, this type of short-term program suffered the same fate as the Adventure Trails program. It required the best staff to establish a healthy group culture quickly and saw far fewer results than

---

[12] Ken Edgar in interview with the author, September 4, 2010.
[13] Loughmiller, *Kids in Trouble*, 56.
[14] Ibid., 58.
[15] Ibid.

the long term program. It closed in 1976[16] and attention was shifted to "bringing to reality one of [the club's] long-cherished dreams – a permanent, fulltime, residential camp for girls."[17] The girls program was begun in April 1976[18] on its own beautiful 1,083 acre piece of property in Palestine, Texas[19], and enjoyed initial success. Ken's experience with Eckerd Youth Alternatives was invaluable in beginning this new program. However, after the program began, African big game were situated next door. It was feared that if a girl ran away she would encounter one of those animals, so the girls program was moved to the same property as the boys camp and eventually ceased operation. Early in 1978, Ken accepted the challenge to begin a camping program in Vermont with Eckerd Youth Alternatives and moved on from the Salesmanship Club.

The End of an Era

On May 31, 2004, the decision was made to close the camp. Those who remain loyal to traditional camp philosophy feel the camp was innovated out of existence. The story I have written is a story of innovation and experimentation. Throughout the experimentation process, consistent leadership had prevented mission drift. When Chief Lock, Chief Mac, and Chief Ken moved on, other directors who did not have a firm grasp of the principles that made the program successful stepped in. Gradually innovations resulted in a drift from many of the principles that had created the success.[20] By 2004, the Club had hired a number of directors with no direct experience in a Loughmiller model camp program. They had reduced the average camper stay to a short six months; kids went home on weekends; free time and sports were introduced; and classroom time had become a daily routine. To allow

---

[16] Lynch, "Investing in Children of Despair," 26.
[17] Loughmiller, *Kids in Trouble*, 59.
[18] Lynch, "Investing in Children of Despair," 26.
[19] Sharon Cobler, "Camp for Girls Planned" *Dallas Morning News*, March 13, 1975.
[20] Interviews with Buford McKenzie, Ken Edgar, Paul Daley, and Bill and Karen Collins all supported this premise.

for classroom time other parts of the program, like planning cookouts, had to be trimmed.[21] The state had also proposed changes "including limited tent camping...to 'address the weather and basically give them more of the modern conveniences of life.'"[22]

An email from Kent Skipper, the President of the Salesmanship Club at the time, shows the program had remained effective until its demise. For up to five years after discharge, 75-80% of former campers stayed in school or graduated, were not arrested for a criminal offense and were not admitted to another residential treatment facility (three of the Board's primary outcome measures, among others). Additionally, support for the program was high and the club was not having financial problems. A number of factors were considered including the severity of children being referred and the cost per child. The primary reason he listed confirms the dedication of the club to innovation. Mr Skipper said:

> the Salesmanship Club made the decision...to pursue new, innovative solutions to help troubled kids and their families. The Club has a proud history of pioneering new approaches...Although our camp was continuing to develop new tools to help children, it was felt that after 60 years, it was time to explore other possibilities to help troubled young people and their families. Seeking innovative solutions remains a core value for the Club. As one Club member said, "Good is the enemy of better."[23]

Nonetheless, the decision to close the program was difficult for the 600 members of the Salesmanship Club. One member likely put it best when he said, "My head understands, but my heart is racing to catch up."[24]

---

[21] Interview with Bill and Karen Collins 3/28/2017.
[22] Kim Horner, "Tough Call for Youth Refuge: Camp program ends as laws change, kids problems grow more complex." *The Dallas Morning News,* May 13, 2004.
[23] Kent Skipper, E-mail to Stephen Ashton dated 10/13/2010.
[24] Ibid.

AFTERWORD

Around 1970, Before the close of the Salesmanship Club Camp, Buford McKenzie, Ken Edgar, and Everett Lindstrom left to launch Eckerd Youth Alternatives with Jack Eckerd. The program was wildly successful growing to over 20 programs stretching from Florida to Vermont. In the late 2000's, the Eckerd Camps suffered a similar fate as the Salesmanship Club.

Seeing the writing on the wall, in 1980 Mac Ken, and Paul Daley, moved on from Eckerd to pioneer a wilderness program for the Baptist Children's Homes of North Carolina. Camps then began to grow independently from one another. Ken Edgar consulted with Fair Play Boys Camp, Fairplay, SC, leading to the founding of Wilderness Way Girls Camp. The Loughmiller model continues to grow and the Wilderness Road Therapeutic Camping Association was founded to preserve the principles as practiced by Campbell Loughmiller and Buford McKenzie. Today Loughmiller model camps exist in Pennsylvania, Maryland, Ohio, North Carolina, South Carolina, Florida, Canada, and Ireland. That is certainly a story worth telling, and the companion volume follows.

WILLIAM S. HOOD
SALESMANSHIP CLUB MEMOIR

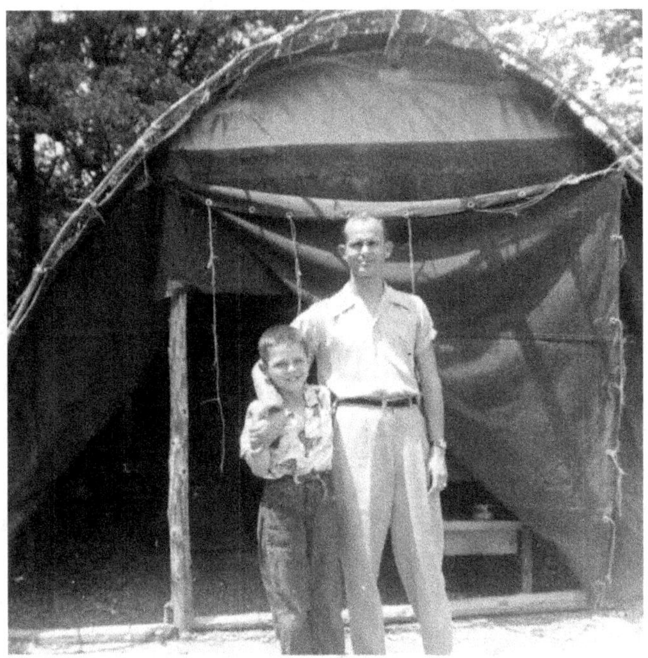

Billy Hood with Chief Sam Inman

Preface

I was born in Oceanside California, in February of 1944, to parents who both worked in the World War II related industries in southern California. My mother's third husband, somewhat uncomfortable with impending fatherhood, apparently suggested an abortion, to which my mother was vehemently opposed. At five weeks old, I was fatherless and on my way back to my mother's home in Dallas, Texas. Not remotely interested in the enlistment of another husband's help in raising me, my mother took on two distinctly difficult and unpopular roles, that of a single parent, and a divorcee.

Initially, I was in the care of my mother's sister, Mary Etta, recently married to a World War II veteran, Bob Sego, but childless in the newness of that relationship. At the age of about three or four years, my Aunt Mary and Uncle Bob bought their own place out in Pleasant Grove for beginning their own family. They moved out, leaving my mother to fend for herself in providing for my care. In addition, mother had to pay for my Aunts share in the home we occupied, which was designed and built by my late grandfather. I understand now, that my mother had few options from which to choose. After getting to know my mother as an adult, I was amazed that Aunt Mary and Uncle Bob stuck it out as long as they did. Mother was not an easy person to live with under the best of circumstances as far as I could tell.

Soon, I became the responsibility of complete strangers with varying degrees of concern for my well-being. As I recall, mother would exchange full use of our house if the person, or couple, would agree to take care of me while she worked. Their only financial responsibility was their food and half the utilities. Our house was located at 3036 Rosedale, adjacent to the campus of Southern Methodist University, in Dallas, Texas. Some of the "care" givers were married students who needed to provide living quarters for their mates while they attended the University. There was no such thing as "background checks" in those days, but my mother did all she could do to ensure I received the best available care. Sometimes our best is just not good enough. Over the next four or five years, and several different care givers, I developed into a seriously maladjusted child. At age five, because she didn't know where else to turn, mother had to take me down to the University Park Chief of Police, for a stern admonition. When I entered the first grade, in University Park Elementary School just north of Dallas, at age seven, I think I may have been the only one in my entire class not traumatized. About half way through the first grade school year, I was expelled.

By the time my mother stood before a Juvenile Court Judge, with her seven year-old son in tow, I was a real problem child. And, it did not look as if I had any intention of making the necessary changes, or that I even recognized that changes needed to be made. Quite frankly, my mother was at a complete loss as to how this all came about, or how to initiate the required corrective action. In retrospect, she had made her choices and was now facing the consequences of those choices. Had I been in her shoes, I don't know that I would have done any better.

Today, I give that Juvenile Court Judge, and my mother's good judgment in making a choice for me, the credit for saving my life and my future. This story is about how that salvaging operation unfolded in those early years.

New Beginnings: Introduction and Overview

If you were classified as a delinquent male child in Texas, circa 1950, and from a single parent home, there was only one solution available. The Juvenile Detention Center in Gatesville, Texas. However, if the Juvenile court could see chance of turning a young boy around, there was one other option; The Salesmanship Club Boy's Camp out east of Dallas.

Living in the woods was going to be a new experience for me. To tell the truth, I was scared silly. I had never even been camping before, and suddenly it felt like I was expected to assume the role of a Daniel Boone! Living with nine other boys, ranging in age from seven to nine years, would prove to be a challenge in more ways than one. I was an "only child", and though I didn't usually get what I wanted all that often, I didn't have to compete with any other kids to get it. I sure didn't have to "get along" with any other kids in my house!

Funny how the reality of living in an environment with Copperheads, Coral Snakes, Rattlesnakes, Raccoons, Opossums, and a number of other wild animals, never presented itself as any big deal to most of us. In fact, there was an animal hospital, treating injured and sick zoo animals, just a short distance away on the banks of the Trinity River. Some of those animals escaped on occasion, and camp-wide alerts were given when a Lion or other dangerous animal had gotten loose. No big deal!

No, we found the greatest challenge and the most difficulty, in getting along with each other. We each had our own special problems and shortcomings, which ran from delinquency to deprivation. Some of us had physical issues resulting from early childhood diseases like polio, and others had emotional issues stemming from physical abuse and other trauma. We each presented a unique challenge to our fellow campers.

Yet, with time, we became a family unit of sorts. Dysfunctional as it may have been, we learned the art of teamwork and the consequences a society pays for the bad behavior of one. We also learned that one has a responsibility to society, and that society has a responsibility toward the one. Any family unit, deprived of the influence of a caring mother or father, is dysfunctional to some degree. Many families, with both mother and father, are completely dysfunctional to the point of incredibility. I found the new society in the camp to be far superior to the one I had left behind, not immediately by any means, but eventually.

We would be living in tents year round, called “Hogans”, and we would build them ourselves from willow poles we cut down on a creek-bed. We lashed them together with binder’s twine, forming several large arches with crossing support poles in a row, and covered them with waterproofed canvas. The ends of the Hogan were open in summer and closed in winter. A large flap of canvas served as a tent door in the colder months. The tent sides rolled up in the hotter periods, providing open-air ventilation.

There were “community” buildings for specific uses. There was a Chuck Wagon building where the whole camp, five “tribes” of ten boys with two councilors called “Chiefs”, met to eat three good meals a day, five days a week. There was an additional building when the camp moved to Hawkins, Texas, and television became a staple in the American entertainment diet. This building served as a community building in which we were allowed some “quality” Television viewing. All live black and white programs, like “The Hit Parade” and “The Honeymooners”, along with various variety shows. As I recall, there was a small library of sorts as well, but you could not remove the book from the building. All of the “tribes” shared the use of this building at differently scheduled times.

Two days a week, in order for the camps only cook, “Mom” Taylor, to have some down time, we cooked our own food on a wood fire in our respective campsites. We used large aluminum pots, cast iron Dutch-ovens and cast iron skillets. Later, as our camping skills increased, we built ovens of red clay and a couple of steel barrels. We had a community mess-tent with a couple of picnic tables and a food locker inside. Our “schooling” consisted of reading the menu of available food items, writing the selected items down on an order form, and figuring the total cost of the meals we were planning. We had strict budget guidelines for each meal. Two boys were assigned to this task on a rotational basis.

Another avenue of education consisted of planning prolonged field trips, and day trips, to various places of interest throughout the state of Texas. A great deal of research was required, regarding destinations, for historical information and our questions were directed primarily to local Chambers of Commerce. Through these efforts, a pretty thorough knowledge of the destination was gained before the first pair of socks was packed. We learned how to ask questions, which would provide the information we needed. It was an education by itself, in the art form of communication. The value of careful preparation was gradually ingrained in all of us, as was the cost of travel and the cost of daily living while on the roads we chose. Other than these avenues, we had no formal classroom teaching. We were, by every definition, woodsmen.

By the age of ten years, I could build a fire without matches. I could design a campsite with proper water run-off, blaze my own trails, camp for days, and leave the land as I found it. I could chop wood using a double bladed ax without cutting my leg off, find a spring for drinking water, build a suitable shelter, recognize edible plant-life and dangerous vegetation, and survive in the wild on my own. I knew how to cook, catch fish, trap rabbits, and had acquired a number of other skills for surviving in the wild, by the age of eleven. I could handle deadly poisonous snakes like a professional. I really was in a kind of "hog heaven" for boys, though I was quite unaware of it at the time.

As you read this, I want you to know that this story is not about hardship, nor is it about being deprived of the normal provisions of society as punishment. It is about excelling as young people in an environment geared to teaching human survival in society. It is about rising to the occasion, in spite of the obstacles. This story is about learning to live in a society of your peers, and becoming a productive member, when no one thought you could. It is about men with vision, and children who had never been given the opportunity to see what they might become. This story is not about individual failure, it is about the wonder of personal triumph.

Chapter One: 1951 Tejuacana: The Youngest Tribe

My introduction to camp life, as I recall the shock of it, was just wonderfully terrible. I remember the sunlight coming down through the majestic oak trees and beautiful cedars as we walked the dirt trail toward my new home, our home. There was the excitement of something new, the dread of the unknown, the anxiety of being among nine other boys in my age group, and where I would fit in the pecking order. There was also the sense of being rejected by my only parent, my mother. Everything I knew about living, changed dramatically in one miserable day. Details are fuzzy now, but the distinct impressions remain. Suddenly, I was in the woods with nine other boys and two grown men I did not know. I was being told what to do, and how to do it. The worst part of the experience, as I recall, was being "bossed around" by complete strangers. These were people I did not know, and had no respect for as a belligerent young boy. There was also the fear factor of not knowing exactly what to expect from these folks. A kid just doesn't adapt to such a radical change of environment overnight. No doubt, at that moment in time, I felt that I would never make the adjustment.

Here I am, walking for “miles” to who knows where, carrying my suitcase on a dusty dirt trail, through the woods. In reality, the distance was probably closer to a half mile, but the urgency of the moment had taken control. Everything I am allowed to have in my possession, while in the camp, is in this suitcase. It is heavy! I was acutely aware, in my over-active imagination, of little beady snake eyes peering at me from both sides of the trail. I just knew I was goin’ to get bit, if I wasn’t awful careful! Oddly, I didn’t notice anyone else being particularly concerned. I don’t believe it dawned on me then, but I was the new kid, and they are glad to have someone else in the spotlight for a change! The beady little eyes did not go away!

After a really long hike, by my standards at the time, we arrived at the campsite I will call home for a couple of years. Of course, had I known that then, I would have run all the way home screaming! I figured maybe a few months, and I'm back home again. I don't belong here!

Chief Sam Inman, and Chief John Spencer, are my first councilors in Tejuacana, pronounced "Teh-walk-in-ee" in Texas dialect. They introduce me to my fellow campers, and take me to my Hogan. What's a Hogan, you ask? To me, it was a long shot from a roof over your head! Basically, it was a big tent. I shared these "living quarters" with four other boys, rain or shine, windy or calm, hot or cold.

The councilors had a wood burning stove in their tent for heat in the winter months. The Chuck Hogan had a wood burning stove for heat, but we had no wood burning stove in our Hogan! For obvious safety reasons, as look back now, there were no thin-walled metal wood burning stoves in our five-camper Hogans. The oak wood fire would turn those thin walled metal stoves red-hot. Everything, with the exception of the Army surplus bed frame and springs, from the dirt up, was very inflammable. Those old metal wood stoves felt really good on those chill northeast Texas nights, but the risk was obvious with small children. But, then and there, it was just one more comfort of home I did not have anymore, warm shelter in winter!

Texas can get bone-chilling cold in the winter! What we had, to ward off the chill, was a bunch of olive-drab wool Army Surplus blankets! Each of us had two, if memory serves correctly. I remember jumping into a cold bed, consisting of a four inch cotton mattress on an Army Surplus steel bed frame and steel mesh springs, in the dead of winter! I'm telling you the "Polar Bear Club" (those folks who jump into the icy waters of January for the fun of it) had nothing on us. It took several minutes of frantic movement to warm up those beds, even in your "long johns"! But sleep? No one ever slept better than we did! No one ever slept cold, and our Hogans never burned down.

We each had an Army Surplus footlocker at the foot of our bunks. Moving in consisted of dumping all my suitcase stuff in the footlocker, or so I thought. I learned very quickly, however, that nothing is done haphazardly in my new environment. Each activity seemed to be related to another, and served a purpose. My footlocker had to be organized in order to facilitate group activities. For instance, if we were going swimming, no one wanted to wait on me while I looked for my swimming trunks and towel! Things had a place for a purpose. There was no one to pick up after me, no one to fold my clothes for me, no one to sympathize with my feelings of hopelessness and abandonment. It was up to me. Under the supervision of a counselor, I repacked my footlocker. It is a horrible thing for a youngster to have to accept responsibility, for their own actions, at such as tender age, don't you think?

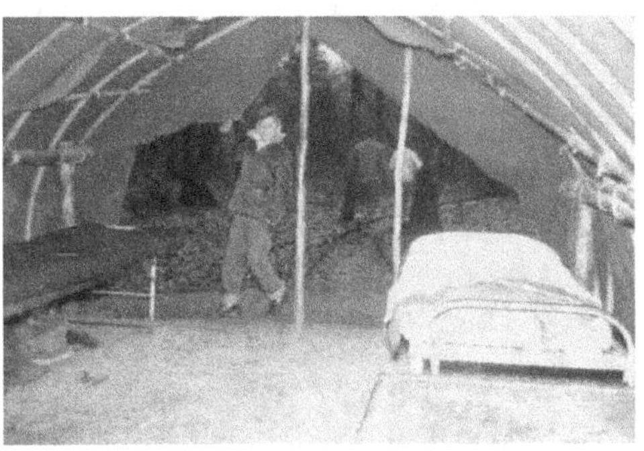

There were things, which you could not keep in your footlocker. Living creatures was one, and creatures no longer living, or parts thereof, was another. Living creatures cannot survive in a completely hostile environment. And, oddly enough, if you place a lower portion of a deer's hind leg in your footlocker, in the summer, it will make itself known to your entire tribe in very little time, your Hogan mates first! Dead animal odor seems to survive long after the fact. It lives well in canvas, bedclothes, wood, your clothing, and any other material found in a Hogan! One of my "tent-mates" learned this by experience, and taught the rest of as well. Some lessons, especially of this variety, are better learned through other people's experience.

Hiking was our primary activity as campers. We walked to breakfast, probably a mile or so, then walked back to our campsite, or to another planned activity. It was the same plan for lunch and dinner. Three square meals a day and six mandatory hikes a day. The meals were always worth the walk! We even walked to the beginning point for a planned hike! The only time we even saw an automobile was when we happened to be in an area where one could drive up, or had been parked by a camp employee in the designated parking area.

Once a month, while at Camp Woodland Springs, we were transported to a Tom Thumb grocery store in east Dallas, where our parents picked us up for the weekend. The weekend consisted of Saturday afternoon through Sunday afternoon. We made this journey in the back of a one ton Chevrolet flatbed truck. Today it would be seen by many as child endangerment, but in those days it was a means to an end and fun! No one was ever harmed on these trips, and I made those round-trips for five years. Our firsthand experiences, with mechanical conveyances, was limited to special trips and the occasional sighting. Everywhere else, we hiked!

You know there will be problems arising among ten little boys with ten different personalities and a wide variety of backgrounds, not to mention their emotional diversities! One of the reasons we all found our way to the camp was our inability to solve, or even address, problems for ourselves. Multiply that by ten, without the introduction of the counselor's personalities, and you have the makings for a difficult row to hoe. Today's American culture knows very little about hoeing rows, but suffice it to say a really hard way to go.

Problem solving is really very simple, as it relates to behavioral issues. If you don't want your child to behave unacceptably, involve your child in an unpleasant activity as a result of their unacceptable behavior. Simple as that! Have them sit on an oak log, with the bark still on, until they change their mind about their behavior. This activity changed my mind more than once, and I have observed its effectiveness many times with many people! It works very well rain or shine, windy or calm, hot or cold. It has been a long proven reality that the brain is closely related to the behind, especially with children! In those days there was no mystery about that association.

Another behavior modification method in a society of unruly individuals, is the group accountability tactic. If one misbehaves and the others overlook the behavior, as if to say it isn't my fault, place the whole group at risk by removing a group privilege. It amounts to the "You knew it was happening and you allowed it by turning your head the other way" approach. It registers as "you are your brother's keeper", and it is very effective in moderating behavior within a group. These are the lessons, which help prepare an individual for responsible living. There were times when I thought I was bleeding for sure, my behind hurt so bad, but oak bark is that uncomfortable. I can tell you it didn't make me want to misbehave anymore, and it sure motivated a body to keep others in line as best you could.

This new life sure had its eye opening twists and turns! However, I do not recall ever feeling as if I was being neglected, or that nobody cared about how I behaved or what happened to me.

The idea of being rewarded with praise for doing a good job, as well as paying the consequence for unacceptable behavior, was relatively new to me. Usually the reward, something purchased, was intended to solicit acceptable behavior, and consequences only reflected anger on the part of the "care-giver" when they were displeased. The learning process was far from over!

Chapter Two: Anecdotes and memories

Not everything that happened in my new surroundings was pleasant or character building. As with any organization, where people are involved, you have your bad apples, and over the years, we had a few wormy human products. To my knowledge we never had a child molester among us, but physical and emotional child abuse is not a new horror on our planet. It isn't necessary to go into elaborate detail, but in this day and time it is sufficient to say the vast majority were good decent people and the rotten cored human few did not last long. I was very fortunate that I only ran into a couple over my long stay at the camp. The oversight of men like Campbell Loughmiller, and Buford

McKenzie, known as "Chief Mac", was largely responsible for weeding out the riffraff.

Chief Mac was our in-house trouble-shooter. He was the Chief of Chiefs and answered to the Director, Campbell Loughmiller. When it was necessary for Chief Mac to come help solve a problem, everybody knew there was going be hard times! Buford McKenzie was a huge man with a golden singing voice and a no nonsense approach to living agreeably with others. His word was law in the camp. There were times I feared his presence, and times I was really glad to see him coming up the trail, with little dust clouds puffing from beneath his huge shoes with every step. Chief Mac had a stiff leg and walked faster than any man I ever knew. To us kids, with our short little legs, he was at a dead run pace most of the time. You could spot him from a mile away, approaching in his quick lumbering gate.

I don't know how he was injured, but I like to think he was a decorated combat wounded veteran of the Second World War with Germany and Japan. As I look back, it would fit him well. He was a hero in real life, a dedicated man, not at all like the fanciful crafted stories of Hollywood writers. His legacy still lives among us today, in the productive lives of once wayward baby boomers. As I think of him now, and his devotion to his work, which was each and every boy in the camp, it was evident in everything he did.

I remember my first Canoe ride on Opossum Kingdom Lake in north central Texas. It would have been in 1952, I believe. The water in that lake was crystal clear. I remember thinking how unstable we seemed to be in the water. There were five of us boys, one with a bow seat and a paddle, and one councilor propelling us through the water from the stern. Still, I was mesmerized by the clarity of the water as I pondered the depth. In some places I could see what looked to be, as I consider it now, fifty feet or better. I don't remember the fishing being all that good, but then I figured the fish could see me as well as I could see them so it was understandable. Then, I thought it was a given that the fish had to be sneaked up on, and kept totally unaware of ones presence, before you had a ghost of a chance to catch one. I guess they must hear pretty well too, because the counselors were always "shushing" us come fishing time. Anyway, these guys lived in the biggest glass fishbowl in the world as far as I could tell. How in the world could a fellow sneak up on them?

I did manage to sneak up on a rattlesnake den one evening. It is still frightening when I think about how close I came! We drew our drinking and cleaning water from the lake, just down a rocky wall from our campsite. After one supper meal, it was my turn to get a bucket of water for cleaning the dishes. On the way down to the lake's edge, I took a little shortcut over the rocky surfaces, jumping from one level to the next on the smooth rocky ledges. No jump was very challenging, it wasn't quite dark yet, and it was the most fun to go that way. We had done it during the day without incident. LESSON #1... Rattlesnakes are nocturnal animals. They hunt and feed at night. They withdraw during the hot daylight hours, into little crevasses between the large rocks, which make up the rocky walls around the lake. LESSON #2... Rattlesnakes do not see very well. They have no need. They seek their prey by heat sensing ability. LESSON #3... Never shine a flashlight into a crevasse when it is broadcasting sounds resembling a thousand angry babies waving their plastic rattles! I did not get bitten, but I did give myself every opportunity.

During my stay in the camp, at both locations, I have gone fishing in Caddo Lake, Lake Whitney, Eagle Mountain Lake, a private lake owned by one the members of the Salesmanship Club, and numerous creeks and rivers. And yes, I even tried to sneak up on the fish in Opossum Kingdom Lake. The experience of catching my first big-mouth Bass on a Hula-Popper still remains fresh after fifty-five years. I would tell you how big and heavy he was, but it has been so long since I caught him that I don't even believe me now! Okay, actually, he weighed around one pound. I caught him on a last cast into the privately owned lake I mention before. We were called to supper, but I had to cast just one more time! I became the fisherman's hero in that one moment of defiant perseverance!

I imagine I have logged more miles in a Canoe, on rivers and lakes, than Davey Crocket, Lewis and Clark, and the most water-born Indian who ever lived. Next to hiking, Canoeing was the only other accepted form of transportation for a camper. On every trip I have ever taken while a camper, with the exception of the trip around Texas taken in late 1957 while in the Tejas tribe, Canoes were part and parcel of the journey. Unless we were taking a local one-day field trip, our destination included water of some variety. That water demanded exploration by Canoe!

Our counselors taught us what we needed to do, if the Canoe capsized, before we ever took to deeper water. We actually practiced making the Canoe flip over in safe places. It was such fun, making the Canoe capsize, then coming up under the Canoe and hanging on to the gunwale braces. Righting the Canoe, after the fun, was another story, and a lot more like work! No camper was ever denied the adventure of exploring the waterways by Canoe, yet we never lost a boy or a Canoe in my eight-year association with the camp! And yes, we always wore life jackets on every Canoe outing!

Pets, while common place in the average home, were not available in the wild where animals were in great number. I suppose there was never a single day, even in the dead of winter, when I did not see one animal in its natural habitat. Cottontail Rabbits were everywhere, Opossums were constantly trying to dig up the garbage we buried in our "Garbage Pit", Raccoons were in abundance, and there was the occasional fox slinking around. We had Armadillos and Turtles, Horned Toads, a great variety of Lizards, and the warmer months brought out every indigenous poisonous and non-poisonous snake you can imagine, from the Hognose Snake to Cottonmouth Water Moccasins and Rattlesnakes. We also had the indigenous Coral Snake and it's non-poisonous counterpart the Scarlet King Snake. Discovering which ones you could mess with, and which were better left alone, was an adventure in itself. Of course, there was instruction! But, as the saying goes, "Boys will be boys!" This concise phrase is universal language for "It doesn't matter what you told them, or how often!"

A Hognose snake is like a Chihuahua with the mentality of a bad tempered Roman Rottweiler with a toothache. The Hognose snake is relatively small, generally no longer than eighteen inches or so. I don't recall catching one longer than about fourteen inches. At a glance, a Hognose looks similar to a Rattler. Its defensive mode makes it resemble a small Cobra. It puts on one great show of force, but the only damage done will be from tripping and falling, on your way out of the Hogan, as you run for your life!

I don't think I was really a mean kid, but one of my great joys was introducing a new camper to a Hognose snake in close quarters! This little pass-time didn't always work out well, but I earned every lump I got in retaliation. Again, I was learning who I could mess with, and who was better left alone. For all of that, camping was a good life for a boy with no direction. It was a learning experience to be envied!

Chapter Three: A Camper's Work

When you live in the wilderness, so to speak, you have certain chores that require accomplishment on a regular basis. There are a number of things that have a sense of perpetuity when maintaining a year-round campsite. Garbage and trash are generated on a daily basis. Human waste must be properly managed. Living quarters, tents specifically, need maintenance, such as waterproofing the canvas, and replacing worn binder's twine, which holds the frame structure together. Since the structures are flexible, and move with the wind, the binder's twine will chafe and weaken. Any structures, such as the mess tent, latrine, and most community tents are built with natural posts secured in the ground. When those posts begin to loosen with decay, they must be reinforced or replaced. There was an ongoing need for firewood, so wood had to be cut and stacked on a weekly basis. There is never a shortage of things to do. It was difficult to find an idle mind, and consequently the Devil's workshop was fairly short-handed, though on occasion, we managed.

Each of these tasks was assigned to one or more campers. We actually did the work, which had become part and parcel of our training and learning process as members of a society. Teamwork becomes key to success. Compromise, that "getting along" attitude, becomes key to teamwork.

Take the simple digging of a Garbage Pit. This is where we dispose of every type of waste material generated among ten boys and two grown men on a daily basis. We dug them with round point shovels, which had four-foot handles as I recall. The hole usually measured about ten to twelve feet across and six to seven feet deep. This task would usually fall to three or four campers. Two would dig the hole, while the other team member(s) would arrange the dirt that was thrown out of the hole. Arranging this dirt around the edge of the Garbage Pit was an important task. This same dirt

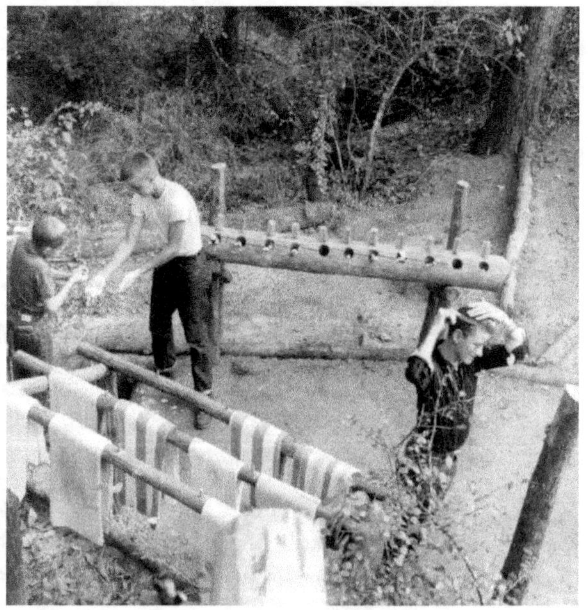

would be used to cover each deposit of garbage/trash into the Garbage Pit in order to keep Raccoons, Opossums, and other animals out of the waste. This precaution was taken for their sakes as well as ours. Animals can spread trash like nobody's business, and they could be harmed by eating the wrong things. Neither of these two options was acceptable.

Now you put two young fellows in a hole ten feet across and four foot deep, each with a shovel, both digging and shoveling for all they're worth, and somebody is going get a bump somewhere before too much time slips by. When you get smacked in the head with a shovel handle, your first considered response is to smack somebody back! The concept of teamwork, completing the task without injury and in the shortest period of time being the goal, you learn how to work in harmony with teammates and within your environment. The sooner the task was finished, and the fewer the problems incurred during the effort, the sooner we went swimming or played "Kick the Can", or launched on some other fun adventure! We knew that rewards were earned, and it was up to us. We set our goals and we succeeded, and sometimes failed, on our own merit. What a remarkably effective concept!

I learned the true art of cooperation on the business end of an eight-foot crosscut saw, like the ones you see in lumberjack movies. I learned the art of using a "Buck Saw" the hard way, by nearly losing my left forefinger. Some lessons are harder learned than others, but I survived. Nobody got sued, and the life lesson was well worth any lost blood!

When I was about nine years old, I was introduced to the "pull-pull" crosscut saw. It was about six feet long, somewhat limber and fairly heavy as I remember it. One had to be trained in its use, or failure was inevitable. The primary objective was simply to produce firewood from large girth trees for the winter. We also fashioned camp style sitting furniture amounting to short sections of larger diameter logs. But, fuel for the heating stove, open fireplace, and Powwow fires took center stage.

There were many other daily chores which needed completion, so you had to develop skill with the crosscut lumberjack saw. That skill was the ability to cooperate with whomever was on the other end of the saw. When your partner finished his pull, you began your own pull as a continuation of that motion. Nobody pushed on their end of the saw, ever, or the saw blade bound in the wood immediately, or jumped out of the cut, bringing the activity literally to a screeching halt. Your only option was to start fresh, pulling when it was your responsibility. If you kept at it, you soon developed a mutual rhythm, the wood piled up, a friendly competition developed with other boys, and everyone benefited. You had a skill to be proud of, the cook had wood, you ate good hot food, enjoyed heat in the cold, and your world was a better place.

Normally, when our chores were finished, there would be some kind of positive reward waiting in the wings. Sometimes, it was the swimming pool and a "moonlight" swim. Other times, there was a special T.V. night, or perhaps a moonlight hike to a special destination. And, sooner or later, everyone was introduced to the midnight Snipe hunt. If your councilors were especially creative, a midnight Snipe hunt was a lot of fun!

Occasionally, when an especially difficult task was completed, we might get to plan a canoe trip on some river or lake. Many times it was being told what a good job we had done together and how proud our "Chiefs" were of our accomplishment. Just as it would have been on any ranch or farm, you benefited by getting the work done well and ahead of schedule. Regularly, as needed after the day's work was done, we took a hike to the communal bathhouse for a good warm shower.

Not all was as it should have been among us, and bumps in the road were a given expectation for our counselors. We would not have been placed in the camp initially if we had all been well-adjusted Citizens. Looking back now, the beauty of the camp's philosophy was in the fact that we faced every obstacle and enjoyed every success, as a group. Though individualism was not erased, by any means, we made up a distinct society. We suffered, or we benefited, from the actions of individuals within our tight little society. Each night, before bedtime, we would meet in a circle around an open fire to discuss the happenings of the day, sing a song or two, and just wind down from the day. This was our end of the day "Powwow", an American Indian term for a meeting. Problems, if any between campers, were openly discussed among all of us. We put those things to rest, for the most part, which gave us difficulty with each other, or some event of the day.

We not only learned how to get along with each other, we learned the art of combining our strengths to accomplish a common goal. In that process, we also learned the concept of personal accountability and how to take pride in a job well done. We learned how to respect one another for our individual contributions to the team effort. What better lessons could a young person learn than these, in today's world?

Chapter Four: Success and Failure, Benchmarking Progress

How can a person know what it means to succeed when they have only experienced failure, or have never experienced failure? Certainly, there would be no benchmark for comparison. One of the things campers were allowed the opportunity to do, was to fail. What I mean by that has more to do with the decision-making processes exercised, than with the actual task, though we did occasionally fail to measure up in certain areas of undertaking. Mostly, our defeats were due to our listening skills, but sometimes it boiled down to anger at an individual, or frustration with the confines of the camp itself. We found that the same personal issues, which had challenged us at home, were the very things placing obstacles in our paths as campers.

"Running away" was not an uncommon goal among campers. Several boys, myself included, ran away from the camp more than once. Of course, today, I would be hard pressed to tell you why, exactly. Maybe it was homesickness, perhaps rebellion against being sent to the camp, the temporary "celebrity" status gained among other campers in having been a fugitive, or some other momentary peer influence. For whatever reason, some of us thought "running away" was the thing to do. My Aunt Mary lived in Pleasant Grove, about two miles away from Camp Woodland Springs, so I never had far to run. My Aunt never waited very long to call the camp and let them know where I was, so it turned out to be more of a short visit with her than an escape!

The thing was, we were not tied to a post, or chained to a railing, nor confined under lock and key. We were given the freedom to make poor decisions and exercise our free will. Running away did not get you out of the camp, nor did it get you locked up as a delinquent. No problems were solved. To the contrary, more were created. We learned individually, and collectively, problems do not disappear when you refuse to face them. Often they tend to fester and grow in their enormity. "Running away" adds another unpleasant dimension, which requires resolution. All of this we learned because we were not restrained. It took some a little longer to digest the meat of the lesson, but we all "got it" sooner or later. To learn a lesson well, sometimes it has to be learned firsthand.

I don't remember at what age I handled my first poisonous snake. As I recall it was a Copperhead, and not much over a foot long I'm sure. We had a pretty fair variety of pit vipers, which included the Copperhead, Rattlesnake, and cotton Mouth Water Moccasin. We also had in east Texas especially, the dreaded Coral Snake whose venom is similar to that of the Cobra. Did we have permission to handle dangerous critters? Absolutely not! In fact, we were admonished to leave all of them alone. Were we taught proper methods of safely handling dangerous critters? Absolutely, and supervised every moment while actually handling non-poisonous snakes. Why, you ask, would an adult teach a kid how to do something they were told not to do? You will remember the "boys will be boys" statement?

Things were a lot simpler then, where child psychology was concerned. Doctor Benjamin Spock was unknown at that time, as a leader in the child psychology field. The recognized experts were the responsible grownups among us. It is far more valuable, in my judgment, and apparently in the judgment of the camp director and councilors, to know what a child will be likely to do, rather than why they will do it. Adults knew, because they had been children, we were going to press the limits and go beyond our verbally established boundaries. In other words, we were going to try to capture and handle poisonous snakes, and the knowledge of proper handling might just save a life. So they taught us, in this instance, how to survive should we make that bad decision and engage the slithering, scaly pit viper population. I don't recall a camper ever being fatally bitten, but I do recall being taught how to treat a poisonous snakebite in the wild.

Building a fire, deep in the woods, can be a very dangerous activity. When children are building that fire, the danger quotient is multiplied significantly. One of the first things I remember being taught was the art of building a fire, and the steps to protect my surroundings from that fire. Building a fire anywhere is a tremendous responsibility, but in the woods it takes on a whole new demeanor. Smokey the Bear wasn't the product of fire safety practices well exercised! We learned about wind, clear space around the fire location, and how to ensure the fire was completely extinguished before leaving the area. We learned both the value of fire and it's unforgiving destructive personality. Then, we built fires and enjoyed the confidence placed in us by others to do it well. In addition, we learned what to do if a fire took on a personality of its own.

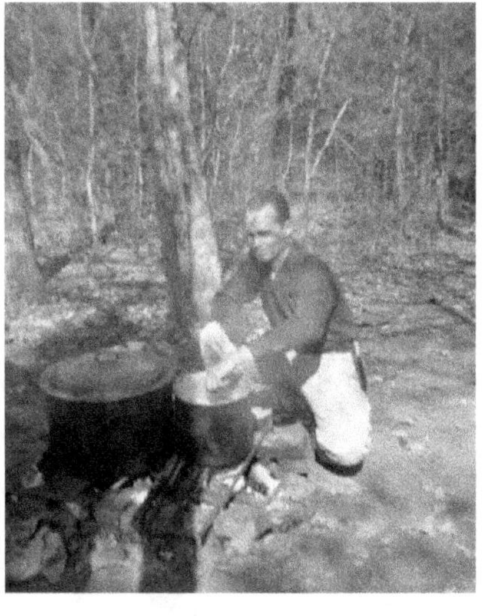

On an extended trip around the state of Texas, as a member of the Tejas Tribe, we had a frightening experience with fire and a camper. Richard, a good friend and fellow camper, was straddling a log, which we were gradually feeding into the fire. He had turned his back to the fire, warming his backside on a particularly chill morning, and the fire crept down the log to his pants leg. Suddenly, he yelled bloody-murder and took off running very fast. He had a good lead on us before we realized his pant-leg was on fire. Richard, unfortunately, was a very fast runner when just fooling around. He was not fooling this day! We finally, out of shear panic and adrenaline rush, caught him and wrestled him to the ground, extinguishing the blazing material. His leg was burned pretty badly, below and behind the knee, and he was taken to the nearest hospital for treatment. He rejoined us, as I remember, several days later and well bandaged, in a new campsite to which we had relocated.

If we behaved in a totally unacceptable manner, and perhaps caused the whole group to suffer unnecessarily, there was a good chance we all might be excluded from the next group lunch or dinner. Breakfast, even in those days, was considered too important a meal for a camper to miss. This personal accountability reminder could occur during the two days we cooked in our own campsite, or it could be exacted during a camp meal at the Chuck Wagon when all tribes and campers met to eat together during the other five days of the week.

I remember this experience, if exacted during a Chuck Wagon meal, as being both embarrassing and somewhat humiliating, not to mention hard on the stomach. The meals prepared by Mom Taylor were always hearty and, to the best of my memory, very tasty. Of course, all that hiking and wood-cutting, building and digging, swimming and playing "kick-the-can", had a way of developing a fairly substantial appetite in a growing boy's stomach! The smells coming from the Chuck Wagon were extremely enticing to a hungry young fellow sitting on a log outside the building, while everyone else ate their fill. Then, there was also the inescapable knowledge that food meant for my belly was being shared by those other nine guys, which added insult to injury. Additionally, an explanation would be required, sometimes several times over by campers of every age, as to why I was sitting outside alone while everyone else was eating! But, you know what? I learned, as did others, that when you break the rules there is a penalty! That penalty is determined by the seriousness of the infraction. There was justice in simple form, made clear and understandable to a wayward kid. It is a true concept in life, which says "Lessons learned hardest are lessons learned best!" When children are subject to injustice regularly, whether too lenient or too strict, the lessons derived are often destructive to the society in which they live. Failure to teach children responsibility for their own actions is perhaps the greatest injustice of all.

Chapter Five: Boys will be Kids..Sometimes for their whole lives...

One of the things young boys do is test the waters, push hard enough to go slightly beyond established behavioral boundaries, on a continual basis. There seems to be this primal need to know who is the toughest, smartest, most likely to "be in charge" guy in your peer group. Don't know why this is, but it is a natural fact. Perhaps it is a reminder that, though we are the highest form of intelligent animal life on the planet, we are still animals. What this produces, among ten boys, is a great likelihood of fisticuffs. I wish I could say that this affliction goes away with the maturing process, but that is sadly not the case for many. Unfortunately, due to the ignorant and criminally minded, there are times when fighting in self-defense is the only option when there is no escape. But grown men fighting to prove their manhood? Must be a warped gene gender thing.

The first time I got into a "fight", if you could call it a "fight", was at seven years of age. My opponent was Dennis who told us he was from Tampa, Florida. Dennis, at that particular time, was an incorrigible liar. Though he may well have been from Tampa, we soon became convinced that Dennis did not know the difference between truth and what he wanted to believe. Many of us had that same problem before we learned the value of honesty. In any event, Dennis had told a story about me, as I recall, which was not true and most irritating.

So, Dennis and I squared off to solve the issue of who could beat-up whom, when Chief Sam Inman miraculously appeared with four large brown leather bags, which appeared to be the size of large watermelons. Turned out these were sixteen-ounce boxing gloves. When Chief Sam had finished asking us what we were doing (which he already knew from observation), and had given us the opportunity to change our minds about our chosen course, he introduced us to the boxing gloves. You haven't lived until you have seen sixteen-ounce boxing gloves strapped on a seven-year old child! From just below the elbow, we took on the appearance of large brown elephants. Chief Sam announced that he was the referee, and we could "have at it" any time we wanted. Having received the "Chief's" blessing, we enthusiastically proceeded to prove our toughness to the gathered masses.

Well, those gloves felt like they weighed twenty pounds each after just a few swings at each other! It was like being hit with a solid leather pillow filled with cotton. The sheer weight of the glove easily knocked me off balance when Dennis scored a roundhouse to my arm, but there were no bloody noses, no pain or bruises, after the fact. Neither of us could continue after about a minute and a half. We could barely lift a glove! Neither of us was declared the winner, which by then was not an issue anyway, we just wanted these huge growths removed from our arms. At an early age, most of us began to see that fighting doesn't solve problems, and there are no real winners in an activity that merely proves superior brute strength.

There were occasions when a camper would fall ill, have a serious cut or some other injury, and a message would be dispatched to the necessary authority by runner. This seldom happened, but it did happen now and then. Sometimes this would require leading people back to the campsite, and other times it was a notification that a camper was being brought to the administration office or Chuck Wagon for treatment. Being a messenger was a kind of honor. You had to be fast and dependable to be chosen. Running full out for a mile was not unusual.

I remember the first time a messenger was sent on my behalf. I must have been around eight years old when it happened. I was using a Buck Saw with another camper, cutting firewood for campsite cooking.

Similar to the larger crosscut saw when used by two people, the saw is designed, and intended, to be pulled through the wood and never pushed unless being used by a single person.. Buck Saws have very sharp and jagged teeth on a thin blade, which is scary enough just to look at. I was gripping this smaller limb with my left hand as we attempted to cut it in two. My sawing partner suddenly pushed the saw, causing it to jump out of the limb and onto my left forefinger. It was an ugly ragged cut, and it looked as if I would need a lot of stitching up. A runner was dispatched immediately, and the proper people were waiting when they brought me to the Administration building. Turned out, upon closer examination, there was nothing to stitch together, so they bandaged it as best they could and we returned to our campsite. Luckily, no tendon damage occurred and my finger, though significantly scarred, was perfectly functional after the healing period.

One of the most favorite of our possessions was a pocketknife. I was introduced to the Case xxx brand as a camper, and carry one to this day. Now, having already talked about fighting amongst ourselves, you probably wonder at the wisdom of allowing us to carry sharp edged pocketknives. Things were different in 1951. One difference was the attitude toward training children. We were taught about knives, their uses, and the dangers involved with handling such a potentially dangerous instrument. I recall someone threatening another camper once with his pocketknife, but there was never an incident when someone actually used their pocketknife as a weapon. Society was more civilized in those days, for the most part.

At eight years old, or there about, I knew to keep my knife sharp, clean, and that cutting toward the body or any of its parts can be hazardous. A knife is a necessary tool in a camper's life. It can be used to cut thin slivers of wood for kindling a fire, cutting binder's twine, carving intricate wood sculptures, and cutting the skin over poisonous snakebite fang wounds to drain out poison. Knives, with three blades, can also be used to play mumble-peg, though that was a forbidden game in the camp. If you cut yourself, playing mumble-peg, you bled quietly and privately, telling no one who might relay your misfortune to a Chief. You wouldn't lose your knife because you cut yourself, but because you disobeyed a rule. It was hard to explain a cut on your foot or your knee! And, after a proper "learning" period, you would get your knife back.

Woodcarving soon became my favorite activity with a pocketknife, though mumble-peg certainly had its allure. I have more than two dozen scars on my left hand (the hand a right-handed person uses to hold the wood being carved) as a result of my woodcarving days. It was an activity that taught me to pursue excellence in whatever I chose to do. I fear it may have induced a perfectionist's perspective at an early age. But, as many have said, if it is worth doing, it is worth doing right! Woodcarving also teaches patience. A hasty cut, in the wrong place, can put a sudden end to a carving project! One has to observe the wood with a view toward the finished product. In woodcarving, haste truly is waste.

I said there was a different attitude toward training children in 1951, but most especially that difference prevailed at the camp. I would never have cut myself if I had been forbidden to own a pocketknife. I would only have cut myself once if it had been taken away from me the first time I made myself bleed. But then, I would have missed out on one of the best lesson sets, learned over a period of several years, about patience, perfection, and perseverance, in my growing-up processes. Now, I would not trade one scar!

Chapter Six: Up through the Ranks

When I came to Camp Woodland Springs I was seven years old. My mother, who had divorced my father when I was five weeks old, had to make a hard choice. Either way, she would lose me to the care and raising of others. Unfortunately, she had proven her inability raise me on her own, and it would be good for both of us in the long run. It really was a moot point anyway, because I had been in the care of strangers for years. With me at home, she could only look forward to being responsible for a juvenile delinquent and eventually a full-fledged criminal. I was already well on my way at the tender age of seven years. Her choice, mandated by the Juvenile Court in Dallas, was limited to the camp or a Juvenile Detention Center in Gatesville, Texas. It was the woods, or the bars and high fences. If my mother ever made a wise decision in her entire life, the camp was certainly that decision! I was assigned to the youngest tribe, Tejuacana, upon arrival at the camp.

We had several councilors over my stay in Tejuacana. I remember Chiefs Sam Inman, John Spencer, and "long" John, by name, and a couple whose names escape me. The men, whom I remember by name, were good men who cared about all of us boys and acted as mentors, as teachers, as protectors and concerned guardians. I remember thinking how lucky I would have been, and how much better my mother would have fared, had one of these men been my father.

I believe I was there about two years before being moved up to the next age group called Frontier. Before I was old enough to move up to Beavers, I was allowed to go back home in 1956, at the age of twelve years, and resume life in the real world of schools and rules which were completely foreign to me. Stonewall Jackson Elementary School, in Dallas, welcomed me with open arms into the sixth grade. It was already the middle of the school year as I recall.

When it was time for the seventh grade, Stonewall Jackson decided I was no longer welcome, and I would be sent to a school better suited for physically advanced and socially inept students. I attended W.W. Spence Junior High in my thirteenth year on the planet, where most problem children in the Dallas area were sent. My problems with other students continued, and I continued to develop an unsavory reputation as a fighter and trouble prone kid. I was literally like a fish out of water on my first return to "civilization". I still had no supervision at home, which I very badly needed. I did not complete the seventh grade, and was returned to The Salesmanship Club Boys Camp in late 1957.

The camp was now located in eastern Texas near the town of Hawkins. I had skipped the Beavers tribe, and found myself in the Tejas tribe, which was the oldest group of the four camping tribes. After a year or so in Tejas, it was decided that I had earned the privilege of going back to school, this time in Hawkins, as a High School freshman, and I was moved up to Ranchers.

I suppose Ranchers were so named because they actually lived in a house, like cowboys. We had a bathroom, a kitchen, and heat in the winter. I don't recall air conditioning, but we may have had that too. In any event, the Ranchers had always been considered the elite group of boys in the camp. We had "arrived" as campers when we were elevated to Rancher! Age was not the deciding factor, behavior and personal progress was. I do not recall a group called "Ranchers" at Camp Woodland Springs, though there may have been.

I was enrolled in the ninth grade in Hawkins High School, and immediately became involved in track and football. I loved going to school in Hawkins and, as it turned out, the ninth grade would be the only full year of conventional schooling I would ever receive. After completing the ninth grade, and doing relatively well, I once again ventured into the world from which I had been rejected. At fifteen, I was going to give it another go. To my knowledge, I spent more time in the camp than any other camper. I'm sure many thought I was a hopeless case and would never so improve as to be successful in the real world. As I look back now, I believe I was happier in the camp than I had ever been at home. It was my "real world". I adapted well to the environment, seemed to excel as a camper, and was comfortable living in the wild. I had developed friendships in the camp, which bordered on having brothers.

Every day in each age group brought new experiences, and new lessons, which prepared me for new responsibilities, as it did for every other camper. I had come from a life where I had no daily guidance, and was left to my own devices, into a world of mutual responsibility and obligation. The transition was not easy, but the challenges were necessary opportunities, allowing me to grow and flourish as a human being on my way to manhood.

By the time I was old enough to enroll in the first grade in University Park Elementary School, I already had a criminal record of sorts. I had stolen a toy wind-up car from the five and dime, for which my mother marched me down to University Park Police Headquarters, and a stern "talking to" by the Chief of Police. That scared me half to death at the time! I never had the urge to take anything else that wasn't mine. I still remember that huge man, on the other side of that big desk, talking about little boys with blood running down their legs.

I had gotten a Red Ryder BB gun for Christmas just before turning seven. No one supervised me in its use. Oh, I'm sure there were the canned warnings about pointing the BB Gun at people or cats, but in the excitement of the moment there was no listening! I was only too anxious to have real BB gunfights with other kids.

An angry policeman confiscated my Red Ryder BB gun, as well as the other three or four involved in the "BB Gunfight At The Not O.K. Construction Site". After a very thorough scolding, he sent me and the other cowboys home with a frightful warning! My mother never inquired with the police about destiny the BB gun.

I once broke a water main pressure gauge under the water tower at Rosedale St. and Airline Drive, causing a terrific geyser to erupt under the tower. Construction crews had been working on the massive plumbing under the tower, leaving the large square concrete bunker containing said plumbing wide open. There was probably two feet of water in the bottom of the bunker, a large pile of broken concrete chunks beside the bunker, and I was having a great time making big splashes with those chunks of concrete. The fun ended when the pressure gauge toppled off its mount on the huge water main, and a thirty-foot stream of water shot skyward.

Once, when probably six or seven years old, and before attending first grade, there was some road surface repair being done in our neighborhood. A Steam Roller, among other pieces of equipment used to finish the blacktop surface, had been left unattended during a lunch break and all the operators were nowhere to be seen. Yep, you guessed it! The keys were in the ignition, and I knew about the floor mounted starter button! Unfortunately, the machine was also left in gear, apparently to prevent it from rolling away on its own. The engine quickly roared to life, and I was off and rolling, without a clue how to steer or stop my forward motion. I turned the steering wheel, but the machine went in the opposite direction and targeted a neighbor's front door! I was so frightened that I didn't think to turn the key off! To my horror I was rolling right up the walkway to the front door of a house! About midway across the yard everything came to a quiet stop. I must have been screaming bloody murder from the git-go! A neighbor man, who apparently was familiar with heavy equipment, had known how to stop the run-away machine. He was also very familiar with corporal punishment techniques, and proceeded to wear my butt out with his belt. I had it coming, I needed it, and no one could fault him for administering it. My mother thanked him profusely for coming to my rescue and saving the neighbor's house I was about to destroy. I remember him telling her he had given me a pretty severe spanking. She was not the least bit defensive of me, and thanked him for that too! Suing him for his physical attention to my behind never came to my mother's mind!

No question about it, I was a wild child with little or no restraint at that age. With no mentoring and no appreciable guidance, I had become a true menace to the society in which I lived. It would not get better, and eventually I would come to a bad end on the present course I was maintaining.

And those are just some of the public issues I was involved in at such an early age! I was definitely headed in the wrong direction, because I had no hands-on direction at home. Camp Woodland Springs changed that significantly, overnight.

Chapter Seven: Fond Camp Memories

One of my fondest memories, of one of my best friends in the camp, is of Paul. Paul had contracted polio as an infant, which gave him some physical problems to deal with. He stuttered very badly, unless he got angry. When Paul lost his temper, he had a phrase he unloaded on the object of his wrath without respect of persons whatsoever. In order to deliver this phrase with the correct enunciation and appropriate force, Paul would rotate at the waist in a back and forth wind-milling fashion, with both arms straight out from his body, building momentum. At just the right moment, he would spin completely around very quickly in a perfect 360 degree spin. While spinning around, he would shout without a trace of a stutter, "You jackass shit-bomb!" Sometimes this performance was very funny to watch, because we knew what was coming. Other times, it wasn't so funny!

I remember one specific event when he applied this reaction to Chief Buford McKenzie. Apparently, Paul did not like a decision the head Chief had made regarding a disciplinary action. This time it was not the least bit funny! We all believed that Chief Mac could call down lightening from the heavens. He didn't, as it turned out, and we were all relieved.

In spite of Paul's challenges, he was a good kid and a good little musician. I remember the first time he agreed to play his Accordion for the whole camp after a supper meal in the Chuck Wagon building. I remember we all applauded his performance, and how happy that made him. After that, he played for us often.

Every once in a while we had an opportunity to perform planned skits, for the whole body of campers, after evening meals in the Chuck Wagon. We would sit around the campfire in our evening powwow in our campsite, and plan what we would do the next night. Our councilors would offer helpful suggestions and advice on the presentations. One time, on the prompting of our own Chiefs, we did an echo skit for the benefit of Chief Mac. Three campers positioned themselves at intervals of about one hundred feet apart, trailing away from the Chuck Wagon front door. One camper stood in the doorway, and would shout something for the other campers to repeat as echoes, falling away into the night. The last echo sequence of the skit was to be "Chief Mac is a good Chief!" Unbeknownst to the camper in the doorway, when he shouted "Chief Mac is a good Chief!"; the echo battalion was to respond "Ba-loney!"... "Ba-loney!"... "Ba-loney!" All went as advertised until that final echo sequence. The look, which contorted the face of the camper in the doorway, brought the house down with laughter from everyone, including Chief Mac.

We had a Chief, and I don't remember his name or the tribe he was associated with, who could play the piano like nobody's business! I remember he reminded me somewhat of Henry Fonda. His name may have been Ed, but I am not sure. Anyway, I don't remember a time, when we all ate in the Chuck Wagon, that we didn't sing several songs after supper. Many times we sang without piano accompaniment, but occasionally we had that luxury. We sang "Oh Susanna", "She'll be Comin' 'round the Mountain", "Red River Cowboy", "Row, Row Your Boat" and many other old time favorites, mostly all taught to us by Chief Buford McKenzie. That man had a voice that wouldn't quit, and a sincere love of music. He imparted this love of music to a number of us. Another of my fondest memories, as a camper, is the sound of fifty kids raising their voices in song.

Mom Taylor was a woman of incredible stamina. How she cooked three hot meals a day, feeding sixty to sixty-five people for five days straight, is beyond me. She did this all by herself. Her meals were always good, always hearty, and always anticipated. On a rotating schedule with other groups, we took turns working in the kitchen with Mom Taylor. Our job was to wash all the dishes and cooking utensils after each meal. When we did a particularly good job, with minimal horseplay, Mom Taylor would sometimes give us an extra treat when we finished up, usually some left over desert. That was always a special moment with her. It was obvious that she loved every one of us. She had a huge roll as the only female influence we were regularly exposed to in the camp. She managed that roll with a simple eloquence, hardly found among most women today. Mom Taylor gave me my first Red Letter New Testament Bible, and helped teach us lessons from the book. I still have the book she gave me.

Among the field trips we planned and participated in were trips to manufacturing businesses, bottling plants, and canning factories. As a boy, I was treated to tours of the Proctor and Gamble facility in Dallas, the Dr. Pepper Bottling plant, Mrs. Baird's Bakery, a jelly canning plant south of Dallas, a pottery manufacturing plant, and a fishing lure production facility, just to name a few. As a camper I enjoyed some real advantages, which were not available to most other children. We were exposed to life, on many levels, as it unfolded around us. This kind of education is not available in a classroom. It teaches lessons not found in books. We were learning from people who were doing, and we were learning by doing. You could say we were being brought up in the classroom of life.

There is one more memory I have, which you may find to be a mite unusual in the "fond memory" department. It involves a serious crime. There were two of us plotting this daring foray. I recall the other boy was Danny H. We were around fourteen years old when we launched our bone-fide criminal careers. At the time we actually did the deed, we weren't even thinking about the gravity of the act we were committing. At about three hours into our caper, we had changed our minds about being real criminals.

Danny and I were in the Tejas tribe. Our campsite was located within a half-mile or so from the Community Building on the new camp property in east Texas. This building also had a special name, but I do not recall what that name was now. I had just recently been returned to the camp, and was still angry about being taken away from my friends in Dallas, though they were in reality part of the reason I had been sent back. The camp's central parking lot was an area in front of the Community Building. I don't recall if we actually planned which vehicle we were going to take, but the plan was to steal a vehicle and drive to Dallas, some one hundred miles west. We waited until the camp had settled down and we were satisfied everyone was fast asleep, then crept out of the campsite and made our way quietly to the parking area.

Once among the cars and one older pick-up truck, we chose the truck. It was a 1950 or 1951 Chevrolet as I remember. Perhaps the keys had been left in the ignition before and we had noticed it. I surely do not recall trying to start the truck without keys, and neither of us had developed the skills, which that would have required! As quietly as we could, we inched our way out of camp and down to highway 80 for the trip west. Just getting to the highway was a scary proposition. Between us, we had no real experience behind the wheel on open roadways. I scared myself silly more than once, and I think Danny was equally frightened on more than one occasion during our journey. Non-the-less, we were on our way and in the process of "escaping" the confines of the camp. As I recall, I was driving when we entered Dallas.

The reality of what we had done began to sink in as we approached the city. I had come to the starkly clear conclusion that I did not want to be a criminal. Danny and I discussed it at length, and he also had misgivings about our crime spree. I also reached another eye opening conclusion at this particular moment. Those friends, the ones I had run away to rejoin, were not important enough for me to ruin my life over. When we reached the city, I drove directly to the Juvenile Detention Center on Harry Hines Blvd. and knocked on the door. When the attending officer opened the door, I explained who we were and what we had done, handing him the keys to the truck. All of those times I had been allowed to fail and recover, over the years I had spent in the camp, had come back in a rush. I recognized the failure, and pursued the recovery on my own.

For me, as for others who continued to observe my progress or lack thereof, this was a long awaited turning point in my development as a person. There must have been some that thought I would never reach this juncture of my own volition. The resulting changes, which took place in my life, would be applauded as major steps in my maturing process. Those who really cared about me had witnessed my passage from delinquency to responsibility. Now, as I look back, it was indeed a fond moment!

Chapter Eight: Realities of Life

A little About Me

I was born in Oceanside, California to Eva Anne and Earl Leslie "Jack" Hood. From what I have gleaned over the years from close family, I was neither expected nor wanted. I am told my father wanted to have me aborted, but my mother would not hear of it. It took less than five weeks for my father to openly demonstrate his inability to cope with a baby son. My mother divorced him at that revelation. She moved us back home to Texas right away. We moved into the house my grandfather, on my mother's side, had designed and built in University Park on the north side of Dallas. She had been raised in that house and it was now jointly owned by my mother, my Aunt Mary Etta and her husband, Bob Sego. It was 1944, and Uncle Bob had just returned home from serving in the U.S. Army.

Early on, the responsibility for my daily care fell to my Aunt Mary. Mother had taken a full-time job with Southwestern Bell, in order to support us, and Aunt Mary was a stay at home wife. I come from old-fashioned stock, but my mother had broken that mold forever. It would appear that the rebellious nature of my youth comes naturally by inheritance.

When Aunt Mary and Uncle Bob decided to start their own family, mother bought Aunt Mary's share of the house and they moved to a new home in Pleasant Grove. Ironically, their home was only a couple of miles north of Camp Woodland Springs just off Loop 12 in east Dallas. I would find that location very handy later on, as "run away" camper!

A new challenge arose now that my mother and I found ourselves on our own. Who would watch over me while she worked? Daycare centers had yet to materialize as a major business entity. Baby sitters were impractical and a last option. I needed someone who could be there every day and that almost mandated a live-in caretaker. Mother began making those arrangements and considering her options right away. She arrived at what she thought was a workable solution. She would offer our home as residence to anyone who would agree to be responsible for me during her required work times. Since she was a telephone operator, her schedule varied from day to day. At best, in retrospect, this was a very inappropriate resolution to a serious problem. However, it was all she could manage at the time, and she did her best to look out for me. There are many stories I can tell from the experiences I endured during the last four or five years of this arrangement. I remember some incidents as if they happened yesterday, which will give a fairly accurate overview of the utter failure of this compromise in child rearing.

I must have been about five years old when this event took place. I was playing in our front yard when a traveling salesman parked his car at the curb. He got out, asked if I lived here, and if my parents were home, threw down a lighted cigarette in the grass and walked toward the front door. I picked up the cigarette and said, "I can do this!" and sucked in a mouth full of smoke. He immediately came back to me, took the cigarette away from me, chided me for being silly, stomped the cigarette out and walked to the door.

We had a young couple from Spain, the San Miguels, lodging with us and supposedly taking care of me at that time. He was a student at S.M.U., which campus was a mere block away. Apparently, Mr. San

Miguel observed my "smoking" feat. After the salesman left, Mr. San Miguel called me to come into the house. He was a cigar smoker. That day, I became a cigar smoker too! He made me inhale, and forbade me to spit the tobacco juice out, making me swallow it. I had already had the mumps and the measles, but had never been so miserably sick before this. My mother later recalled I had been a sickly shade of green when she came home one evening, but had no idea what caused it. I was so afraid of Mr. San Miguel that I never told her what he did to me in the course of a day. He was a brutal man. I was never sexually abused, but certainly physically and mentally abused during this period of my life.

One couple, which were very short lived as my caretakers, would go out drinking and dancing with me in tow. They had a wreck on one such excursion and well could have done me great harm. The older two door cars had front seat backs that tilted forward to allow passengers to enter the back seating area. When the collision took place, the seat back tilted forward and somehow I got lodged in the opening between the seat back and the seat bench. All I remember about it is that I was very scared, I thought I was going to be pinched in half, and they were gone the next day. I also recall my mother being very upset over the incident. These early years must have been very difficult for my mother.

I can't recall who the people were that did this to me, but I recall the way it happened. I could not have been more than three or four years old. The person, or persons, taking responsibility for me had devised a simple plan to ease the burden of caring for me. Put me outside, in an unfenced yard, warn me not to leave the yard and that they were watching me, and refuse to allow me into the house until just before my mother was due home. By bringing me into the house early, they had time to clean me up for mother's arrival. That was exactly what they did. Bathroom needs, feeding needs, all put aside for the entire day. This didn't go on very long because neighbors still had the "get involved" attitude, especially where children were concerned! There were some unpleasant details, but the picture can paint itself.

Needless to say, by the time I entered the first grade, I was a difficult little mess to deal with. I am the only person I know who got expelled from the first grade of Elementary School! Of course, a lot has changed over the years, and I imagine I am no longer alone in that particular boat, but it was relatively unheard of in 1951. It was becoming apparent to me that I was not a child people wanted around. Little did I know then, there was a campfire light at the end of this particular tunnel!

Chapter Nine: In Retrospect A Camper Looking Back

There is no absolutely perfect method of dealing with all of society's problems. It has always been so and will continue to be so. You approach one, try to think it through, and initiate the actions you believe will correct the problem or at least change its course for a better opportunity later. There are no guarantees, only honest efforts toward resolution.

Some campers may not have benefited as I did, and some may have derived more benefit than I did over the years. Whatever the case, I would not change my history with the camp in any manner. I believe the camp was what I needed most at that time in my life, and that my life has been richly rewarded as a direct result of the widely applicable life lessons I learned as a camper. One does not have to look very far, nor labor his eyes overmuch, to see the deficit we face in this country where our children are concerned today.

It was my profound pleasure to discover that the Salesmanship Club of Dallas is still doing what they can do for the children of Texas! I am blessed today by the insight of those men who, more than sixty years ago, conceived of Camp Woodland Springs and its mission for the wayward and emotionally unstable boys of my day.

As we grow older, we grow away from our roots in this modern age of high-speed travel and cutting edge technology. We forget where we came from. With lost roots, we lose our heritage. Camp Woodland Springs, and the Salesmanship Club Boy's Camp, represent my roots in our society. I am delighted to rediscover them at this time in life. It has been a pleasure looking back and recalling those most influential early life events that have brought me to this day in this time.

William S. Hood

LYNN LOUGHMILLER: GREAT OAKS FROM LITTLE ACORNS GROW

The story of the development of the Salesmanship Club Children's Camp as seen through the eyes of the Director's wife.

It all started when Mr. McCallister came to Campbell and asked him to go with him to look at a piece of property that the Salesmanship Club (SSC) was thinking of buying to start a boy's camp. Mr. McCallister was Chairman of the Welfare Board of Dallas and also a member of the SSC. Campbell had been Director of the Dallas Welfare Dept. for about three years and Mr. McCallister was familiar with Campbell's ability to organize and direct an organization. Campbell went with Mr. McCallister, reluctantly as he had a very bad cold. Being a country boy, Campbell was smitten with the beauty of the property, especially lying so close to the city of Dallas.

The Club had conducted a summertime recreational camp for underpriviledged children for seven years, but had turned the property over to a group for their use during the war. They now wanted to get into something more vitally affecting children. They had become familiar with the Salesmanship Club in Houston who was running a camp and picked up the name from them – not only Salesmen but anyone interested in providing an opportunity for youth to grow up and live productive lives.

Mr. McCallister, owning the oldest largest Chevrolet dealership in Dallas, was a good Salesman and persuaded Campbell to meet with the SSC. board. This eventuated in his being hired as Director of the camp.

We owned a very small farm in Irving. We had bought it so our children could have the experience of farm-life, because this sort of childhood had meant so much to both Campbell and me. We had a horse, cows, pigs, and chickens, and a large garden. The house had been built by a Frenchman and the main room was log, and it was sturdy, over a hundred years old. When we told our children of our pending move, they asked if we could take the animals with us. They were very involved in their care. So we had to sell them all, and eventually the homestead, taking only the dog and two tom cats.

Mr. Bryant and his family lived in the only house on the property as caretaker. We camped in a one-room storage room attached to the car shed, until we could arrange to leave for L.B. Sharp's camp in New Jersey. The SCC arranged for us to attend it as it was the nearest thing to an outdoor, educational experience for youngsters at that time.

We stored our furniture, arranged for Camelia, 11 and Grover, 10 to be in a camp not too far from ours. We left the dog and cats with the Bryants. While we were gone a house was built for them on the property.

The experience at L.B. Sharp's camp opened up many avenues of interest and help for our pending experience at camp. It was fun. We lived in a "hogan" (a tent structure), did some outdoor cooking, learned how to use nature in craft projects, how to teach in an outdoor setting, and a little about group work – at least the importance of getting along in a small group. The whole experience was educational, helpful for our own planning, and fun.

When we returned Campbell found Mr. Bryant "clearing" an area and stopped his axe in mid-air until he could contact Mr. Mac, the Camp Board Chairman. Mr. Mac came out and they went to the area and he said to Campbell, "Now don't you think this (where he had cleared out the underbrush) looks a whole lot better than that?" (where he had not cleared) Campbell said, "I'll tell you what we'll do, Mr. Mac, we'll bring some boys out here and if they head for the open area, we'll clear it, but if they head for the area with the undergrowth, we'll leave it." Mr. Mac said, "I see what you mean and we're going to have just one Director, and you're it." Campbell felt very fortunate to have Mr. Mac as his first Camp Board Chairman.

Another time the use of tents was questioned. Campbell took Mr. Mac out to the camp where we had set up teepees for housing the boys. I say "we", I read the directions for setting one up while the men did the work. Mr. Mac said, "Could we go in?" The boys were out of camp at the time. Campbell said, "sure." They had a left a little fire going. That did it. Mr. Mac was sold on the camping program forever after. But I'm ahead of myself here.

Settling In

We moved into the home the Bryant's had occupied. It was log too but didn't have the craftsmanship in building that our farm house had. It was architecturally very pretty, but the logs were sealed with concrete, and as the logs dried the concrete pulled away. Also the living room and dining room had no ceiling. It was very pretty, but impossible to heat or cool. A large fireplace added beauty and helped when you stood in front of it. It was set deep in the woods and an eight foot porch on three sides made it so dark that a light was needed on the brightest days. Because of the cracks we kept company with the rats and mice, a wren, and a copperhead snake in the broom closet. Also, spiders and once a swarm of honey bees. I recall one night three box turtles woke us up playing tag around our living room – really they did. They came into our bedroom, crawled up on the treadle of my sewing machine, went to the other edge, fell off, and made another trip around the living room.

The house was too hot to eat supper in the summer. The ceiling fan just didn't get the job done, so we ate in the front yard. The Screech Owls were so tame they scooted up and down on the railings – not 15 inches from us – bending at the "ankles" and turning their heads to scrutinize us. A faucet at the corner of the house dripped. They would hang upside down to drink from it. We had a bird feeding shelf on a post in the front yard. Swamp rabbits as large as jack rabbits would chase each other round and round it. The raucous barn owls would wake us, telling us, "I cook at our house, who cooks at you alls?"

The area was unbelievably covered with Copperhead snakes. The campers would come by for a gallon glass jar on their way to Vespers in case they camp upon one – and usually did. It was an interesting place to live – never a dull moment. My mother had taught me to fear snakes, and I knew the boys would run me out of the woods if they found I was afraid, so I "set-to" learn about them and teach our children. We learned to distinguish the poison from the non-poison, we kept them in jars and cages, and fed them, skinned them, and made belts from their hides, and learned to respect the dangerous ones, but not to fear them. And the non-poison ones we enjoyed and respected.

Camping on Purpose

Campbell was hired to run a camp for boys for the three months in the summer, and weekends when the weather was good. Campbell hired a boy (19) who had been a camper at the Big Brothers program. He was strong and willing and lived in a tent we set up near our house for him. We prepared for the first "week-end" campers after the tepees were up. Campbell had hired two Theology students from S.M.U as they had the weekend free to go to a community of their choice and minister to them. John Spencer was one of these. We had cots, mattresses, sheets, towels, etc. for their use. I dispensed the sheets, etc. to them as they arrived by bus after school. Food and a menu was provided also our refrigerate being the only refrigerator we had.

The counselors had been out for a training session the weekend before. The Health Dept required that they have Typhoid shots. A nurse came out and taught me how. When I got to John, and hit the needle into his arm, it just bounced and John laughed at my being upset. He was an outdoor person, with skin tanned and tough. I didn't see how I could, but I tried again with success.

Our house, the log house, was headquarters, commissary, hospital, first aid station, laundry, storage room, office – what have you, and I was nurse, cook, dispenser of food, clean linen, etc., etc. And this log house was our home. Those were busy days. Our children were involved in any way they could help. Campbell, did, however make an effort to keep his family separated from the job, but in the early days every willing hand was needed.

Once the Camp Board met at camp – where else? At our house. I wasn't at home and the phone kept ringing. Mr. Mac said, "who answers the phone when you aren't here?" "My wife", Campbell said. "You need a secretary", he said. So a desk was installed in one corner of the 20 x 30 living room, and we had our office and a part-time secretary – and she fit right in and was a good one.

I don't remember the exact order of things, but a dining room, kitchen, and store room, and an office – library – craft shop was built so the boys could invest more of their time in something besides cooking. A dietician was hired, but she had just graduated and asked if she could have her friend join her and split the salary. They shared a tent and our house was where they did their washing and ironing and "primping". They were good girls, but those hungry boys and young counselors thought some of their well-balanced summer menus were a little "light".

Our house was the recreation spot for the counselors and the meeting place for discussions. I was secretary in the new office building until a full-time secretary could be hired. Also, for about five months I was business manager – during the war – when it was hard to find help. At our option, I never received pay, even though the SSC was more than willing to pay me. Campbell always operated the camp as if it was our money supporting it. Also he wanted to keep it at a level that other communities could afford to duplicate it.

Camp Memories

Memories abound. I will never forget the night a boy at camp got a 105 degree temperature, the counselor carried him to our house (the lodge), Campbell was away. The counselor and I took him to emergency; the faster I tried to go the carburetor flooded, I guess, and we slowed down. I ran red lights, blowing my horn, trying to attract a policeman to take him and got all the way to the hospital without disturbing a policeman. The boy survived without incident.

All types of boys came to camp. Once three brothers from a West Dallas home came together. They huddled in a corner of our living room like frightened animals. When Campbell needed to see their mother about a problem, he located her working in a bar and the latest baby, a girl, in a box on top of the boxes of beer bottles. Another brother came later. To live to see these boys reverse the pattern of poverty and degradation made every effort we made more than worthwhile and very rewarding. Campbell should have written a book on the success stories in our experience, but we were all too busy in those days trying to discover ways to be more helpful – yes, even just to stay one jump ahead of some of these boys.

On another occasion, the visiting teacher called about our taking a boy: he had pushed an old lady off the sidewalk, he climbed on top of his house and threw rocks at people as they passed by, drove road-working equipment into a house, etc., etc. Campbell said, "I'm afraid he's too old for us to tackle." "Too old, "he replied, "he's six." We took him. One day the business manager took him to the doctor. When he returned he said, "I believe Tommy is improving." "How's that," Campbell asked. "He just kicked me in the shins once on the whole trip," he replied." This same child came to our house with an unusually large rat snake around his shoulders and holding each end of it, "Take my picture Chief." He began holding the snakes head near his face and making faces at him. He let him get too close and the snake bit him on the nose and it bled. "Now take my picture Chief," he cried jubilantly. We had and invitation to his high school graduation. Years later Campbell ran into his brother who was a dentist, and he reported that Tommy was married, was working, and had no problem.

There was no pattern to go by. Campbell inquired through every avenue he knew to find someone who had experience in working with the most acting out boys on the one hand, and the most withdrawn on the other (we took both) in a group, outdoor setting. There was none to be found. Group work, as we now know it was non-existent.

We were fortunate in having dedicated young men. They and Campbell spent untold hours discussing problems. One outstanding memory, John Spencer, very late one night, came into our hose, pulled up a chair beside our bed, and proceeded to expound his latest problem. There was this sort of rapport between us all – and we learned. In the final analysis, it was as Campbell often said, "You just love the hell out of them." This has to be, of course, what is now known as "tough love". There was never a dull moment. We had to hang on to keep up.

The experience that made Campbell realize that there was "dynamite" as he expressed it, in our program more than any other was when we had two boys with serious speech impediments. One had been give up on by a Speech Therapist. The fetters on their personalities were erased and they become normal beings.

In all our experience we had only one boy snake bitten, one nearly drowned when he had a seizure in the pool, one nearly lost an eye as he ran into a barbed wire fence, running from a counselor. When Campbell took him to the doctor he said, "Chief, I've learned my lesson," and Campbell was pleased until he added, "Never look back." He had looked back to see how close behind him the counselor was. This was one of the three that huddled like frightened animals in our living room. There were outstanding experiences, but by no means uncommon.

We learned about bed-wetters, liars, thieves, those with low self-esteem, speech defects, hate, poverty, fear – the whole gambit of human disorders. But most importantly Campbell and the counselors had their own "wells filled" by participating in the successes – and the success rate was phenomenal. I wished that every child – including the well-adjusted – had an opportunity to live in a group with a staff as well-trained and well-motivated as these were. The world would not be in the shape it is today. To learn to get along with one another – to "love God and love thy neighbor" is a lesson that one learns slowly.

Remembering the Wilderness Road

Stories from the

Founders of Therapeutic Camping

Vol 2 – The Real People: Eckerd and Beyond

Stephen Ashton

CHAPTER 1: NEW BEGINNINGS ECKERD YOUTH ALTERNATIVES

Jack Eckerd was

> born in Wilmington, Del., in 1913...graduated from Boeing School of Aeronautics in 1933. He flew cargo planes to India and China for the US Army Air Corps during World War II. Starting in the 1950s, he transformed the retail drug store business, creating self-service stores and the national drug store chain bearing his name.[1]

"Because of a deep interest in finding ways to relieve community ills and to better the lives of people," Jack and Ruth Eckerd "established the Eckerd Foundation in December 1961."[2] "Over the next several years, varying amounts of Eckerd Foundation money were channeled to such organizations as the United Fund, Y.M.C.A. and the Children's Home."[3] However, the couple desired to do more. Their large family of seven

[1] Martha Chamberlain, "In Memoriam Jack Eckerd Founder of Eckerd Youth Alternatives," *Journal of Therapeutic Wilderness Camping* no.2 (2004): 9.

[2] Jack and Ruth Eckerd Foundation Program and Policy Manual Vol 1 10/16/1976. p. 3.01

[3] Ibid., 3.01.

children prompted a desire to help children. Jack stumbled upon a study on children placed in correctional institutions in the State of Florida that showed 25 to 30 percent of children in placement had emotional problems and were there because, "no other program was available to meet their needs."[4] Being a shrewd businessman who cared about children, Jack saw a problem he believed needed to be solved. As a result, in October 1967, Jack Eckerd commissioned Floyd Glisson to help him "find a unique program for meeting the needs of 'emotionally problemed' children...not being provided for by current community or state services."[5] Proposals were submitted and evaluated from many sources, but one in particular, written by Dr. George H. Finck, Director of the Pinellas County Juvenile Welfard Board, caught his eye. He described a year-round camping program for emotionally disturbed boys, sponsored by the Salesmanship Club of Dallas, Texas" and the next day, "Floyd Glisson flew to Texas to observe it first-hand....About two weeks later, Mr. Eckerd informed Mr. Glisson that this was the type of program he wished to pursue."[6] They both began spending their weekends exploring the state for a suitable tract of land. In 1968 Eckerd Family Youth Alternatives Inc. was established[7] and "880 acres of what seemed a primeval forest [was purchased] south of Brooksville in Hernando County. It was an area rich in history, yielding Indian arrowheads, and containing the roadbed of an old stagecoach line between Gainesville and Tampa, Florida."[8]

Mr Eckerd, and the Eckerd Foundation, then set out to find a director. They, "first asked Chief Lock if he would start the program. He was retired and felt he was not the one to do that. Next, they asked Chief Mac (Buford McKenzie). He was not interested because he had just returned to the Salesmanship Club."[9] Chief Lock talked with Ken Edgar about going to Florida to help Jack Eckerd. He said, "You should go down, Chief. You can go to college anytime, but this is a unique opportunity to start a brand new camp."[10] Ken was not convinced that

---

[4] Ibid., 3.01.
[5] Ibid., 3.01.
[6] Ibid.,. 3.02.
[7] Jack Eckerd, *Finding the Right Prescription*, JME Inc: Clearwater, 1987, p. 147.
[8] Jack and Ruth Eckerd Foundation Program and Policy Manual Vol 1 10/16/1976. p. 3.02.
[9] Ken Edgar, *Starting Wilderness Camps*. Unpublished document given to Stephen Ashton on 4/18/2013. 1.
[10] Edgar, 49.

was the direction he wanted to go. Finally, "they asked Pat Stanford, who was directing a summer camp at the time. He was hired as director in 1967. Pat had only 18 days experience in Therapeutic Wilderness Camping, but he was very interested in learning the program."[11]

Pat headed to Florida, but the idea of working with Jack Eckerd continued to come up in conversations around the Salesmanship Club Boys Camp. Ken Edgar recalls the conversation that finally changed his mind:

> One evening, in early January of 1968, I was loading canoes with Chief Gary Johns. When out of nowhere, he turned to me and said, 'So I hear you're going down to Florida.' I said, 'O, no I'm not! I'm going to stay here and get my degree.' [After further goading, Ken recalls,] 'I told him that Flora and I would pray about it. The very next morning I told Eckerd we would come. God had changed our minds that night.[12]

In February of 1968, Ken Edgar left Flora in Texas to begin to work as Assistant Director under Pat Stanford.[13] Flora stayed back in Duncanville, to fulfill her duty to the first grade children she began the year with. Looking back Flora recalls, "It was probably one of the hardest things we ever went through. If we hadn't both felt so strongly about our mission, we wouldn't have done it. But we felt like God was calling us to do this and we are glad we followed him. As a result, more than twenty-five other camps were started"[14]

Ken took a late flight from Dallas to Florida. There were only three people on the rather large airliner and the stewardess allowed him to make a bed crossing the isle. When he awoke, the sun was rising over his new home. The State of Florida. Upon his arrival, he met Pat Stanford and they went to an Eckerd Drug Store. There, on a bar stool at the soda fountain, Ken interviewed a young man who worked in the Eckerd Warehouse and hired him to be the first counselor. The trio headed to the property that Mr. Eckerd was thinking of buying. On the way, they stopped at a camping store and bought two pup tents, two

---

[11] Ibid.,. 1.

[12] Edgar 49, and Unpublished document, Starting Eckerd Camps (Edited at 3/27/17 interview).

[13] Interview with Chief Mac 8/17/2010 edited by Ken and Flora Edgar 4/17/2013.

[14] Edgar, 49 (this number includes the camps started by the WRTCA).

bedrolls, and a lantern. Pat dropped them off, then Ken and the new counselor spent the night down a little two-rut road on that property. The next day, the pair drove into town and purchased two more pup tents and used one for a warehouse and the other for a trading post. It was there that Ken discovered his first counselor had stolen his camp boots from the Eckerd warehouse. Camp had just begun and Ken had to terminate his first Chief. After that, they began interviewing for more counselors and campers. Both Shep Young and John Watson were hired in the early days and trained by Ken and Mac.[15] A few days later Mr. Eckerd came out with the land owner and finalized the deal.

They decided to name the camp E-How-Kee, a Seminole Indian translation for "His Open Door" [16] or "opportunities."[17] To Ken that is what it was, an answered prayer...an open door...an opportunity.

E-How-Kee: The First Eckerd Camp

Without a single building constructed or any significant staff orientation, in February of 1968, E-How-Kee welcomed its first camper. As campers came to visit, Ken would take them down into the woods on an interview. He would talk about opportunity and adventure, and show them where the buildings would be located. Then they would hike down to the 'big tree' where the campsite was to be built, and he would share the dream of what was to come. And campers came. The first campers slept in pup tents and use fly tarps to get out of the weather.

The first thing the new group constructed in the campsite was a log table under a fly tarp so they could eat off of the ground. Sitting around the table they began to discuss what was next. It seemed every boy wanted bigger tent and a chance to sleep off the ground. Soon it was decided they would build a sleeping shelter large enough to fit every boy and Chief inside of comfortably. As it turned out, this project was not as easy as they thought. They quickly discovered beginning a camp in a new state provided its own unique challenges.

---

[15] Interview with Ken 3/27/2017.

[16] Jack and Ruth Eckerd Foundation Program and Policy Manual Vol 1 10/16/1976. p. 3.02.

[17] Ken Edgar, Starting Eckerd Camps, Unpublished Document, 8/31/2016, 3.

Building Relationships

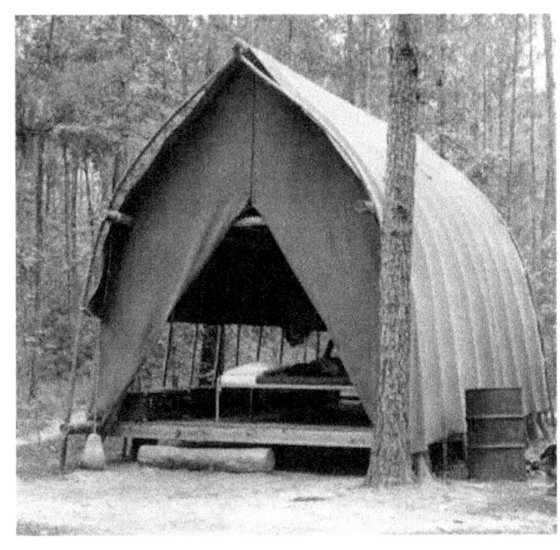

There were no building codes for a camp of this sort, and the inspectors felt they had to follow the rules. One of those rules dealt with ensuring enough "air space" for each boy. To meet the regulation, the footprint of the tent they were planning to build would have be extremely large! Undaunted, the group began problem solving. The solution they came up with? Instead of building the tent seven feet tall, they created a structure twelve feet tall to provide enough "air space." Admittedly, it made the tent impossible to heat, required too much tarp to cover, was more dangerous to build, and used more trees. But they had solved the problem and had sufficient cubic feet of air space to meet the code![18]

This type of creative problem solving became paramount to growing the program. The next problem involved building a bathroom. The high water table made digging a casita nearly impossible. At one point, they feared they would have to build a bathroom and sewage plant for the campsites. While they did build a sewage plant for the buildings. They managed to keep campsites simple and just build up the ground around where the casita would be and stay above the water table.

Other smaller issues continued to present themselves. One had to do with putting exit signs in the tent so the boys would know how to get out in case of a fire. Ken recalls, "It seemed a little silly to us to have an exit sign when the campers could roll over twice and be out of the tent."[19] The fire marshal who enforced the code, with time came to love the camp idea. He would come to visit and be intrigued with the work.

---

[18] Edgar, 52.
[19] Ibid., 52.

> He developed a friendship with camp and began to refer to it as 'his camp'...and started bringing friends and family to show them 'his camp.' One day, while down at the campsite, he said, 'Ken, take those exit signs down. It looks a little ridiculous.' After that, Florida started to write new regulations for outdoor childcare.[20]

Once a partnership was established with the state, they set out to continue to build their campsite and discovered a benefit in a state mandate requiring wooden floors instead of gravel or dirt. As spring rains came, the wooden platforms proved valuable in keeping kids out of the wet conditions. Initially, building platforms slowed things down, but as they figured these details out the group began quickly to build their campsite.[21] Within one month, they had a full group of ten campers and a campsite well underway.[22]

No buildings on the property, meant no dining hall. No dining hall meant no kitchen. In the early days, they had to be creative. The camp cook fixed the meals ten miles away in the kitchen of her mobile home in Brooksville and would bring them out in her car on the service road to serve the boys. This went on for a month or two, and amazingly she never got stuck. When the warehouse was finished they ate meals there. It was several months before they had a Dining Hall.[23] By the end of March, there were two groups of ten boys and the camp cook cooked for both.[24]

They learned a great deal adding the second group in March of that year. This was the first time anyone had tried to duplicate camp from scratch. Ken was unsure about how to begin a second group. Should he begin an entirely new group or divide the functioning group he had? He made the decision to split the group in two and add boys to each. The first of many lessons learned the hard way. The two new groups struggled and instead of one group that could model off of the other, there were two groups in disarray trying to learn to live together. He discovered it is much easier to leave the first group largely intact and let the second group model off of the first. Starting a new campsite is hard,

---

[20] Ibid., 52-53 (Edited by Ken and Flora on 3/27/2017).
[21] Interview with Ken and Flora 3/27/2017.
[22] Ken Edgar, Starting Eckerd Camps, Unpublished Document, 8/31/2016. 2-3.
[23] From Ken Edgar's notes on an early draft of this book. 4/18/2013.
[24] Interview with Ken and Flora 3/27/2017.

and in dividing the group, power structures change and boys vie for position making a difficult task even more so. Further, groups help each other just like individuals help each other. A functioning group is of more benefit than two non-functioning ones.

They also had to figure out how to balance the problems boys had in a new group. At times it is hard to tell what problems boys would have when they arrived. In the process of working that out they went through a number of boys and staff. As they balanced the groups with kids who had varying problems, the groups began to settle down.[25]

A Camp in Every State

Within six months, a lot of progress was made. "Camp E-How Kee had a Chuckwagon (dining hall), shower house, warehouse, roads, a staff house, and a sewage plant."[26] Not long after that, Mr. Eckerd and Ken were walking down a camp trail and Mr. Eckerd started talking about putting a camp in every state. Ken knew the program worked and wanted to help get it started. But he also knew for sure that he needed help and support developing and running a therapeutic camp.[27] The prospect of starting one in every state scared him to death.[28] Pat Stanford had little experience in therapeutic camping and after six months was having trouble directing the program.[29] There was both a desire to see it grow and a realization that without an experienced director, the program would have to be changed. As they continued walking, Mr. Eckerd mentioned he would like to see a camp for girls as well. Ken said, "If you want Chief Mac to join us in this project, you only need mention a girls camp!" The next day Jack Eckerd had Mr. Glisson get on the phone and pitch the idea to Chief Mac.[30] A letter dated August 13, 1968 outlines goals and objectives set forth by Chief Mac outlining a program run under his direction. A consulting fee of $100 was paid, and a second letter from Floyd Glisson closes with the phrase, "I will be looking forward to having you as part of the program and

[25] Interview with Chief Mac 8/15/2008.
[26] Edgar, 55.
[27] Ken Edgar, Starting Eckerd Camps, Unpublished Document, 8/31/2016. 2.
[28] Edgar, 55.
[29] Interview with Chief Mac 8/17/2010.
[30] Interview with Chief Mac 8/15/2008.

working very closely with you in its overall development."[31]

On October 1, 1968, Buford McKenzie officially resigned as Resident Director of the Salesmanship Club Boys Camp.[32] Mac writes in his resignation letter that, "an exciting opportunity has been offered me to head up a year-round camping program for both boys and girls."[33] On October 15, he began his duties as Program Director of two groups at E-How-Kee Boys Camp in Florida.[34]

Buford McKenzie Joins Ken at Eckerd

During his first week at camp, Hurricane Gladys hit. As a result, his first day was spent boarding up windows.[35] Once the dust settled, Mac got to work at camp. It quickly became evident that Pat Stanford and Mac had two different visions for the program and Mr. Glisson decided that Pat needed to move on. Chief Mac became the Director and Chief Ken the Assistant Director. Mac and Ken began three more groups by setting up squad tents in campsite on wooden platforms and bringing boys into the group. They would then build the campsites. At one point, Jack Eckerd was concerned they were moving too fast.

---

[31] Letter from Floyd Glission to Buford McKenzie dated August 13, 1968.
[32] Buford McKenzie, Resignation Letter submitted to Salesmanship Club Boys Camp August 31, 1968.
[33] Buford McKenzie, Resignation Letter submitted to Salesmanship Club Boys Camp August 31, 1968.
[34] Jack and Ruth Eckerd Foundation Program and Policy Manual Vol 1 10/16/1976. p. 3.02.
[35] Interview with Chief Mac 8/15/2008.

At Christmas all the groups came back and were raising cane in the Chuckwagon. I had a Chief guard each door and went around to each group working with them one at a time. Finally little Billy Aikers stood up and yelled to the biggest boy in camp, 'Bobby, sit down and shut your mouth!' and he did! Later Bobby said it was the best thing that happened to him. After that, we sent camp to bed and sat up with the three boys still raising cane. I walked around with a Chief and one boy dropped off to bed around 1:00, a second around 2:00. Finally about 3:00 in the morning the last boy got with his group and into bed. I told them, 'you can't raise enough cane to run me off! I'm here on business! Gradually, camp became camp and we had peace. No one was cussing out the cooks and things began to make sense.[36]

[36] Interview with Chief Mac 8/15/2008 and 8/17/2010.

CHAPTER 2:
E-NINI-HASSEE
THE FIRST GIRLS PROGRAM

Group a Ready Logs at E-Nini-Hassee

By December of 1968, one of Mac's dreams was becoming reality. The search had begun to find property for a girls' camp. "The day after an old phosphate mining area was put up for sale, a real estate friend alerted the Eckerd Foundation and shortly after a tract of 847 acres near Floral City in Citrus County was purchased from the Loncala Phosphate Company."[1] The land was located about an hour from the first camp. Chief Mac knew just the people to help start the first girls program.

[1] Jack and Ruth Eckerd Foundation Program and Policy Manual Vol 1 10/16/1976. p. 3.02.

Everett, Helen, Chuck Swindoll, and the Perfect Storm

Everett at far left and Helen at opposite far right

Everett Lindstrom has been the first Chief hired after Mac returned to the Salesmanship Club after his time in Colorado. Everett had graduated with a sociology degree from Texas A&M and seen a flyer about the camping program in East Texas. He could not believe a job like that existed. He later would comment that during his interview he was so curious and amazed by the program he was not sure who was interviewing who. Everett began as a Chief on January 31, 1964.[2]

He had been working at camp for nearly four years when Helen arrived. Helen had been working at Goshen College in northern Indiana and was ready for a change when Mac invited her and Ruby Horst to return to camp as a Chiefs in the fall of 1967. Not long after Helen began, she and Everett found themselves spending more time together. There was a general agreement at the camp that there would be no dating within six months of the employment date, so things did not progress quickly, but they would often go to church together.

---

[2] Club and Camp News, September 29, 1966, Vol 40, No 1.

Everett had known Chuck Swindoll when the latter led singing at Second Baptist Church of Houston. After church, Chuck and Cynthia would frequently have lunch at the Lindstrom home. About the same time Everett came to the Salesmanship Club Boys Camp, Chuck Swindoll became the Assistant Pastor at Grace Bible Church in Dallas. Everett would travel over 100 miles round-trip to attend services on Sundays. In 1965, Swindoll left to serve as senior Pastor in Massachusetts. However, in 1967, when Helen joined the Camp he had returned and was Senior Pastor at Irving Bible Church. On Sunday mornings, they attended chapel at camp, but Helen recalls driving on Sunday nights to Irving and back (over 100 miles) to go to church. Everett would say, "we drive long distances for entertainment, why not do so for good Bible preaching."[3] On those long trips, the pair grew closer and by November of 1968, the pair drove to Iowa to meet Helen's Family, then drove to College Station to experience the Aggie Bonfire.

The pair arrived in time to watch the bonfire being built and watch the tankers hose it down with aviation fuel. Then the band came out with torches and, at just the right moment, the torches were thrown onto the wood and the fire ignited. The evening was cut short, because after the fire was lit, a torrential downpour drenched everything and Everett and Helen were forced to watch the bonfire continue to roar from their car. Because of the rain, they made the decision to leave the event early and drive to Houston to spend the night with Everett's parents as they had planned. While driving to Houston that night in the pouring rain, Everett asked, "can you think of any reason why our trails should ever part?" Helen was stunned a little bit by the question. After considering things for a while she responded, "I can't think of any reason why." The next morning they saw Everett's parents at breakfast, who then took them to the airport to meet Chief Mac in Florida where they would discuss the possibility of helping to start E-Nini-Hassee Girls Camp.

Upon arrival in Florida, Everett, Helen, Mac, and Lois toured the property and interviewed with Mac and Eckerd executives. After the interview, Mac pulled Everett and Helen aside and said, "There is one unanswered question, if hired will you come as single adults or a married couple." That moment the fact that they really were engaged

---

[3] Interview with Helen Lindstrom 3/22/2017.

sank in and they announced to Mac that they would begin the girls camp together. That was the first time they had ever told anyone about their engagement. Not even their parents knew!

Quickly discussions began about wedding dates and planning ensued. Helen had hoped for a May wedding in Iowa, but Jack Eckerd wanted to begin a group at E-Nini-Hassee in April so they moved the date up to March 8 in her hometown in Iowa. Everett's only condition was he wanted Chuck Swindoll to officiate their wedding and do their pre-marital counseling. They spoke with Chuck and he was agreeable. Because of their situation at camp, he even combined six premarital counseling sessions into three so they did not have to make so many trips to Irving.

The entire wedding weekend was a whirlwind. Helen flew to Iowa two weeks for the wedding to prepare, and Everett arrived one week before. To get their marriage license Helen's sister drew Everett's blood, and Everett drove it to the lab himself. The weekend of the wedding Pastor Chuck flew to the North East US, back to Iowa, then immediately after the wedding, one of Helen's cousins got him to the airport so he could preach Sunday morning. Chuck Swindoll recalls,

> My recollection of Everett is nothing but outstanding memories of a man of strong integrity and sincere dedication to his calling. I always admired his determination and discipline to "stay at it," regardless the sacrifice! My life is richer for having known this fine man with a warm heart for those in need and deep devotion to his Lord. He was truly a fine husband, a loyal mentor, and a devoted disciple of Christ.[4]

The wedding was beautiful and despite the whirlwind came together wonderfully. After the wedding, they drove to Hawkins and picked up the mobile home Everett had been living in and towed it to Houston for a reception at Everett's parents' house. Monday they left and pulled the mobile home to Florida.

Getting Camp off the Ground

On March 23rd, they arrived and planned to spend a week on their honeymoon and begin work April 1, 1969. However, when they arrived

---

[4] E-mail correspondence from Chuck Swindoll 4/5/2017.

they saw the property was bare and nothing was done. Instead of honeymooning, the newlyweds found themselves mapping out campsites and buildings, creating trails, doing initial family visits for intake, and building tents for the girls. Much was to be done to have girls in camp by June 3. Everyone did all they could to help get it started. Chief Mac, Mom Lois, Chief Everett, Helen Lindstrom, Chief Ken, and the E-How-Kee staff all pitched in.

Helen recalls,

> While we were holding to the model and knew what to do with groupwork, we were experimenting with so many things like structures and living in an environment that was not East Texas. All the original sleeping shelters were teepees. We learned quickly why the plains Indians had teepees and not the Florida Indians." She continues, "It was extremely hard to keep the beds dry when the top was opened for ventilation. Then, when it rained, we could not close them up right to keep the rain out. To make matters worse, we used eight-inch sections of tree trunks to form floors. Things fell between chunks of trunks and made for a real headache. After that we did not build any more teepees.[5]

By June 3, 1969, shelters had been built in two campsites – the Cliff-Dwellers and the Kalapakans – and the first seven girls arrived at Camp E-Nini-Hassee, which in the Seminole Language meant "Her Sunny Road."[6]

Water had not been run to campsites yet, so it was hauled in for the first five weeks in 55 gallon drums. Showers were taken, "behind a ponchos, out of a hose in the middle of the woods"[7] until a shower house was built. On July 4, 1969, the first camp newsletter was published chronicling the early days of Camp E-Nini-Hassee. The girls were excited about building their campsite and taking trips. The stories below illustrate the spirt among the girls at camp:

---

[5] Interview with Helen Lindstrom – 6/23/2020 and 9/23/2021.

[6] Jack and Ruth Eckerd Foundation Program and Policy Manual Vol 1 10/16/1976. p. 3.03.

[7] "Our Showers," The Whispering Pine, Camp Newspaper of E-Nini-Hassee Girls Camp, Vol 1 – July 4, 1969.

A Windy Awakening

Going to bed that night was hot and sweaty but waking up the next morning was cold, windy, and wet. In fact it was so windy, Tent 1's tarp blew off. The girls from Tent 1 and Tent 3 came running over to Tent 2 with blankets, all bundled up. Then here comes Chief Mac up the trail singing "Oh, What a beautiful morning!" But in the end we had a pretty good day. We got all the tarps tied up and still had plenty of time for relaxation.

How We Have Fun

Kalapakans have been having a lot of fun. We went swimming, we went on hikes for turtle shells. We have fun doing things in campsite like making trails and cooking during cookout. We like making pow-wow fires and we like to go to pow-wow every night. We have done lots of things in our campsite this month. We fixed up our toothbrush rack. We dug our garbage pit, and we built a tool rack.

In Only Three Weeks

We have been in camp for 3 weeks and have made our campsite really look good. First of all we built our alter fire and got our chuck tent fixed up. Then we got our pow-wow logs up and fixed Pow-wow steps and trails. Then we got our ready log. After completing all this we put our trail logs in and finally we got our shower fixed. We now have our toothbrush rack up. We have had a lot of problems in these 3 weeks but we managed to solve every one of them. And we have learned to have more than one friend and to be a friend.

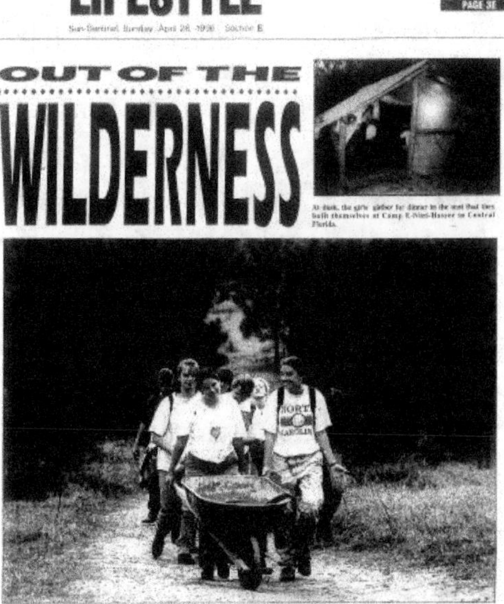

LIFESTYLE

FASHION

OUT OF THE WILDERNESS

Story by Staff Writer LISA J. HURIASH Photos by Staff Photographer HILDA PEREZ

A Poem

There is a place called E-Nini-Hassee,
Sometimes I think it's made for the Nazis.
But since it's made for problem solving,
I know I will have to start my solving.

Two Day Canoe Trip
Starting Tuesday afternoon, June 30, the Cliff Dwellers will be leaving for a two day canoe trip on the Withlacoochee River. We are looking forward to it.

Kalapakans
Our group is named the Kalapakans. Kalapakan is the Seminole word for "seven." There are seven oak trees in the middle of our campsite. Mr. Eckerd, who sponsored our camp, has seven children so we call our group the Kalapakans. There are five girls and two counselors in our group.

The Rat Snake
While walking to the Chuck Wagon one of the girls in our group noticed a snake. We surrounded it and Chief Everett caught it. He let us hold it while he took pictures of us. It was the first time for some of us to hold a snake. Since then we have seen black snakes and one hog nose snake.

By Thanksgiving, the girls were dreaming about a long raft trip. Chief Everett remembers the spot of the trail between the shower house and Cliff Dweller campsite where the idea was hatched. "Chief Helen, Mary Ann, Debbie Post and I sat, about 3:30 AM and set our hearts on something big like a raft trip. The full moon straight above us...made the whole meadow a silvery dreamland."[8] Shortly after that, they showed the girls slides from the raft trip "the Tejas Boys took a few years ago. Someone got the bright idea that girls can do anything boys can do."[9] The girls did several short river trips, including a two-day trip on the Withlacoochee River, and a Bus trip to the Smoky Mountains to prepare the group for a big adventure. They wrote letters to the cities on the Ohio and Mississippi River from Louisville, KY to New Orleans, LA. Then they got started on the drawing a design for the raft.

By May of 1970, the group had designed a raft they named, "The Real People" and planned out the trip. The story of their journey, narrated by Chief Everett Lindstrom and containing excerpts of articles written in the camp newspaper by the girls, is available at the end of the book.

---

[8] Everett Lindstrom, Log for First Cliff Dweller Raft Trip, Unpublished Document, July 1970.

[9] "Things are Happening," The Whispering Pine, Camp Newspaper of E-Nini-Hassee Girls Camp, Special Raft Trip Edition.

Chief Mac, Mom Lois, and Daughters with staff at E-Nini-Hassee

The third group, the Achenas started in the fall. E-Nini Hassee functioned for a long time with three groups, and then the fourth, the Palmettos was added. Then, in 1973 a fifth group, the Apalachees was added.

During that time a great deal of work was done around camp. Trails were cleared, water lines were dug, and pine trees were planted in the open meadow areas. Everyone pitched in. There were two lakes on the property that were old phosphate mining pits. One toward the center of the property, and the other at the back. The lake near the center of the property, Lake Ruth, still had pilings from the trains that took phosphate out of the mines. It was perfect for swimming, but was filled with algae. The entire camp spent days at the lake trying to solve the algae problem. Finally, they discovered they could strain the algae between two canoes and pull it to the edge of the lake where campers would rake it out of the water. All of camp got involved. A plan was made to spend an entire day "raking the lake." The groups gathered in the morning to begin cooking beef roast on a spit for lunch. The girls worked until the algae was cleared and the lake was ready for swimming.[10]

Jack Eckerd's wife was known to campers as Chief Ruth, she loved to spend time with the girls and would often spend the day with the groups. One day, when Ruth came to visit, the girls were working to move rocks too big for comfortable driving from the road entering camp. Because of who she was, the staff who greeted Ruth offered her gloves to work with. She took them and asked, "will the girls be wearing gloves?" Then she handed them back and said, "Then I won't either." She spent the day with that group moving rocks to a drain ditch. That was her pattern when she came. She wanted to join the group in whatever they were doing.[11]

The Eckerd's had a huge heart for the children in the camps. Each summer they would invite two groups at a time to their beach house in Clearwater beach until all the girls had an opportunity for a visit. The campers would come for the day and swim, look for shells, and cookout with the Eckerd family. Helen recalls fondly days ending together singing and sharing stories around a fire.

Gradually word about the program continued to grow. Mr O.J. Keller, the Director of Florida Health and Rehabilitative Services heard about the success of E-How-Kee and E-Nini-Hassee and asked for a visit. Jack and Ruth sent him to E-Nini-Hassee. When he arrived, Everett knew who he was, but did not tell anyone at camp. The Cliff Dwellers gave him a tour of campsite that ended at the pow-wow logs where he asked questions and they gave answers. Afterward, Cliff Dweller campers talked with Chief Everett and told him they thought Mr. Keller was really interesting and would make a great Chief at camp. Knowing what was happening, Everett and Helen chuckled. That day a seed planted for the state to ask Mr. Eckerd to begin a state-funded program.

---

[10] Interview with Helen Lindstrom – 6/23/2020 and 9/23/2021 – during the interview Helen mentioned a newspaper article from July 15th 1973 in the Tampa Tribune Florida Accent section entitled, "Wilderness an Antidote for Troubled Youth" that mentioned both E-How-Kee and E-Nini-Hassee.

[11] Interviews with Helen Lindstrom – 6/23/2020 and 9/10/2021.

I REMEMBER CHIEF MAC

The following letter was found in Mac's home addressed to Jack Eckerd with the date September 2, 1978 written on the top. On top of the letter was the following note from Jack Eckerd to Mac dated September 12, 1978 that said, "Chief Mac – Know this has been repeated often but know you would enjoy. Jack" The letter later became a new article published in the Independent Press.

SEP 12 1978
from the desk of
Jack Eckerd

Monday
Chief Mac -
Know this has
been repeated often
but know you would
enjoy
Jack

Mr Eckerd,

My name is Laura O'Neill and I am now 21 years old and have just had a beautiful baby girl. My husband of one and a half years is a fine Christian man and God has greatly blessed our home and family. I am writing and telling you this because this is a happy ending to a story that could have not had an ending at all. A lot of this I owe to one man and friend, Chief Mac, and to my Lord Jesus Christ whom I was introduced to through him.

I went to camp in 1971 a very disturbed little girl. I hated everyone and trusted no one. I had first been discharged from a psychiatric ward at a county hospital which I had been put in for trying to commit suicide. I had not will or reason for living. I was terribly shy and afraid. There seemed no way out for me at all. The only talking I did was the rebellious kind and I made it clear I respected on adults at all.

When I was small, I had been pampered by my father, yet when my parents left one another, my mother moved us all to Florida. I grew up in utter rebellion over this. So you see, camp took on a big job when they took on me.

I was put in the group Cliff Dwellers, and my first encounter with Chief Mac was not a joyous one, but it was one of the things that started my life turning around. Chief Mac confronted me. I look at it now with a smile because the love I saw in his eyes then is something I didn't understand, and yet now I am able to love others in that same way.

For a long time I was afraid of Chief Mac. The fear was not caused from discipline, rather it was caused from the love I saw I his eyes. If my fear had been caused from the discipline, I might have understood it, but this love was something I couldn't shake off. How could someone love me, a rebellious teenager? I can answer that now. It's because Christ loves me and still does. Christ was loving me in and through Chief Mac.

When a Chief (Ann Young) who was also an asset in my camp stay found out about my fear, she took me to Chief Mac. He put his arms around me and hugged me. That scared me a little, but it was the beginning of a life-long friendship with not only Chief Mac, but also Jesus Christ.

I've told you how I was then, let me tell you how I am now. I am open and honest. I can relate not only the things that are bothering me, but I can help others I've run into to more understand themselves. Before I left camp, my shyness had disappeared to the point that I wrote three songs for camp and taught them in the dining hall. That's a change!

Chief Mac is Camp. That is a statement that was said by everyone who was in Camp at that time. He related to us with stories and laughter and music. Most of all he gave us love. Not only have I remained in contact, but most of the girls still end up on the phone or at his doorstep and he never turns them away – even when he is tired or busy. He's sat for hours in problems with us, hugged us when we need to cry, and helped us years later when we needed to talk.

The other night, when he held my little girl, I thought how I want her to know him. Another lucky generation. And most of all, she'll know Jesus Christ.

Yours in Christ,

Laura O'Neill

'I Remember Chief Mac'

Independent Press, Wednesday, September 20, 1978 – 3A

EDITORS NOTE: Confused and troubled. Laura O'Neil ran away from home when she was 15. She was placed in a camp for almost a year and there she met Chief Mac, who gave her needed guidance. Now, 21 and married with two chidren, Mrs. O'Neil wrote this story. She entitled it, "I remember Chief Mac."

He stands six feet two and weighs 215 pounds. When he walks you may notice his shoe, which is specially made due to an accident he suffered when a child. But when you look in his eyes, all you see is the love that radiates from them. This is Buford McKenzie, better known to me and hundreds of other kids as Chief Mac.

I first met Chief Mac at Camp E-Nini-Hassee in Floral City, a camp which is privately funded for girls who need guidance. I was fifteen. Camp would come to life when he walked into the dining hall. His rich voice would lead us in Christian songs and tell us stories which always had a moral we could learn by. If there was a problem in a group in which he could help, he would sit for hours until it had been talked through and a solution had been found. "No problem is too big when given to the Lord," he would say and then he'd break out into a smile which made us all light up. We respected him and he never let us down.

Years later when I needed someone to talk to, he was there. I could always depend on him. Those long talks helped me grow up. Hundreds of campers to this day who have known him from camp either wind up on his doorstep or on the phone. What makes a man give up his whole life to help kids?

He once told me that his one dream had been to sing professionally. I often wondered why he never made that dream a reality. The answer lies in Jesus Christ. The Lord had a path for his life and he chose that path rather than his dream.

Since the day I met Chief Mac my life has turned around. When I gave my life to the Lord, he blessed me with a Christian husband and two beautiful children.

The other night as he held my children I thought another generation will know Chief Mac, but most important, another generation who will learn of Jesus Christ.

CHAPTER 3: E-MA-CHAMEE THE FIRST STATE FUNDED PROGRAM

Kekewhs Group at E-Ma-Chamee Boys Camp

In early 1973 many changes began to take place across the Eckerd programs. Shep Young took over as director at E-How-Kee, Ken took on a new role evaluating programs around the state of Florida and did intake for the first campers in a new Eckerd Camp named E-Ma-Chamee.[1] Everett Lindstrom was selected as the director and Paul Daley worked under Everett to help begin the program at E-ma-Chamee.

This was the first state funded program and was birthed from E-How-Kee. State funding brought new concerns and a new level of oversight. A primary concern early on was about the role of spiritual

[1] In August of 1973, Ken and Flora accepted two new challenges. They adopted their son Tim, then moved to begin a new camp at the Hope Center for youth in Houston. They spent a year in Houston, then Chief Lock requested that Ken return as director of the Salesmanship Club Youth Camp to help get things back on track.

teaching in the program. Jack Eckerd and Floyd Glisson made a trip to Tallahassee early on to address this. Jack Eckerd said, "our program addresses the whole boy the whole time: physically, emotionally, mentally, and spiritually. This is our program. If you are not interested, we will find other funding sources."[2] The state was sold on the effectiveness of the program and allowed him to run the program and include spiritual principles and teaching.

To prepare to launch the new program, two new groups were created at E-How-Kee Boys Camp. In March of 1973, three E-How-Kee campers moved into two 16' x 32' army tents down by the lake at E-How-Kee. These tents served for "sleeping and eating...Chief Lee Williamson, Chief John Jenkins, and Chief Everett Lindstrom began the nucleus of Kekewhs, the first group at the new camp. Right away, they began building a campsite and making preparations for new campers. Within a few days, seven additional campers joined the group,"[3] two campers came from E-How-Kee and three were new to camp. "During March, they set up...a cook area, a latrine tent, cut a trail to the dining hall, cut four sets of ready logs, laid a water line, and did some minor campsite repairs and constructions."[4]

Everett reports,

> Kekewhs have enjoyed the group program from the start. They have climbed trees, swung on rope swing, explored, made crafts, sung songs, and gone on camp-outs. The first trip was a two-day camp-out on the back side of the property. They canoed, fished, and thoroughly enjoyed the experience. Next they spent a day off the camp property, swimming at Silver Lake on the Withlacoochee River. This time, they had such a good time, and got such a case of 'river fever' that they took a notion to go on a three-week river trip down the Suwannee River. By the end of the month, they had menus, equipment lists, and

---

[2] Interview with Helen Lindstrom 4/3/2017. Helen would later become instrumental in beginning the North Carolina Program and serve as Executive Assistant to Gerald Rehm. Helen says our whole time at E-Ma-Chamee we ran the spiritual program and never had a ripple of conflict."

[3] March 1973 Letter from Everett Lindstrom to Chief Mac on Progress at E-Ma-Chamee Boys' Camp, 1.

[4] March 1973 Letter from Everett Lindstrom to Chief Mac on Progress at E-Ma-Chamee Boys' Camp, 1.

goals made and were ready to go. Departure time was set for a week after homesday.

The first homesday was momentous, some of the new campers had not been home in two to three years and were excited about visiting their families. During the first homesday, "not a single camper got out of hand."[5]

This does not mean the new group did not face problems. There were issues with following camp routines, schedules, and a few violent threats. Everett records on such problem,

> The group was packing for the three-week canoe trip and was having the typical 'pre-trip jitters.' In addition, one camper was deliberately trying to cause enough problems to undermine the whole trip. Toward the end of a hectic lunch, the group decided to leave the dining hall to discuss a problem. On the way, one camper insinuated a knife threat toward another. The explosion erupted and feelings flew pretty high. As soon as things could be simmered down and the original problem resolved, attention was turned to the still angry, knife-threatened camper. When asked, 'What would make you feel comfortable?' he responded with a caustic, 'Take away all the pocket knives!' The counselor responded by asking the group if we all cared enough about his feelings to let Chief hold everyone's knives. The tide being already turned, the group members immediately began handing over the pocket knives. However the offended camper interrupted the process by backing down from his position with, 'Never mind, I know I can trust everyone.' At this point, the camper who had made the threat in the first place broke, and with tears of repentance, asked for forgiveness. Spontaneously, the offended camper jumped across the circle to give him a hug, and the whole group broke into tears.
>
> Sessions as graphic as this one have focused on other discoveries. One day, the group discovered that most problems of anger and aggravation would not exist if each group member would be willing to give up his rights so that group or individual needs could be met. Related to this discovery was the

---

[5] Ibid., 1.

advantage of treating other people right whether or not they treat you right.

> When Kekewhs left on the Suwannee River trip (April 10, 2913), they were excited, not only by the trip, but also by what they were learning about 'sticking with a line of action.' They were realizing that when they make a plan and stick with it, all sorts of good things can happen...Problems are to be solved![6]

The first river trip for the new group was a success. Chief Pat Stanton, a Group Work Supervisor from E-How-Kee came went with the group for most of the trip. The group became more settled in its spirit and gained a new confidence that could handle almost any discipline problem. "The counselors, too, moved closer into a position of secure leadership, which freed the campers from the role of competing for unfair group leadership."[7] A few hard feeling remained after the trip from a section of the group who wanted to do more fishing and exploring and felt they were not heard.

> As a result, every member suffered from feelings of being 'pushed around.' From small incidents, these feelings grew to the point of causing some of the members to want to be transferred out of the group. Hope and trust in the group had been undermined. By the end of the evaluation, each member had realized the cost of not taking his share of responsibilities. Each one knew what to do about it. Once again, hope was re-established. The camper, who had wanted out of the group most made the following summary, 'Before this discussion, all I wanted was to get away from Kekewhs. Now, I wouldn't leave if someone offered to pay me to leave![8]

By June, a second group, the "Tococos [group] began to take form and Kekewhs had to do some reshaping to assimilate three new members plus a new Chief. Both groups completed successful short trips that were useful in building group history, identity, and

---

[6] Ibid., 2-3.

[7] April 1973 Letter from Everett Lindstrom to Chief Mac on Progress at E-Ma-Chamee Boys' Camp, 1.

[8] Ibid., 1-2.

confidence."[9]

> The Tococos started the month by building a dining tent, and therefore, got the focus in the group on something outside themselves and their problems. Being an older and more sophisticated group, Tococos have kept the counselors hopping to keep ahead of the group. Several members have excessive anger and temper problems. If words could kill……! Forgiveness has been one of the biggest needs in the group, but it will come a little easier when rivalry for position in the group has been satisfied…With more time and experiences, they will develop greater loyalty and deeper feeling for each other.[10]

Mud Slide at E-Ma-Chamee Boys Camp

Toward the end of June, the need was felt for the E-Ma-Chamee groups to move to their own property. Everett writes,

> E-Ma-Chamee's development at this time is both helped and hindered by being at E-How-Kee. The advantages of operating within the security of an established organization are clearly obvious, however, part of the months was spent with six or

[9] June 1973 Letter from Everett Lindstrom to Chief Mac on Progress at E-Ma-Chamee Boys' Camp, 1.
[10] Ibid., 1.

> seven groups together in the dining hall, at chapel, and around the warehouse. The number of people assembled together has been a hinderance in establishing individual identity, holding all-camp discussions, and maintaining order. Normally at camp, each child knows every counselor and camper. No one is a stranger. Knowing seventy-five people representing five groups is far more possible than knowing a hundred and five people.

The next month, the Tococo and Kekewh groups planned to spend "ten days exploring and having fun in the forest property on which E-Ma-Chamee Boys' Camp" would be built. The boys were excited to see "our forest."[11] When they arrived, they "found a camping area near the creek and began setting up a ten-day campsite." They pitched tents, built an alter fire, created food prep tables, a cooking area, and organized food supplies.

> Soon, we had the absolute necessities under control and were playing in beautiful Coldwater Creek. Both groups found themselves directing a great deal of effort toward building a dam across the creek. They pulled in some heavy logs and piled on the sand. The activity became an all-day project. At the end of the day, an evaluation revealed some startling facts to both campers and group directors. For one thing, twenty-one people had been working in a united effort and had accomplished a pretty good feat. What power was great enough to motivate them to lay aside all those petty arguments, forget all those personal problems, move all those heavy longs in the rain, and work together? The group directors couldn't have possessed that much power. Neither was the job itself important enough to provide that much motivation. Everyone began to realize that the spirit of building a dam had been present and that he had been willing for that spirit to influence him. Through this experience, we all became more aware of the power of a spirit, good or bad. In the light of this positive, constructive, group spirit, each person present could more readily identify negative, destructive, thug gang spirits. Either type of spirit can be powerful enough to get people to do things they would never otherwise do. Kekewhs and Tococos had to face the question,

---

[11] July 1973 Letter from Everett Lindstrom to Chief Mac on Progress at E-Ma-Chamee Boys' Camp, 1.

"Which type of spirit are you willing to let influence you?"[12]

Throughout the two weeks, the two groups took turns cooking meals. In the spirit of building E-Ma-Chamee, they also peeled pine poles for future tents, explored possible permanent campsite locations and each chose a suitable one. The Kekewhs even staked out the position for their sleeping shelters, dining tent, and all other features for their small group campsite. Everett closes the July letter with the following story,

> The real climax for the month came on the last night before we left our new found haven. The creek had become partially plugged with trees and snags, and someone suggested a bonfire. Both groups got involved in piling on the wood scraps pulled from the creek. By the last day, there was a large bonfire ready to light and an appropriate ceremony was planned. The campers decided that each one would light a torch and place it in the center of the pile. Each torch would represent a spirit that person had grown to know and understand during the trip. The bonfire itself would represent the spirit of E-Ma-Chamee.
>
> After the lighting took place, both groups sat on the other side of the creek to watch the fire and reflect...The spirit that each camper and group director chose to represent proved to be strikingly revealing. For example, one camper had received much pressure to solve a problem of dishonesty. He chose to represent the spirit of honesty. Another camper having a problem of doing quite well one day and quite poorly the next, chose to speak about the spirit of consistency. Other spirits chosen were helpfulness, friendship, problem-solving, working together, communication, adventure, opportunity, hope, participation, and many more. One camper had been away from home for five years and had lost all hope of living with his family. That night at the bonfire, he expressed renewed hope by thinking of the spirit of home. All were well chosen and were without a spirit of hypocrisy...The spirit of E-Ma-Chamee has begun.[13]

---

[12] Ibid., 1.
[13] Ibid., 1.

By the end of October 1973, Tococos had taken a Raft Trip on the Chattachoochee River during which they planned a three-week river trip on the Ocmulgee and Altamaha Rivers in Georgia. Everett noted this as "a real mark of accomplishment" because they had been able to "look ahead to plan a trip while they were on a trip." On October 17, 1973, the group, led by Chief Everett Lindstrom, Chief Lou Barrington[14], and Chief Chuck Davis left for the Georgia River Trip. Kekewhs returned from a Smoky Mountains backpack trip on October 22, 1973. Additionally, a training program was completed for three counselors who would serve at E-Ma-Chamee camp and Miss Braxton was able to move into her role as family worker. The foundations for the new program were being laid.

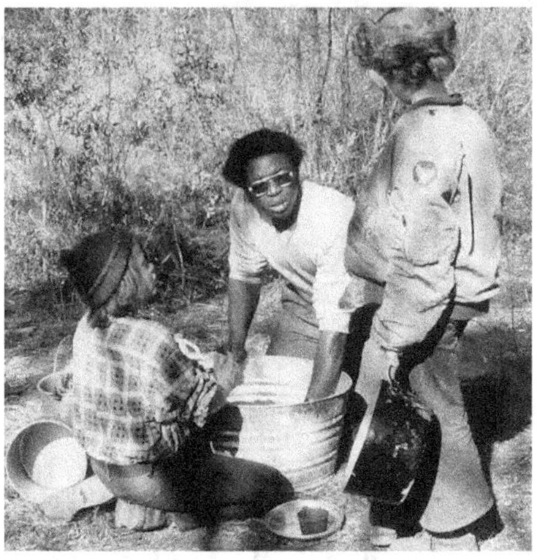

On New Year's Eve 1973, the land and the groups were ready and the director, Everett Lindstrom, led the two groups to their new site.[15] Chief Paul was a Chief in the Kekewhs group at that time. He recalls that, they left after lunch and drove all day and arrived at the campsite at midnight. They set up their pup tents, and dropped into bed.

The next day they set up two squad tents. One for the cook tent and one for the dining hall. Those tents were the only thing there. In the beginning even the director and his wife (Everett and Helen) slept in pup tents until they could bring the mobile home to the new site. [16]

---

[14] **Louie Barrington Jr** (known as Chief Lou), is shown in the image above. He was a very effective chief and Camp Director. He worked at Eckerd for over 35 years and was Paul Daley's first supervisor at E-Ma-Chamee. Paul was later thrilled when he was reunited to work under him at E-Mun-Talee in Low Gap, NC. Staff from Eckerd programs remember Lou as a "Gentle Giant." Chief Lauren Clark reflections perhaps characterize him best, "I'm pretty sure if God had a smile...he borrowed it from Chief Lou Barrington! Lou was one of those rare individuals who you would try to put out the fires of hell with an eye dropper for. He was a confident leader who never let anything rattle him. I could always depend on him for words of wisdom, a laugh and will never forget his delicious tea cakes. My life is so much richer for having known Chief Lou."

[15] Interview with Chief Paul 5/21/2012.

[16] Interview with Helen Lindstrom 3/22/2017 and 4/3/2017.

Later, they brought in a tractor trailer for a warehouse and set up gas and electricity in the tent for cooks, and that is where they cooked. From there they began picking out and building the campsites. That first winter there was no shower house. Paul recalls walking down to the clear, cold water, ducking in, lathering up, rinsing off, and rushing back to the fire to warm up. The first year the group spent building their campsite and taking four trips.

Paul Daley: Heaven, Hell, Mosquitos, and Scorpions

In 1973, Paul Daley began a career that would span over 40 years in wilderness therapy at E-How-Kee Boys Camp. Paul had been serving in the Air Force and was stationed at Bergstrom Air Force Base in Austin, TX. At that time therapeutic camping was the last thing on his mind. As a matter of fact, his father was outright concerned about his son and was looking for help. He wrote a letter to Paul Hensley, a Navigator Representative at the University of Texas, to ask him to come talk with Paul about the Lord. Amazingly, the young man received the letter made contact. One day Hensley drove out to the Barracks. Paul recalls the young man stood at his door and asked, "If you died today would you go to heaven or hell?" Paul said, "I'd go to hell." He responded, "do you believe that?" Paul said, "Yes." He said "do you want to do anything about it?" Paul said, "no." And that was the end of the conversation.

Three months later, Paul attended Northwest Baptist Church. While Bob Tedley was preaching Paul began to feel convicted and accepted the Lord that night. Soon after, Paul was deployed to the Philippines where began doing Navigator Bible Studies. After returning to Austin, he looked up Paul Hensley. Mr. Hensley got Paul into a training program over the summer working with college students. There he met a couple starting a ministry in Tampa, FL. As part of the training he moved with them to Florida. Six people lived in that house. Three guys, a girl, and the married couple. It was a rich time of learning to study scripture and do ministry together. It was while he was there some of his roommates met Everett Lindstrom at church. They told Paul about camp. Intrigued by the opportunity, he called E-How-Kee and set up an interview with Chief Mac.

During the interview he stayed a couple nights in the woods and spent time with the boys. The mosquitoes were so bad, he recalls rising the next morning having not slept a wink with blood all over his sheets. He knew two things: he wanted to serve the Lord, and he did not want to live in a mosquito infested swamp. He decided he would spend the summer at Eagle Lake Camp in the Mountains of Colorado Springs with the Navigators organization.

It was an incredible summer of ministry and personal growth. As it was coming to a close, Paul spent a day on top of a mountain praying about what was next. That evening, he had dinner with a co-counselor he had spent the summer with. The counselor told Paul about a family who had picked him up after hiking earlier that day. They had been kind enough to give him a ride 26 miles up a dirt road back to camp. During their ride they told him they were on vacation from Florida. He and the family swapped camp stories on the ride. Before they left they gave him their name and phone number and said to keep in touch. When Paul saw the name, he could not believe his eyes! "It was Buford McKenzie from that camp in Florida!" After dinner, Paul went to a church service where the Pastor asked, "What is the hardest thing the Lord would have you do?" Paul thought, "go work at that camp in Florida." Then the pastor said, "will you do it?"

Paul made up his mind then and there he needed to go work in Florida at Eckerd Youth Alternatives. He put in his application and joined Mac at E-How-Kee at the end of the summer in 1973.[17] The first night he spent in training in the woods, he woke up in the morning and read from Ezekiel 2,

> The people to whom I am sending you are obstinate and stubborn...do not be afraid of them or their words. Do not be afraid though briers and thorns are all around you and you live among scorpions. Do not be afraid of what they say or be terrified by them, though they are a rebellious people.

---

[17] This section taken from an interview with Chief Paul 3/15/2017.

After praying, Paul rolled out of bed and when knocking out his boots before putting them on, a scorpion crawled out of his boot.[18]

Wet Sleeping Bags and Widowmakers

Paul Daley was a Chief in the Kekewhs, the youngest group, when they took their first river trip from the new camp, Paul Daley recalls that he forgot to count the sleeping bags before they left. Because it was cold, Paul let a boy borrow his sleeping bag. The boy happened to wet the bed that night and both of them spent a miserable cold night. A couple days later a supervisor dropped a sleeping bag off of an over pass into their canoe. Paul never forgot to count the sleeping bags again. A second trip to the Yellow River in Florida brought excitement as well. It rained consistently the whole trip and the rain gradually became harder and harder. The director, Everett Lindstrom had been watching the weather closely and realized trouble was brewing. He contacted the Whiting Field Naval Station north of Milton and they took him up in a helicopter to find the group.[19] That night the group could not believe their eyes when Everett showed up on the side of the river. He instructed them to pack up and get out of there! A hurricane was on the way! After that, Paul was convinced Everett was a super-Chief. Everett never told him how he found them until much later.[20]

After this the group took a three-week backpack trip and a month-long DC bus trip went by without incident. However, on Paul's first long river trip, they learned a thing or two about widow makers. That day had been especially breezy – gusts at times reached 60 mph. The boys made the best of it by stretching out their ponchos and using them as

[18] Interview with Chief Paul 3/15/2017 and 9/11/2021.
[19] Interview with Helen Lindstrom 3/22/2017.
[20] Interview with Chief Paul 9/11/2021.

sails. The group made a ton of mileage that day. That night they pulled in to camp at a boat ramp. As they were gathering up, Paul heard a loud snap, and before they knew it, a tree had fallen in their midst and directly impacted two boys. One boy had a shoulder dislocated. The other boy suffered a severely broken foot. They splinted and tied a tourniquet on his foot and Paul's co-Chief ran for help. 45 minutes later an ambulance arrived and provided medical care to the boys. Both boys made a full recovery.[21] It was after that month-long trip that the boys returned to camp and got to experience their first showers in their new shower house.[22] Showers had never felt so good! Paul recalls those day fondly exclaiming that they were able to help some of the roughest kids in the state truly become successful.

It was about this time that Mac realized a need to improve the work the Eckerd Foundation was doing with families and he was able to persuade Segred Belcher to come out of retirement to give, "three years of specific effort in developing the principles and methods of family work for Eckerd Wilderness Camping."[23] Segred Belcher did intake and family work at the Salesmanship Club Boys. She was a trained social worker who had grown up in North Dakota. She had worked under Campbell Loughmiller and Chief Mac and was versed in family work. When she retired in August of 1976, she left behind a manual for staff working with families that in use to this day.

---

[21] Interview with Paul Daley 3/15/17.
[22] Interview with Paul Daley 3/16/2017.
[23] Jack and Ruth Eckerd Foundation Program and Policy Manual Vol 1, 10/16/1976. p. 3.03.

CHAPTER 4:
E-WEN-AKEE:
CAMP GOES NORTH!

Building upon the success of the camps in Florida, Jack Eckerd had a dream of developing camping program in the Northern United States. In 1978, while Ken Edgar was the Director at the Salesmanship Club Boys Camp, Jack Eckerd approached him with a new challenge. He was interested in seeing if this type of therapeutic camping program could be implemented in colder climates and asked if Ken would be willing to try his hand at the experiment. Ken and Flora accepted the challenge and moved to Brooksville, FL where they spent a month planning and writing a proposal to do the camp in Vermont.[1] Then, in September of 1978, Ken, Flora, and their son Tim packed up and moved to Vermont. They searched the whole state over and found an old boy scout camp and recommended it to begin the program.

The camp was centered on a beautiful glacier lake and the first inhabitants of the camp were a family of beavers. As they explored the property they discovered the beavers had built a dam on the natural spillway. When the lake was dammed up, the water covered much of the property they desired to use. So Ken painstakingly deconstructed the dam. The next night, the beavers rebuilt the dam and Ken would go out and tear it down. Ken inquired about relocating or discouraging the beavers but was told he was not allowed. So part of Ken's daily routine began by deconstructing the dam. If he waited more than one day to break it apart, they constructed it so well that he found it twice as hard to pull apart. Eventually, the beaver group moved on and Ken was able to turn his attention to the other groups at camp.[2]

The plan for human residents involved using the 20 x 20 buildings the Boy Scout Camp had constructed near where they planned to locate each campsite. The boys lived in those buildings until tents could be built. For the first two months, the Edgar home served as the kitchen,

[1] Interview with Ken and Flora 3/27/2017.
[2] Ibid.

dining hall, office, and shower house. The first group ate at the family kitchen table and Flora volunteered to cook the meals and do the shopping. The living room couch served as three offices. One person per couch seat. When a second group was added they ate on the back porch. By the end of October, there were three groups at the camp.[3] An old three story barn on the property was converted into an office building/dining hall/emergency shelter. One floor served as the office, one as the dining hall and kitchen, and the hayloft was used the first year as a place for the boys to sleep during cold weather. They only used the hayloft one or two times before they realized it was unnecessary.

> To have camps further north, we had to build the tents a little different from the way we were used to building tents. We used two tarps on the tents with a thin layer of insulation in between the tarps. We also put insulation under the floor and bales of hay around the outside at the bottom of the tent tarp. We used more posts and larger rafters to hold the snow's weight. Other than that, the tents were built the same as the tents in the other camps. The group drew the plans and did the building. We quickly learned not to leave anything on the ground. Any tool or item that was left when it snowed was not found until spring.[4]
>
> Water lines were buried six feet deep. But even then, if you walked over the water line, or a car drove over it, it would freeze. In the south, campers would have to use ice and insulation to keep their cook-out food from spoiling. But not so in Vermont. In fact, the camper would have to use insulation to help keep the food from freezing as we got the food for the two days when meals were fixed in the campsite. We really didn't want frozen eggs.[5]

The first Thanksgiving the boys went home for homesday and Ken and Flora got snowed in. No one could get in or out of the property. Then one evening, much to their surprise, they heard a hard knock on the door. A man from the local store knew they were stranded and

---

[3] Ken Edgar, Unpublished Document, Vermont. Given to Stephen Ashton 8/31/2016.
[4] Ken Edgar, Unpublished Documet, Vermont. Given to Stephen Ashton 8/31/2016 and interview with Ken and Flora 3/27/2017.
[5] Ken Edgar, Unpublished Documet, Vermont. Given to Stephen Ashton 8/31/2016.

drove his snowmobile up to them to check on them and drop off an apple pie. By the time the boys needed to return, Ken and Flora had devised a plan. They found they could get around in the snow with the camp bulldozer. So they hooked up 4WD vehicles to the bulldozer and in that manner transported boys around the property. Every morning, Ken would meet the camp cook at 4 AM at the bottom of the hill with the bulldozer and pull her up. Ken also became adept at driving a snowmobile and it became quite an attraction for visitors to the camp from the south. Ice fishing also became quite an event.

> The camp lake would freeze over and the ice would get to be about four feet thick. To fish, we would have to drill a hole through the ice. I remember a fun time when one of the Vermont State Senators came to visit camp and he wanted to take the campers and staff ice fishing. He started us walking out on the lake. Me being a southerner, I kept telling the boys to spread out so that we would not break through the ice. He laughed at me and kept walking to the center of the lake.
>
> He asked me to have the boys build a fire. What!!! I couldn't imagine building a fire right there on the ice in the center of the lake. He just laughed at me. He had a small sled that he had been pulling behind him. It had firewood on it. I was so worried that the fire would melt the ice. He laughed at me again.
>
> The fire did melt a small bowl shape in the ice. But it only would melt so deep, then stop. The fire would keep above the melted ice water. So we had a warm fire to huddle around and we caught a lot of fish that day. And so it went. We had a lot of different experiences in that cold northern country and a lot of fun with all the winter sports and activities.
>
> A report went back to Mr. Eckerd that it was very possible to have an outdoor camp that far north. Because of that experiment, other camps were started.[6]

---

[6] Ken Edgar, Unpublished Document, Vermont. Given to Stephen Ashton 8/31/2016.

CHAPTER 5:
MISSION DRIFT

Over the next few years, several factors led Mac, Ken, Everett, and Paul to choose to leave the Eckerd program. Chief among them was Gerry Rehm's growing insistence that God should not be any part of the program. On more than one occasion Gerry told Mac to, "put away his Bible and just run the program."[1] Two other closely linked factors also became a clear problem: centralization of the program, and an emphasis on academics over the group and the development of healthy relationships.

Losing Faith – Finding Hope

Ken and Flora remained at E-Wen-Akee until May of 1980. Around that time, Gerry Rehm came to visit the program and see its progress. During the visit, he told Ken that people were complaining and he would no longer be allowed to say anything to the boys about God or Jesus.[2] Chapel and Vesper services should focus on moral lessons and spiritual discussion needed to be left out. Ken responded saying, "That is like discovering chocolate ice cream and not being able to say anything about it."[3]

Ken and Flora prayed about the situation and decided they could not do the program without mentioning God. As a result, the pair moved back home to Longview, Texas and planned to, "just work a normal job and be a normal family." Ken got a job as a salesman. He was successful, but hated it. He wanted to help people, not think about margins and money. Ken was miserable, and because Ken was miserable, Flora was miserable.

In July of 1980, Chief Mac called the Edgar's to ask them to join him at the Baptist Children's Homes of North Carolina to work toward starting a Therapeutic Camp there. Ken and Flora made the move and

[1] Interview with Paul Daley 3/16/2017.
[2] Interview with Ken and Flora 3/27/2017.
[3] Ibid.

worked in an Emergency Cottage where they successfully applied camp principles in an indoor residential setting. After three years in North Carolina, the Florida Sheriffs Ranch asked Ken to help begin a residential program and summer camp. They spent two summers at the ranch with Art Dagg and his family. Ken and Flora ran the summer program and Art began the year-round program. After the first year, boys from the summer program were selected for the year-round program.

During the second-year, Art took the group to land the Florida Sheriff's had in the Okefenokee Swamp while Ken ran the summer program. In the long run, the Florida Sheriffs thought a summer program better accomplished their goal of building relationships in the community, and the year-round program was ended.[4]

At that time the Georgia Baptists reached out to Ken and Flora about starting a program. Ken and Flora moved to the Georgia Baptist Children's Homes. Soon a collaboration between South Carolina and Georgia Baptists was underway. While they were getting the land ready, and the Chuckwagon was under construction, the Children's Home leadership asked Ken to share camp principles they had applied successfully during their time in North Carolina around the state. Then tragedy struck, the Presidents of both the Georgia and South Carolina Children's Homes were killed in separate accidents. The prospects of a joint partnership between states to begin a camping program dimmed. However, God was still at work, while in the area, Ken made contact with Floyd and Harvey Yoder. That meeting would result in Ken becoming involved with Fairplay Boys Camp in February of 1987, and eventually led to the founding of Wilderness Way Camp School for Girls.

Centralizing Around a Classroom

The second significant factor that led Mac, Ken, and Paul to choose to leave the Eckerd program began to creep in before the spiritual mandate was given. A foundational camp principle is that adults and children consistently work together in a group to solve problems. As problems are solved, children build trust, feel secure, gain confidence, and develop meaningful relationships. Without those critical bonds, life does not have meaning and learning cannot happen. Campbell

---

[4] In 1988, Everett and Helen spent two years at the Florida Sheriffs Ranch after leaving Eckerd Youth Alternatives before Everett passed away in a motor vehicle accident on October 18, 1990.

Loughmiller used to say, 'the only thing worth a quarter at camp is a healthy relationship between a boy and his Chief.'"[5]

Many experiments were done to try to help boys and girls transition out of camp while leaving the traditional camp group intact. The first attempt began with the girls at E-Nini-Hassee. A joint effort with the Pinellas County Juvenile Welfare Board in September 1971 resulted in, "a lovely home on five lakeside acres...[60 miles from camp being] set up as a transitional facility to help those E-Nini-Hasee girls who had special need in adjusting to school and community before returning home for good. Eight girls lived in the home with two 'houseparent chiefs' to help with lessons and living needs." [6] Girls went to public school and returned back to their Chiefs. "Although many girls received an effective 'finishing touch' in the Townhouse, evaluation showed the best use of staff effort was within camp itself. Consequently, the townhouse closed at the end of December 1974."[7]

In early 1976, a second attempt was made by setting up a transition group as a sixth group at E-Ma-Chamee,[8] and one followed at E-Nini-Hasee.[9] "It would not duplicate the previous concepts of a school group, but would be a classroom located within camp itself."[10] This group lived in campsite with 40 x 40 tent in the middle.[11] This was a pilot program with the Santa Rosa County School Board, and a teacher for the classroom was hired using state educational funds. The students woke up, did morning routines, went to breakfast, then attended school in the classroom in their campsite. They would break for lunch, and return to their studies. After dinner they would create their own evening plan.[12] This was discarded because it was judged that students were not any more successful in this transitional classroom than they were in the schools. It seemed that students moved from the success of camp to marginal success in a classroom, and they lost momentum in

---

[5] Interview with Paul Daley 9/28/2021.

[6] Jack and Ruth Eckerd Foundation Program and Policy Manual Vol 1 10/16/1976. p. 3.02.

[7] Ibid., 3.02.

[8] Ibid., 3.07.

[9] Interview with Paul Daley 3/15/2017.

[10] Jack and Ruth Eckerd Foundation Program and Policy Manual Vol 1 10/16/1976. p. 3.07.

[11] Interview with Paul Daley 3/15/2017.

[12] Ibid.

their transition to home. It was better to help a boy or girl transition directly from camp to home without this intermediary step.[13]

Gradually, camp began to drift from a de-centralized program where groups decisions and solved problems together to a centralized program. Financial and governmental pressures began to increasingly shape the program instead of core principles of effectiveness. The problem here was twofold:

- First, most boys and girls who enter camp have failed in a traditional educational model. The primary thing they have learned in traditional classroom is that they can't learn. That is both tragic and untrue. Consider how much the average child learns in the first 5 years of their lifetime without chalkboards, textbooks, lesson plans, or computer screens. The work of L.B. Sharp and John Dewey proved that, "we learn most through direct experience, we learn faster, the learnings are retained longer, and the appreciation is greater."[14] Education is not maximized through regurgitative learning experiences. Classrooms make academic learning efficient for those can memorize facts and regurgitate information on tests, but it is entirely ineffective for those who do not. Why would camp choose to mimic a model that has already failed these students? Historically, camp has been extraordinarily successful in helping children failing in traditional school see tremendous growth through an experiential education model.[15]

- The second problem is that, in the camp model, true life-wide education happens within a healthy group who is responsible for meeting needs in the context of relationship by maintaining their campsite and running their program. The group exists to meet individual needs, and individuals are given responsibility and learn from each other. The spirit should be, "I love my group and my group

[13] Interview with Ken 3/27/17.

[14] L.B. Sharp, "Why Outdoor and Camping Education," *Journal of Educational Sociology* 21 (1948): 314.

[15] Interview with Ken 3/27/2017

> loves me." In the group, learning is multiplied as problems are solved. When individual needs are met consistently apart from the group, the group fails to be a group, and the heart of the work at camp is sacrificed. Campbell Loughmiller writes, "[In a group], if this [democratic] process is not used *all* of the time, it will not work *any* of the time."[16] "[Group work]...is not something employed for an hour or two a day. It is a method consistently used from the time a boy gets to camp until he leaves. It is the most effective tool we have found."[17]

By the dawn of new millennium these core values had been forgotten in the Eckerd program. Notions of group balance were negated by financial pressure to accept a maximum number of Department of Juvenile Justice placements. To remedy a lack of group balance and provide for pressures surrounding education; counseling, classroom time, and imposed schedules were introduced. In 2011 a North Carolina newspaper wrote,

> EYA education services follow the N.C. Department of Public Instruction course of study, and the camps provide 30-33 hours of instruction per week. Each camp is budgeted for four certified teaching positions, one education coordinator and one teacher certified in special education services. EYA educational services are accredited by the Southern Association of Colleges and Schools Council Accreditation and School Improvement (SACS/CASI) as a special purpose school[18]

By 2011, group process was further undermined as length of stay was shortened to under six months. Instead of a group process, the program centered around the classroom. Groups no longer designed their own shelters, rather campers choose from a list of pre-approved designs. Educational trips had been shortened to the point they were nearly non-existent.[19]

---

[16] Loughmiller, *Kids in Trouble*, 65.

[17] Loughmiller, *Wilderness Road*, 72.

[18] Julie Hubbard, Wilkes Journal-Patriot, *Eckerd Camp to Close*, 5/15/2011 - North Wilkesboro, NC

[19] Another experiment in education revolved around the training of chiefs. As camps continued to expand, the need for well-trained chiefs expanded as well. A four week full-

"Trusting relationships are the basis for the whole program."[20] As the program was shortened, relationships suffered, camper ownership diminished, experiential education was abandoned, and groupwork was minimized – as a result, effectiveness plummeted. In mid-2011, Eckerd programs across the nation, with the exception of E-Nini-Hassee,[21] closed citing a shift across the country from residential services to community based services.[22]

Difficult Endings and New Beginnings

Chief Mac recalls "I worked with Mr. Eckerd for 11.5 years and started 10 camps." In March of 1970, Gerald Rehm was hired as the Executive Director. Mac recalls, "I was told several times I needed to see Mr. Eckerd at least once per week. However, I felt that if I did, I wouldn't have a camp when I got back."[23] The few times Mac did make the trip, Mr. Rehm made it clear he did not appreciate Mac not following the chain of command.[24] Soon, Mac began to find he did not have influence in major decisions effecting camp and a rift in philosophy began to develop. Founding directors: Mac, Ken, and Everett wanted to hold to core values – the other Directors they had trained were willing to go along with Jerry Rehm's desire to compromise in the name of efficiency.

"Jerry attempted to run camp as a business," Mac recalls. "He wanted efficiency, profitability, and results. However, there is no easy way to love the hell out of a kid." Mac understood that efficiency and effectiveness were often inversely proportional. Conflicts and tensions

---

time course, called Catatogas was executed through a partnership with St. Leo's College that offered 12 hours of undergraduate credit to new chiefs and provided the basic skills for moving into their new roles with confidence. Chiefs lived in a campsite, built tents, planned, and lived as the boys. The training culminated in a two-week canoe trip the group planned and executed. This program continued to grow, and in August of 1976, "the first graduate-level senior counselor course training course was conducted by Dr. Edward Garlitz and Buford McKenzie."

[20] Interview with Paul Daley 9/28/2021. Paul was quick to point out the result of a healthy trusting relationship with an adult is an enduring transformative relationship with Jesus.

[21] E-Nini-Hassee has endured in large part due to Ruth Eckerd's great love for the program and the girls whose lives have been transformed there.

[22] Donna Jordan, The Colebrook Chronicle, *Camp E-Toh-Anee Is Set to Close Next Month*, Colebrook, CT., October 21, 2011.

[23] Interview with Chief Mac 8/5/2008

[24] Interviews with Mac and Karen Collins

of this sort boiled over in 1978 and resulted in the death of a girl at E-Nini-Hassee.

In 1977, Paul Daley became the Assistant Director at E-Nini-Hassee. He worked there one year. During his time there, the Director insisted he build a six-person casita in the Cliff Dwellers Campsite. Paul refused saying that it was unsafe and would cave in. The Director at the time complained to Gerald Rehm and Paul was relocated to the Candor, NC camp and a supervisor at E-Nini-Hassee was the promoted to take his place. After he left, the casita was built and it fell in trapping two girls. According to an August 3, 1978 News-Press article, "By the time rescuers arrived, camp personnel had removed sand from both girls' faces, but it was too late to save the Larson teen-ager."[25] This news surfaced as Jack Eckerd was in a heated race for "the Republican nomination for governor."[26] He lost that fall to Democrat Bob Graham.

Gerald Rehm attempted to place the blame on Chief Mac for not specifying in manuals the dimensions of the casita. That was simply not the case, Paul had already objected to the practice and been over-ruled. Soon after the accident, Mac was promoted to a position where he was removed from direct supervision and consultation for camp programs and was asked to travel, evaluate the camp programs, and report back to the main office.[27] Mac found himself in a position where he felt unable to reach out to Jack Eckerd and unable to effect a camp program he felt was careening in a dangerous direction. After a final four-hour heated meeting with Mr. Rehm, Mac looked at Jerry and said, "I love you Jerry!" and left. Mac came home broken, and shortly after that, he resigned.

Mac says, "it took the Lord three years to move me from Eckerd."[28] It deteriorated to a place where directors were, "doing the recipe with no spirit. They would go to chapel and not talk about Jesus, they would talk about being good."[29] When Dr. Wagner from the Baptist Children's Homes of North Carolina contacted Mac about starting a program, it seemed the Lord was leading. Mac would have the freedom to run the program as he saw fit. He adds, "one of my failures was not effectively

---

[25] "Girl is Killed After Ditch Caves In," New-Press, Fort Myers, FL. Aug 3, 1978, p. 19.
[26] Ibid., 19.
[27] Interview with Paul Daley 3/15/2017
[28] Interview with Chief Mac 8/5/2008
[29] Ibid.

selling camp at the top level."[30] When Mac announced his resignation, Jack Eckerd scolded him, he said, "Why didn't you tell me?"[31]

In July 22, 1979 article of Charity and Children, Mac's new position as, "Consultant in Wilderness Educational Therapeutic Programs with the Baptist Children's Homes" was announced. Dr. W.R. Wagoner observed that, "Mr. McKenzie is one of the most knowledgeable men in America in outdoor wilderness education camping." Chief Mac worked out an office in Thomasville and consulted with the existing work at Wall Home and Kennedy Home with the vision of expanding the program to Cameron Home near Vass. Chief Paul and Chief Ken followed. Ken and Flora worked in a group home for boys at Wallberg. Chief Paul came to North Carolina March 17, 1980 and began to work in an emergency home. They stayed there two years before they came to Cameron Home in March of 1982.

Life has an odd way of coming full circle. In the early 1980's shortly after Mac left Eckerd, Jack Eckerd became a Christian. His book, *Finding the Right Prescription* chronicles that journey. In April of 2006, Mac received a call from Jerry Rehm. Jerry apologized and told Mac he had become a Christian. Mac standing up to him, not cussing back, and saying I love you stuck with him. He asked Mac if he would help him get camp back on track. Jerry realized camp was not working and wanted to reclaim the program.[32] Mac felt strongly he needed to care for his wife Lois who had developed Alzheimers and there were no other staff at the time ready to take on that challenge.

---

[30] Ibid.

[31] Ibid

[32] Discussions with Mac's family: Karen Collins and Tim Gibson and with Ken and Flora Edgar.

CHAPTER 6: THE WILDERNESS ROAD THERAPEUTIC CAMPING ASSOCIATION

As Cameron Boys Camp, Fairplay Boys Camp, and Wilderness Way Camp School began successful operation, Chief Mac and Mom Lois found themselves often in South Carolina consulting and encouraging. Gatherings in South Carolina for all camp staff became a commonplace occurrence for mutual encouragement. These events became tremendously helpful in establishing camp spirit and culture across the camps.

In the early 1990's; Mac, Lois, Ken, Flora, and Floyd Yoder were eager to see camp continue to grow. Chief Lock was doing some consulting work with Bald Eagle Boys Camp, Bob Griffin left as Assistant Director of Wilderness Way to begin working in Florida with the goal of starting Gator Wilderness Camp, and discussions began about how to preserve the Wilderness Road Model. The Fairplay team had gone to great lengths to re-discover a model that worked, and Mac, Ken, and Paul were mourning the detrimental drift that had occurred in the Eckerd programs.

Among the Camp Directors, there was a general recognition that it was healthy for each of the programs to have their own personality, but there was also a desire to distill and preserve the foundational principles to help camps thrive in the future. On May 11, 1994 the Wilderness Road Therapeutic Camping Association (WRTCA) was incorporated in the state of North Carolina, and the first annual conference was held in 1994 at Fairplay Boys Camp. Cameron, Wilderness Way, Fairplay, and Bald Eagle all attended.

In January of 1995, Bald Eagle Boys Camp would begin with three campers and five staff. David King was the Director, and those men were excited to attend the conference and "rub shoulders" with other camps successfully running the program. From the beginning, conferences were held at camps and the entire staff are invited. There has been a general understanding that every role is important. Camp history is filled with stories of cooks, maintenance men, secretaries, and other support staff who were able to connect with a camper and bring about transformation in a way that direct care staff never could.

In 1998, the association was officially established with Buford MacKenzie president, Ken Edgar as vice president, Paul Dailey as secretary, and JD Miller was treasurer. On October 18, 1999 - with four founding camps - the WRTCA was approved as a 501c3.

Since that time camp has continued to grow and annual conferences, quarterly directors meetings, and regular training sessions have been held. Camps adhering to the model have begun and continue to operate in:

- North Carolina – Cameron Boys Camp
- South Carolina – Fairplay Camp School
- South Carolina – Wilderness Way Girls Camp
- Pennsylvania – Bald Eagle Boys Camp
- Florida – Gator Wilderness Camp School
- Canada – Crane Lake Discovery Camp
- Ireland – Comeraugh Wilderness Camp
- North Carolina – Camp Duncan for Girls
- Ohio – Ohio Wilderness Boys Camp
- Maryland – Allegheny Boys Camp

In an effort to preserve and perpetuate the Wilderness Road Therapeutic Camping Model, the WRTCA laid out The 16 Crucial Components for WRTCA Camps below:

Crucial Components for WRTCA Camps

As members of WRTCA, each camp is expected to support in principle and practice the following camp components:

1. **Christian Values and Biblical Truths are Integral to All We Do.**

   Some of our core values:
   - ***<u>All</u> people are created in the image of God and have great worth.***

- ***God loves people, created them for relationship, and desires for them to live in truth and experience, meaningful lives.***
- ***We learn to have proper relationships with others by following the guidelines that Jesus taught.***
- ***Finding forgiveness for yourself and forgiving others is necessary for a successful and happy life.***
  Feelings of guilt and regret often plague the children and families we work with. We teach them to seek forgiveness from God, reconciliation with others they have wronged, and to forgive themselves.
- ***The truth that we reap what we sow: If you do "well" you will be rewarded with good but if you do "wrong" you will receive the same (Gal 6:7).***
  Jesus taught us to "love the Lord your God with all your heart and with all your soul and with all your mind...and to love your neighbor as yourself (Mat 22:36-40)." We teach campers that God created the world in such a manner that when we do what is "right" and "good" we experience a more happy and satisfying life. Even when circumstances are difficult, it is best to do the right thing. "The fruit of righteousness will be peace, and the effect of righteousness will be quietness and confidence forever. (Isa. 32:17)"

2. Relationship building will be the emphasis and impetus for change and healing.

There are many ideas about how to best help youth with problems. For families at camp, psychotherapy and clinical counseling have often proven ineffective in assisting young people in overcoming their difficulties. It seems that even when the child is surrounded with professionals, their negative behaviors often continue.

We have a different approach. In our camping program we seek to build healthy, appropriate relationships with the children. Many of them do not have a strong, positive relationship with even a single adult. In the beginning they usually reject our efforts. Often, they set out to chase us away by escalating their negative behaviors. When we "hang in there" with them they learn to trust us. This, of course, takes time and that is why we bring them to camp. This allows us to live with them on a daily basis and give them our time and effort.

In professional therapy sessions, camp youth often avoid dealing with their issues. They simply don't tend to take responsibility for themselves or their problems in a clinical setting. At camp however, we employ and carefully train "non-professionals" who are willing to live with the youth and assist them with their life's journey. This takes a great deal of commitment from our child care staff (Chiefs). They experience the young people at their worst - which is just when they need help the most. Gradually a relationship of trust and mutual respect is formed which allows the camper to receive help with his/her problems.

Our hope is that everything the child learns during this relationship building process will be reproduced at home so they can experience healthy relationships with their parents, teachers and others in the community.

3. **The campers and their families choose to participate in the camp program.**

For our wilderness camping program to work effectively it is necessary for each young person and their parent(s) to "choose" camp. We have a pre-admission process that includes a thorough description of the program. As well, the expectations for both parties are discussed. Everyone visits the campsite where the youth will live. They meet the Chiefs and campers. The child and his family are encouraged to ask questions so that "no stone is left unturned." The seriousness of the commitment is highlighted during this time.

Expectations for the camper and family that are highlighted during the preadmission process:

- The length of stay for the camper will not be preplanned but will depend on the campers and guardians progress.

They will help evaluate their own progress on a regular basis. The camp team and the family will decide together when it's time for the youth to graduate.

- The young person must be willing to work on resolving his/her own problems and must be willing to help the other members of their group.
- Parents are expected to make payments as agreed, attend meetings such as evaluation conferences and write the child every week.
- The parent(s) are expected to have the child at home for a few days every six weeks or so with more extended visits during certain holidays.
- While the youth is at camp, phone calls and visits to the youth will be limited to planned interactions.
- The young person is expected to write home every week.

When there is a clear understanding of the camp process and expectations it is time for a decision. The parent(s) and youth are each asked if they think camp would be a good thing for their family. If they feel this is a worthwhile venture they are asked to make a commitment which includes full participation by the camper and his/her family. We want the youth and family to understand that coming to camp is not punishment for bad behavior. It is instead an opportunity for a fresh start.

We often see the camper waiver on his commitment after coming to camp. This is what we expect. After all, if the youth were able to easily keep such a commitment they probably would not need camp. This is when the parent(s) and camp staff must resolve together to help the child live up to his/her decision to graduate from camp and not give up.

4. Family reunification is our goal but if this is not possible, we will support the youth in the most family-like and least restrictive environment possible.

From the first day a child comes into our care our goal is to get them back home with their family. Our hope is that every child who completes our program will return to a family situation suitable for a happy childhood.

While at camp the young person is learning many lessons that will help him/her become a better son/daughter. Attitudes and behaviors that required them to leave home are being adjusted. Most importantly, the child is engaged in mending their relationship with his/her parents.

While the child is learning and growing to become a better family member the parents are also in a learning process. They are learning how to structure the home and create a healthier environment for their child. They are also engaged in mending the broken relationship.

5. **Problem Solving will be part of daily camp life and will be taught to the campers and their families.**

Most of our families have come to a place where they are "stuck". They cannot move forward until a problem or perhaps many problems are resolved. Sometimes the problems are so "big" and have been going on for so long that both child and parent have lost hope.

In the process of living in the camp group the child learns that problems "can" be solved. Our differences "can" be worked out. There is now hope for mending his/her relationship with his/her parents.

Both the child and parent(s) are taught a simple problem solving method to assist them in overcoming conflict and other barriers to their relationship. The family can begin to get "unstuck" by implementing the steps of our problem solving process.

<u>How to Solve a Problem</u>

1) Identify what the problem is.
2) Consider possible solutions to the problem.
3) Choose the solution you want to try and follow through with applying this solution.

4) Evaluate the effectiveness of your solution and if necessary choose a new solution.
5) Consider how you will prevent the same problem from happening again.

6. Each youth and family will be taught to develop their own goals and to evaluate their progress.

One old saying says, "If you shoot at nothing you are sure to hit it." Another says, "If you shoot for the stars you may at least hit the moon." The point is that you must know where you are going to get there. We help the youth and their parent(s) develop goals for what they want to accomplish in the camping program.

We don't create their goals for them. We give them the freedom to set their own goals. This is, of course, with our assistance since most of our families have never written goals for themselves.

Three or four goals for the young person and three or four for the parent(s) is usually enough for getting started. The children write goals that will help them overcome the behavior problems that are causing their difficulties. Their goals address the issues that were preventing a proper relationship with his/her parents as well as problems related to school and the community. At camp in the group setting the child receives daily help with accomplishing the goals. The parents write goals that will help them create a better atmosphere in the home and build a healthy relationship with their child.

The camp staff help the child and family evaluate their goals on a regular basis during scheduled evaluation conferences. This helps keep the family and child moving forward on their goals.

7. Work with the youth will be accomplished in age appropriate groups of 8-10 campers with two or three Chiefs in each group.

That we work with the children in "groups" is important. Isolating the child is normally ineffective, if not detrimental to his/her well-being. By keeping the young person engaged in a group process we can accomplish much more.

<u>Some advantages of a group process</u>

- The child is required to consider the well-being and happiness of others.
- They cannot avoid having to deal with their own problems.
- They get to practice "problem solving" in preparation for returning home.
- They get to practice social and relationship building skills.
- They learn teamwork.
- They learn to properly respond to authority.
- They have pressure from the group to be a helpful member.
- They learn what their strengths are and that they do have something to offer society.

This group process must, of course, be facilitated by caring adults (Chiefs) who are considered members of the group. Conflicts arise, and youth often do not have the perspective necessary to help move the group forward in a healthy direction. The adults are part of every decision in the group. But when problems arise, they play a special role in facilitating to set expectations, engage every member, give each camper a voice, ensure that group plans are successful, and secure healthy attitudes and relationships within the group. These elements are critical for the group to take ownership and function in a healthy manner.

It is also necessary for camp supervision to ensure that groups stay "balanced". If there are too many youth with certain kinds of problems it will become overly difficult to manage the group in a healthy way. For example, if there are several young people in a group who have issues with running away then it will be difficult to prevent repetitive running from the group.

Working with the youth in groups is not the easiest way to do things but it gives us the best chance to help them overcome their problems.

8. **Campers help decide what their groups' plans will be – both long range and daily.**

   When a child comes to camp we are not trying to punish or confine them by putting them in a tightly controlled environment. While we do maintain a structured schedule, we also strive to give them as much control over their environment as possible. Many of them have experienced the discomfort of circumstances beyond their control. We try to give them back some control they may feel they have lost.

   One way we can give them control is by giving each camper a "say" about the groups plans. In group planning sessions every youth is encouraged to verbalize his/her ideas about the group's activities for the near future. Of course there must be "give and take," but in the end, we have a plan that every group member agrees with.

   One benefit of helping the young people plan their own future is that it teaches them responsibility. The activities must be balanced between necessary work and ways to have fun. Along with hiking, fishing and games there must be chores. The campers are learning what it means to live responsibly.

9. **Campers are given a voice in the daily functioning of the group as they strive to find the best way to live together.**

   At camp we do not want our groups to be controlled by adult authority. While adult authority is needed, we believe it is good leadership to ensure that everyone has a voice in helping decide what kind of group we want to be and how we can best live together.

   When a child comes to camp and joins a group, he/she is wondering how things will go for them in the midst of all the other personalities. Some are natural leaders who will tend to dominate the group. Others, who are more passive, may feel intimidated and be fearful of speaking their mind. It is our goal at camp to help each camper learn to speak for themselves in ways that are appropriate.

A more aggressive child will be taught to respect the ideas of others. A passive child will be taught that his/her ideas are just as important as anyone else's.

When a problem arises in the group we appeal to **every** member to help solve the problem. When the group is deciding how they need to improve their attitudes **every** member is expected to help formulate an improvement plan. If there is a question about what work should be emphasized in the campsite **every** campers opinion is valued.

We are teaching the youth to think for themselves, verbalize their ideas and to be helpful group members. These characteristics will serve them well at home and in the community.

10. Camp groups will end each day with an informal evaluation of the day called pow-wow.

In our modern culture we stay very busy. We often do not take time to "smell the roses" or participate in other more contemplative activities. Things that should get celebrated do not get celebrated. Lessons that should have been learned get forgotten. Resolutions that should have been embraced are lost. For these reasons we make a point of ending each day with a time of contemplation and evaluation.

Just before going to bed each night the group gathers around a campfire for a time of informal discussion related to processing the day's events. We call this time pow-wow a term borrowed from Native American culture.

The children have a chance to express their feelings about the day. The Chiefs direct the conversation to keep things on the positive side. It's OK to express negative feelings about an event but that should be followed with some insight from a group member about how we could do better tomorrow. Everyday should have one or more "gold nuggets" that can be celebrated. Gold nuggets are things that happened during the day that we can feel good about. Any progress that a camper or the group is making can be brought to attention. Group successes can be evaluated. "What helped us have such a great accomplishment?"

At the end of the day every camper should have a good feeling about something he accomplished, something he learned, a bit of progress he made on his goals or how he will improve tomorrow. Couldn't we all benefit from this kind of daily evaluation?

11. **Youth will be taught life skills and will gain an appreciation for learning through an experiential education process.**

At camp we say that education is happening "all day, every day". We like to think of education in broad terms not just in terms of academic subjects. While academic subjects are good, they are seldom the key to any child's success. There are things even more important than academic accomplishment. We like to teach the young people "life skills". Consider the list below.

<u>Life skills learned at camp</u>

- A strong work ethic
- The ability to resolve conflict by problem solving
- The ability to set personal goals and evaluate your progress
- The ability to make a plan and execute the plan while evaluating how you can do better next time
- The ability to maintain healthy living routines
- The ability to handle social interactions appropriately
- The ability to communicate effectively
- The ability to work with others as a partner or team member

A child equipped with these tools has a good chance of success.

We do teach academic subjects at camp but in a nontraditional, experiential way. Most of the young people who come to camp are not successful in the traditional class room. They need something different. The camp setting and program lends itself to engaging the children in an experiential style education.

Led by the Chief, the group members learn to explore subjects they are interested in. The Chief appeals to their natural curiosity by asking questions about things in their surrounding environment. "What kind of bug is that? What does it eat? What are its enemies? How does it reproduce? Why is it here but not in other places? Where does it go in the winter? What is its proper name?" As the group members search for answers they are learning things they will not soon forget because they **wanted** to learn about the bug. Most of what gets learned in the classroom is forgotten because the information was spoon fed without having developed an appetite. At camp we use a camper's natural curiosity to help him/her develop an appetite. Then, true learning can take place.

12. Living quarters, when possible, are designed and constructed by the group members using native materials and without the use of power tools.

Some professionals would look at our small group campsites and conclude that we are keeping the youth in unacceptable living conditions. But I have yet to see a professional who spent time in a well-established campsite with a well-established group feel our campsites are inadequate. In the beginning stages of a camps development the campsite is especially rustic and the campers are still not "sold" on this whole idea of building and maintaining the campsite. This soon changes as the campers build more shelters in the campsite and care for its daily maintenance.

Eventually, the campsite comes to belong to the young people. They exhibit a great sense of pride and accomplishment about their campsite. Children who viewed themselves as failures begin to believe they may have hope. They have at least one "big" thing to feel good about. It is a huge esteem builder for a youth to be part of a group that is successfully able to build and maintain its own living quarters.

Many life skills are learned through the process as well. Can you imagine all the planning, team work, communication and problem solving involved?

Once again, this is not an easy way to work with youth but it is a good way to help youth who have a low view of themselves and need a big success in life.

13. Each camp will teach daily routines that promote discipline and healthy living.

Most of the children who come to camp have been living in unstructured environments and have little discipline. They have difficulty meeting some of their basic needs.

We structure camp in such a way that each day is composed of specific routines that teach and discipline the youth to take care of themselves, their belongings and their surrounding environment. This helps remove some of the chaos from the child's life and creates a secure setting where they can experience emotional healing.

Parents especially appreciate our routines. Conflict in the home is often precipitated by the young person's lack of discipline related to basic living skills. We encourage parents to adopt routines similar to ours at camp so the home will also have proper structure and discipline. What parent doesn't want their children to be able to keep their room clean or take care of their personal hygiene? The routines help the young people build healthy habits into their lifestyle. Personal hygiene, meal times, campsite chores and bed time all have proper routines that will work just as well at home.

14. Singing will be incorporated into daily camp life.

Singing has proven itself to be a useful tool for lifting the human spirit. It can cheer a hurting camper, calm unsettled nerves or bring laughter to a sad heart. As well, the campers learn to work together by singing together. Singing can bring unity to a divided group.

We sing many types of songs: spiritual, folk, contemporary, patriotic, and silly songs are examples. Some are even written by the campers and Chiefs. These, of course, carry special meaning to camp.

When used properly where can you find a more healthy form of self-expression?

15. With the help of the campers and their families each camp builds and maintains a healthy community.

In all that we do at camp one of our main goals is to develop an environment where the youth, their families and the camp staff all feel safe and valued - an environment where everyone can learn and grow. This requires an understanding on everyone's part that we are all in this together. Camp will only be as good as we make it.

A new camper should know that he has a role in making camp a "good" place. If he/she decides not to help, everyone suffers. Each day is filled with opportunities to build a healthy camp community. Because the youth come to us with destructive behaviors, the camp must be prepared to absorb a great deal of resistance in the beginning. As the new camper experiences an environment of care and forgiveness, and begins to build trusting relationships, he/she realizes they are a valued part of the camp community and becomes a partner in creating and maintaining a healthy camp culture.

<u>Some key components of a healthy community</u>

- We listen to each other and value each other's ideas.
- We work together for common goals.
- We treat each other with respect.

- We seek reconciliation when conflicts arise.
- We care about the well-being of everyone in our community.
- We forgive each other for our faults.
- We have fun together.

As we build and maintain a healthy community all members are enriched. Like a plant rooted in rich soil, each member can more readily grow to reach their potential.

16. **Camping outdoors is used to provide optimal opportunities for positive change.**

Camping-out in the woods allows many advantages that benefit young people with behavior problems. For that matter, camping is a great opportunity for families or any group that would like to better themselves. The outdoors provides safe challenges which require the group and every member to learn life-skills and mature in character.

Advantages of our outdoor camping model

- It requires campers to work together to meet needs.
- It absorbs a lot of negative and hyperactive energy.
- It gives the youth control and ownership of their living environment.
- It provides a great sense of accomplishment and gives them a feeling of competence and self-worth.
- This environment sets the stage for positive problem solving.
- The youth have more opportunities for responsibility and for learning a good work ethic.
- It requires a great deal of social interaction which gives the campers practice for life outside camp.
- It provides challenges which require the group and every member to learn life-skills and to mature emotionally.

Concluding Remarks

The components of camp are not in order of importance and are not to be thought of as steps. Rather, they are like the ingredients of a cake. When all of these ingredients are mixed up together they make an excellent cake. If you begin to remove ingredients your cake will not be as tasty.

This model/recipe empowers boys and families. Though a team of experts could scientifically study the chemical composition and molecular structure to determine the best cake recipe, in kitchens across America the best cakes are made in loving families experimenting with the right mix of ingredients. The 16 principles above outline these ingredients, but there is no magic recipe. Each boy, family, and group is different. Different circumstances will require different measures, but the ingredients are the same.

The 16 principles are camp's essential ingredients. For nearly a century they have proven effective when applied by competent non-professionals who love children and don't mind investing their time and energy toward helping them.

E-NINI-HASSEE GIRLS CAMP RAFT TRIP

Louisville, KY to New Orleans, LA – May 13 – July 17, 1970

Everett Lindstrom's Trip Journal with excerpts from the Special Raft Trip Edition of the Whispering Pine Camp Newsletter written by girls on the trip.

Finally, at last, at 3:00 PM on May 11, 1970, we pulled out of Camp with "THE REAL PEOPLE" in many pieces and loaded in an 18 foot rented truck. The group once again was the subject of stares by people who were surprised at seeing a Boy's Camp bus full of girls. Just before dark, on the second day after leaving Floral City, we crossed the bridge over the Ohio River into Jeffersonville, Indiana (just across the river from Louisville, KY)..

12:45 AM, May 13, 1970, Jeffersonville, Indiana

Cliff Dwellers first pow-wow on the Ohio was a late one, but we felt like giving ourselves three good "hows." They are quiet now and in bedrolls under the stars. I can hear trucks in Louisville, right across the river, and a tug on the river. Some of the plentiful driftwood is burning behind me, making a soft crackle and a familiar odor. A light breeze keeps the leaves rustling and the mosquitoes down. The lights of the city make many streaks across the water. Our side of the river is well lighted with street lights. We are in a camping area along the river, but plan to find a better place to rebuild "THE REAL PEOPLE" in the morning.

> The most exciting feeling I had while riding up to Kentucky was as if I was on top of the world. While we were riding through Northern Georgia I could look down off the mountains and see for miles. It was a spectacular view that I will never forget. - Mary

A Way to Find a Campsite by Deborah

(In the morning) we got up as usual and had breakfast. Chief Everett and Chief Hubert left and we (the group and Chiefs) got started (taking down) pup tents. Not too long afterwards a policeman on a motor cycle came up, than a patrol car, then another one. We were talking with them and told them Chief Everett and Chief Hubert...had gone looking for a campsite for us to put our raft in. The one policeman on the motor cycle, Officer Rogers, said he'd check for us. He went back to headquarters and around lunchtime he came back. We invited him to eat but he said he had already eaten. After lunch it began to rain and Officer Rogers helped us to put up a shelter. We put the green trailer up to the Ryder truck and put a pole in the middle. Then we began to spread the tarp over the pole. Boy, it was just in time too! It began to pour down rain!

> The first night we spent at the Ohio River we were stopped at a beautiful campsite. We were in Indiana, but as we looked across the river we could see all the lights and majestic buildings of Louisville, Kentucky. It made the group feel really good to know the next day we would begin building on our raft. It had been months of hard work but as we sat and looked at the river and the sparkling city in front of us, we knew it was well worth it. - Mary

A little while later Chief Everett and Chief Hubert returned. We introduced them to Officer Rogers! He told them he had made several calls but on the last one found a place called Admirals Anchor Marina. He and Chief Everett went to look it over. When they returned he said he liked it but it had a very steep bank and we'd have to slide the raft down on poles. We said we'd like to see it so we went to look at it. As it turned out we like it too.

This all goes to show you that police officers will help you in terms of finding places as well as come to your rescue.

11:45 PM, May 13, 1970, Jeffersonville Indiana

Admiral's Anchor Marina

My feet are wet and muddy and the lightning promises more rain. Chief Hubert and I drove all over the Louisville area and the Indiana side of the river looking for a place to rebuild the raft. When we got back to the group, we found that a very helpful policeman, Patrolman Rodgers, had gotten permission here at the marina.

Many of the conditions are not ideal but maybe that is good. The bank where we plan to build is about ten feet above the water, and makes a straight drop to about one foot above the water. Then, there is a muddy beach extending about twenty feet to the edge of the water. It's going to be real tricky to "make it work." The rain hasn't helped make it look any better, and it's starting up again. In fact, it's really become a gully washer with all the lightning and thunder you could want. I like the sound of rain on a metal roof. But, as for the group, I'm sure there is some good that will work out of the bad conditions.

While eating lunch one day on the banks of the Ohio we were talking about how to get the raft from the high banks into the water. One of the group members looked out in the water and spotted a light green boat with two people in it. Someone made the remark, "they're coming to see our raft." About that time a guy pulled up and jumped out of his boat and right into the muddy bank. We all stood amazed that someone would walk through that much mud just to take a closer look.

He climbed the tall bank and walked over to the raft and said, "Wow, that's great!" He was really shining with excitement. Then he called the girl he was with over to see.

Their names were Liz and Tim. We told almost everything about the raft. We also told them about camp. They were almost speechless...the interest they took was unbelievable and the group grew very eager to tell them even more than before...We made an impression that we hope will never be forgotten. - Karin

11:00 PM, May 14, 1970, Jeffersonville, Indiana

"THE REAL PEOPLE" is taking shape pretty well, surprisingly well considering the little touch of a bug most of the group has had. We have most of the materials carried down a couple hundred feet from the truck to the building site. In addition, we got most of the floor joists in place and bolted. We even got a barrel or two strapped on. The campsite itself has begun to take a little shape. A few visitors have stopped by, but not really enough to interfere. The sun has really been great for drying things out a bit after last night. More storm warnings for tonight.

10:30 PM, May 15, 1970, Admirals Anchor Marina

"THE REAL PEOPLE" now has all its floor joists in place and half its barrels strapped on. The group is working in a fairy good spirit, but it is necessary to keep them primed. It seems that they can think of so many good reasons to be doing things other than building on the raft. Edie, however, has impressed me with her faithfulness. Tonight, in pow-wow, she announced that, because of the wind, she could believe in God. The whole group ended pow-wow in a really sweet spirit. A young couple, Tim and Liz stopped to see what we were doing, and were quite bubbling over with excitement and enthusiasm. The group responded to them as would come naturally, and really got Camp explained well.

The biggest moment that I know of Cliff Dwellers have ever had, happened on May 16, 1970. This was the day we pushed our raft into the water for our trip...We got some long poles for levers to raise the raft to slide down. Four people used two levers and the rest of the group pushed. They had the framework tied to a tree so it wouldn't slide down too fast.

As the last row of barrels hit the edge of the bank it took off by itself and finally hit the water. Everyone ran down the hill to push further into deeper water. Everyone was very excited...some of the group members were so excited they started crying. Even though there was about four feet deep of mud, everyone ran through all of this to get to the raft so we could sit on the floating framework and give three "Hows". -Edie

May 16, 1970, Admirals Anchor Marina

"THE REAL PEOPLE" is afloat! It was quite a splash, both emotionally and physically, when Cliff Dwellers edged the framework with barrels over the side of the embankment. We had cut four saplings of hackberry about six inches in diameter and twenty feet long. These made a runway down to the water's edge. Shortly after noon, we pushed and pried until the raft slid down to the water. The girls were so happy-excited they were crying and holding onto each other. I took pictures.

In the morning, we will put up the canopy, sweep oar mounts, load supplies, etc., and be ready to push off as soon as the "back rope is coiled." The group is with higher spirits than even last night. They are really getting closer together and are working more like a single unit. It has rained several times today and is dripping now. Even this has not dampened spirits.

12:45 AM, May 18, 1970, Admirals Anchor Marina

"THE REAL PEOPLE" is ready to set sail in the morning. It has been a fast moving four days, and the group looks really good. We are all excited and looking forward to pushing off.

Chief Mac is here and will see the group in the morning. It was good to see and to talk to him when he got off the plane tonight. I think his being here will add importance and magnitude in the group's eyes.

There was a quotable today. A visitor in a boat was asking the group about the raft and adventure and asked, "What sort of a field trip are you taking anyway?" Edie responded with, "We're not! We're taking a river trip!"

The Grand Push-Off by Becky

It was Monday, May 18th, 1970. We were about to push off and found out that we were stuck in the mud. Mr. Tuell, a friend that we had met, came by to see us off. Chief Mac had come down to see us off and float down the first few miles with us. We got on the raft and put on our life jackets. We then got the push poles and tried to push off. That is when we found out that we were stuck.

Mr. Tuell was out in the river waiting for us to push off. Little did he know that we were having trouble. Chief Hubert then signaled to him to make waves with his boat so that we could push off from shore. Mr.

Tuell went by two or three times and the group worked together and we pushed off. We floated down river three miles. Chief Mac and Chief Hubert then had to leave. So we signaled to Mr. Tuell and let Chief Mac and Chief Hubert board his boat. We said our good-byes and thanks and floated away.

I thought it was a very exciting experience, and everyone enjoyed knowing Mr. Tuell and having Chief Mac and Chief Hubert seeing us off.

5:20, May 18, 1970   Mile 610

I'm on a raft trip again!! We pushed off at 1:00 and everyone had to help push. The river had gone down a little and we were stuck in the mud. Chief Mac and Chief Hubert rode with us for a few miles and then went back with Mr. Tuell. We had a good session with Chief Mac before he left. No we are floating along, feeling a little seasick, and writing articles and letters. The busy schedule of the past few days has pretty well kept us from doing much writing.

Passing through the Locks by Edie

On Monday, the 18th of May, the first day of our raft trip, we came in sight of Alpine Lock. We approached the lock at a slow speed and tied up to a lockage pole. Then Chief Everett blew one long and one short blast from the horn to let the men at the lock know we were ready to go through. We pulled into the middle lock and behind us big iron doors closed. Then a man tied our raft on to the side of the concrete wall of the lock. Then rapidly the water drained down the river. Then the door opened on the other end, and once again we were floating. A little bit wiser, for we learned the reason for locks is to make a boat the same level as the river so the boat won't have to go over rapids, and a little lower, for we

This morning we washed our clothes on the raft. We got the fire going and put a tub of water on to heat. Then we started putting our clothes in until we had a tub full. We put our soap and bleach in. We found a stick to plunge them down into the water. They began to come clean. Afterwards we took them out and rinsed them over the side of the raft. Then we put them on the food box until we could stop to dry them. I learned that problems can be solved if you look for a way to solve them. We needed to find a way to wash them so we could have clean clothes to put on when we needed them. The way we washed them was the best way to solve the problem. - Cathi

were thirty-seven feet further down the river.

8:20 PM, May 18, 1970 Mile 616

12:35 AM, May 19, 1970 Mile 616

It's still too cool for mosquitoes, yet not too cold. Our Camp is on the south bank and not too ideal in some ways. However, it has seemed to be private enough and the group is in good spirits. In fact, Mary was so happy after a pow-wow on the subject of "self-government" that she burst into tears. They really are loving.

10:15 PM, May 19, 1970 Mile 637

I can hear water running, Chief Susie's clock ticking, and a far distant truck. The moon has just come over a hill across the river and is almost full. The river is smooth, so the raft is quite still. I'm writing here on the raft instead of in the tent as usual. This was our first full day on the OHIO, and a full 12 hour day it was. We did stop to swim for an hour, but stayed consistently on the current otherwise. That means we do about two miles per hour. We had a pretty full day, at least there were no signs of boredom. A water pollution control agent helped us get interested in water pollution. There are still plenty of improvements to be made in the raft, and some plans to be made.

2:40 PM, May 20, 1970 Mile 647

As we were floating down the river, we met two men from the Federal Water Pollution Control of the Ohio River. They showed us some water samples they had gotten from the water near factories and power plants. I never realized how dirty industry made the water. They also told us some facts about pollution and what is trying to be done about it. It never seemed important before that people had to use this river for drinking water until we had to do it also. I hope someday soon, people will begin to realize the great need we have to stop pollution. - Mary

7:55 AM, May 21, 1970 Mile 647

Most people sit on the ground and lean up against the trunk of the tree when they want to sit and think. But, this time, I'm sitting on the trunk of a big maple leaning up against the ground. It's the same tree that "THE REAL PEOPLE" is tied to with the three-quarter inch rope. The sun is directly in front of me and I can gaze right at it because a heavy fog makes it look like a full moon. When sticks float close by, I can see them, but I can't see where the river ends and the atmosphere begins. "THE REAL PEOPLE" is quite busy now. Breakfast is being cooked, a few repairs and improvements are being made, Melody and a couple others are combing their hair, firewood is being cut and stacked, and they just finished the flag raising ceremony. They are moving along pretty well as a group. We stopped early yesterday to get clothes dry. We had washed them during the morning and didn't want them hanging all over the raft. Everyone took turns with the wash, but it was Melody that really took over the job.

8:00 AM, May 22, 1970 Mile 667

10:00 PM May 22, 1970Mile 687 Flint Island

I can hear a good many frogs and a distant barge and a few camper snores. A day is done and I'd love to have a bath. It's still cool enough to keep down mosquitoes but that can't last forever. The group is really lovable. They are working very hard at their goals and I really can't complain about a thing. Oh, we have little "run ins" as I hold lines, but they always seem to take it well. Teresa is really making an attempt to "come out" and is doing a good start. Tonight she spoke up well in pow-wow. We worked on her article about what she expects to get out of the raft trip, and she seemed to do a lot of good thinking. The group is able to give her some real good support.

Chief Susie hasn't gotten any better so we've been looking for a doctor. We camped tonight on Flint Island, Kentucky. There is a huge pile of driftwood and the group has found a delight in looking for interesting pieces of wood. Mary has been particularly thrilled.

The River

The river sometimes gives me a quiver. It's big and green and very keen
All its beauties stand out and when I'm around I can't stand to pout.
It's big and it's bold and it always seems to be cold. It makes me wonder about God above and all the love He is showing for us all by giving us the skies, and the trees, the birds and the bees and last but not least, the River

- Ann

What I Want to Get From the Raft Trip

On this raft trip I want to become a better person and to know what kind of person I want to be. To do this I need to know my group better and I need to help solve my group's problems. Most of all, I want to be able to express my feelings to the group. By doing this I hope I will become a real member of the group. I want to learn how to be me and how to bring out my own personality. I want to have fun with my group and be with them in spirit too.

There are several other things I want to learn on the raft trip. I want to be able to read river maps and use the sweep oars. I especially want to know how to cook. I also want to learn what to do to help the group push off and land the raft. I just want to be able to do things right so they won't have to be done over. Finally, I want to learn not to feel too bad when I make mistakes. - Teresa

2:40 PM, May 23, 1970 Mile 703

Everyone is busy. Edie is on the bow sweep oar and Melody is at the stern. Karin is putting mosquito netting on her tent and Becky is starting to prepare supper. Cathi, Debbie, Mary, Edie, and Teresa are writing articles. Chief Lynda and Cindy are checking to see that laundry marks are on the clothes. We left Chief Susie at Derby, Indiana with Mr. Hubert Etienne who will take her to Tell City to the doctor. We will pick her up when we get there.

8:00 PM, May 23, 1970 Mile 708

Once again pow-wow was an experience. Several times during the day, campers had mentioned how good they felt about the day. I had laid the law down that the doors had to be finished or else. Right away, spirits jumped up a notch or two and pretty well stayed for

On May 23, 1970, Cliff Dwellers stopped in Stephensport, Indiana, to get some water. While we were there we saw a big boat coming so we went down to the river and we saw the Delta Queen. It was as big as the Belle of Louisville. It was red and white, and it had a lot of people on it. Delta Queen and Belle of Louisville are the last two steamboats left in the United States.

While we were watching the Delta Queen she came right up beside a big barge and passed it. It was very interesting and historical and Cliff Dwellers were lucky enough to see both of them. - Ann

the day. They surely do feel better when they are hard at work. Mary began reading "Tom Sawyer" and the whole group sits completely spellbound. There is a lot of enthusiasm for article writing and study. If they can continue growing the way they've started out, it's really going to be interesting to see what they will be by the time we get to New Orleans.

1:00 PM, May 24, 1970 Mile 719

11:30 PM, May 24, 1970 Mile 719

KERPLUNK!! That's all there was to it! The same camera I'd taken on the Tejas Responsibility and a five hundred mile canoe trip. The Nikon had broken so I was using my faithful old Yashika. Someone knocked it off and there was a kerplunk and that as the last of my picture taking for this raft trip. At least for a while. It was the regular lens on the Nikon that broke, so perhaps I can use the telephoto lens. Want to bet I'll try?

I suppose it made me more real to the group because it hit me pretty hard.

Arrival in Cannelton by Becky

While the Cliff Dwellers were coming down the Ohio River, we notified Cannelton that we would be passing through their town someday soon. As we passed the dam some men were watching us. They then called Mr. Cummings (the editor of the newspaper in Cannelton, who is descendent of Patrick Henry, to see if he wanted to take pictures and) to let him know we were coming...We landed and introduced ourselves to Mr. Cummings and Mr. Baker. Mr Cummings told us that he was having some land cleared for our stay at Cannelton. Mr Baker then invited us to the Kiwanis luncheon...Later the Mayor of Cannelton, Mayor Hafele, came out to see us and talk...About one half an hour later Mr. Cummings came back with two other cars to take us to see some of their sites. Some of these include the dam (, an old cotton mill, a safe company,) and the airplane crash site. This experience was very beneficial for us all. We learned that there were more "Real People" than just Cliff Dwellers, who are learning to become real.

11:15 PM, May 25, 1970 (Monday) Mile 724 Cannelton

We have really met people today. Mr. Cummings met us when we got to Cannelton and we spent a large part of the day with him and his friends. They took us to see the dam and lock and several other points of interest. It was worth a whole day just getting to know them

We are camped just outside the flood wall on a patch of ground prepared especially by the Mayor. It used to be a ferry boat landing, but is not used as a boat ramp. The word of our presence has spread and we have had plenty of visitors, some good, some bad. We took a walk over the bridge to the Kentucky side and ran into a group of teenagers. It really tested the group, but they held their lines well and won the strangers over to Camp Spirit.

Up With People by Karin

One night while we were docked in Cannelton, Indiana, we decided to take a walk across the bridge to Hawesville, Kentucky. We looked at some landmarks in Hawesville and started on our way back. On the way back, we passed a group of young people our own age. They were singing some of their school songs.

We walked on and listened to the singing. Soon they waved and we started talking. Pretty soon we were sharing our raft trip. At first they didn't believe us, so we pointed the raft out from the top of the bridge. They gazed in disbelief.

Then began once again to sing for us, and for just about anyone willing to listen. Their voices were strong and clear. After they sang to us for some time we asked if we could sing for them. Of course the chance was given. We sang songs like "Day is Done", "Songs in the Daytime", "If I Had a Hammer", and "It's a Long Road to Freedom". We tried to sing songs that would help them catch the spirit we had.

We invited them to come see our raft and we offered to answer any questions they might have involving it and camp. They were beginning to see clearly what we stood for.

We told them our group name was The Real People. That's when we found out they were a group called "Up With People". It's their school band's name. We were also surprised.

By the time we were at the raft we had decided this was an opportunity if we ever had one. We talked about camp and how we solve problems. They really asked interesting questions, ones we really had to think about before attempting to answer.

We ended up singing two of our favorite songs, "Do You Know", and “Pilot Me”. After they had left we could just barely hear them say good-bye.

2:45 PM, May 26, 1970 (Tuesday) Mile 724.5 Cannelton

I’m running the motor because the wind is too high and we need to make a few miles. The group is simply overwhelmed by the indescribable hospitality of the people of Cannelton, Indiana. I, too, am touched and Chief Lynda said that she had some of the most wonderful feelings she had ever had in her life. The group felt strongly like they didn’t want to leave, and some had trouble keeping back tears. I think each one has vowed to return someday.

Not meaning to brag, but it’s only fair to point out that we stole the hearts of not a few natives of Cannelton. I can recall host and hostess comments like, “Never have I seen so many smiles, “ “Every kid in the neighborhood is envious,” and “They certainly are a fine group.” We were invited to put on a program for the Kiwanis Club (and)…we put on (quite) a program.

Push-off From Cannelton, Indiana by Edie

We had a lot of fun in Cannelton but the time came to push off. We were down by the Cannelton Dock and it was two weeks after we left Florida. It was about two o’clock and we had just come back from the Kiwanis luncheon. A lot of Cannelton people had come down to the dock to take a last look at the raft and to say good-bye. We talked for a while, then said we had to go. We all got on the raft and prepared to push off. The Mayor’s son and two other boys wanted to push us off and we were happy to let them. As we went off from the bank we saw our push pole stuck in the mud. The Mayor’s son was real nice and brought it to us. We said good-bye and went on down river. As we were going we saw people waving to us still. We all wanted to go back, but we knew we couldn’t stop here because we had other places to go and other people to meet. I found out there are wonderful people all over the world. All a person has to do is look around.

10:30 PM, May 26, 1970 Mile 734

The Cliff Dwellers really outdid themselves with the singing. Never have I heard them sing so beautifully. One man asked if they had professional training. During the meal and the performance they all presented themselves like well-trained young ladies. After the meeting was over, the girls mingled with members and their wives and discussed the raft trip and Camp. I really couldn't ask for anything to have been better.

The city of Cannelton made us feel welcome and important. We met preachers, lawyers, doctors, a newspaper editor, a lock master, U.S. Department of Agriculture workers, a service station manager, a shop foreman, the mayor and his family, and many others...The mayor and others gave us special invitations to come back. Although each personal was special, it was Mr. Robert Cummings, the newspaper editor, who really played host to us.

It would take the rest of the night to finish telling about all the happenings at Cannelton, but even at that it isn't as interesting reading as doing. Besides, it isn't too comfortable writing while lying on a bedroll inside this little green tent.

10:50 AM, May 28, 1970 Mile 751

We are approaching Owensboro and doing the constant routines of putting everything in order. There is little room that, if anything is out of place, we can hardly function. Great for built-in discipline! Chief Ann arrived last night and was "howed" in this morning. She is busy observing the group functioning and getting to know the campers.

4:15 PM, May 28, 2970 Mile 764

The group is making plans for next week and I'm running the motor. We don't like to run the motor this much, but we must get to Evansville by noon tomorrow if we are going to meet the water pollution control people. We are having a little difficulty maintaining a high spirit after our days at Cannelton.

A little while ago, we went through the lock at Owensboro. It was a pretty good experience, and the lockmaster, Mr. Book English, was especially helpful.

5:00 PM, May 28, 1970

Oops! We (got stuck) on a sandbar at French Island #1 (and) the whole group (got off the raft to push. We managed to get off the bar)...at least for a while.

Chief Ann is pitching right in and getting involved. After last night, I suspect she is brave, resourceful, and persistent. I was to have a cab to meet her at the airport at 8:30, but the cab driver failed to show up. I waited at the agreed upon place until nearly midnight and decided there must have been trouble. I couldn't raise anyone at the airport but the dishwasher, so I called the Evansville police to look for her. Meanwhile, a Rockport City Policeman was circling my phone booth. I went to identify myself to him and mentioned my problem. When I told him the counselor was stranded in Evansville, he said, "Oh, she's in a cab on her way here now." Then I learned she had given up on my cab getting there and had found a ride. She called the Rockport police and they told her, "Sure, we know where they are, we took one of the girls to the doctor for a cut foot." Anyway, we got together and got her to the group. Now, she is really fitting in.

12:30 AM, May 29, 1970   Mile 780

Just finished evaluating with Chief Lynda and Chief Ann. Both were considerably boosted after a real group low today. Around lunch we had a long wait before going through the lock. Then the lockmaster, Mr. English, pushed "THE REAL PEOPLE" to the lock with a real tug boat. That was a new experience. We took a tour of the facilities and he explained all the systems of the lock and dam. After that we put on our skits and made a good many miles. The spirit began to pick up and, by time to put up tents, we were on top again. Put tents up in ten minutes!

7:25 AM, May 30, 1970 Mile 798

This old willow tree has been here a long time and under water a good many times, I'll bet. It's right at the edge of the water, and almost horizontal, sticking out so that most of it reaches over the beating waves. The wind has kept the water whipped into plenty of action all night. The bank is a sandy, ledged one with several levels. Part of the sand has been washed away from the roots, reminding me of the great cottonwood trees along the river. Some of them have twelve to fifteen feet of ground washed away, leaving them standing on hundreds of stilt-like roots. Anyway, this bent willow gives me a good vantage point from which to observe Cliff Dwellers.

They are a little sluggish this morning, partly because I'm not in the middle, shouting, "Let's go! Is everyone ready to push off? Let's get the garbage buried and the tents packed away and the breakfast started and the rope untied. Do we have enough wood to cook on today?" However, they are almost ready to push off, so they are not really doing badly. I've purposefully stayed on the sidelines to observe, so I can start evaluating the Chief's work.

Today was cold and wet so we got the fire barrel inside. We read Tom Sawyer by the fire. Then we had siesta. Then we made taffy even when none knew the recipe. It was delicious. The day ended with me making "spinach pie' and it was good. I feel everybody had a good attitude when it was raining. Everybody was sleepy and tired, but everybody did really great. I was really happy about the whole day. - Teresa

8:10 AM, May 30, 1970 Mile 799

We've pushed off and are doing our morning routines. Becky and Debbie are sawing wood, Edie is straightening the equipment box, Cathi and Cindy are putting draw strings in Mary's bedroll, Mary and Melody are cooking blueberry pancakes and bacon, Edie #2 is working with the food box. The wind is blowing so that the flags are standing out clear and bold.

10:00 PM, May 30, 1970 Mile 822

I'm writing by the light of the remains of our pow-wow fires. We built a big bonfire and sang for a good while. Then, Chief Lynda led a good pow-wow on the subject of the songs we sing.

The wind blew hard all day, and rain came in short, hesitant showers. At times, the wind was so strong against us that only the use of the motor would keep us getting closer to New Orleans. Then about the time we met up with Mike and Larry, the river made a bend which put the wind in the right direction. The two boys, high school aged, kept us company for more than a couple of hours. They were wholesome and refreshing to have around. We talked about everything from teacher-student relationships in school to hobbies and interests. The girls sang quite a selection of songs and even coaxed the boys into singing a couple of their own school songs. It was the type of situation in which both parties benefited.

A Storm Filled with Sunshine

The dark clouds bring a sudden burst of tormenting rain.

It seems bleak and dreary, yet the warmth of my group can make the dreariest day bright.

A cheery smile, a helpful hand, can make the rain turn into drops of sunshine

-Mary

I guess I was so tired last night I forgot to mention even the highlights. All the pushing to go to a water pollution control lab was to no avail because of a holiday (Memorial Day). However, I did get into Evansville to K-Mart and bought a new Yashica Electra 35!! I'm not sure who was the happiest, the group or me. We also went into town and spent a most enthusiastic hour in the museum of Art and Science. This was the first item some of the group had even been in a museum, and all responded quite favorably. We had tied "THE REAL PEOPLE" at a public dock and when we returned a small boy had boarded with full determination to go along with us. It was only with much insistence on my part that he finally consented to leave.

Our last visitor of the day was a friendly deputy sheriff named Jim Neighbors. He was quite fascinated by our story and tried to make arrangements to get a reporter to us. Failing to succeed at that, he finally settled with taking the information for a story himself.

The fire is about to get too low to see by, so I'll guess it's time for sleep.

9:15 AM, June 1, 1970 Mile 838

10:30 PM, June 2, 1970 Mile 870

I was almost too busy today. I was standing at the motor and reading a paper when Edith came up and stood for a while beside me. "Thank you," she said. But I didn't really stop to think what for. "Thank you," she insisted. This time I realized she was trying to tell me something, so I gave her my full attention. "Thank you for letting me come to Camp. I'm just so happy to be here!" She had quite a warm look in her eyes, and I know she felt deeply happy.

Yesterday and today have been rough days, as far as the weather is concerned. It has been terribly windy, and today has included quite a bit of rain. It rained several times last night, and off and on all day. The group, however, has remained high-spirited and solid. Sometimes, I wonder if they could really have problems. I know the people we meet have doubts about the girls having problems. But, now and then, when we aren't in public, a problem comes up and is handled, and we move on.

Yesterday, we stopped and kicked up our heels on a sandbar island. Today we went into Shawneetown and got a few supplies. We bought a 15 pound catfish and had a really good fish fry.

History Relived by Mary

On June 2, The Cliff Dwellers stopped in Shawneetown, Illinois for water and supplies for our anniversary party. We docked and climbed up the bank to the main street. Although it was the main street, it wasn't anything but closed down stores and old buildings. There were very few people and it reminded me of a ghost town.

We talked with some people and learned that it is the oldest town in Illinois. The streets are very wide in order to let the horses and carriages, which the town once used, pass through them. In this same part of history, Jesse James robbed a bank in Shawneetown, which is still standing. In my mind I could picture Jesse and his gang, running out of the bank, jumping on their horses, and riding through the town shooting as they escaped to find a hideout. It wasn't very hard for my imagination to go to work in such an interesting town.

9:30 PM, June 3, 1970 Mile 883

12:20 AM, June 4, 1970 Mile 883 Near Cave In Rock, Illinois

Chief Ann came on down to the raft, so I didn't get much written at 9:30. Now, the fire in the fire barrel is just live coals, but I'm warm enough. The old kerosene lantern is flickering almost enough light to write by. The fumes from the fire aren't so painful as they were. Beside me is the pot of yeast dough giving off a few yeasty whiffs. From where I'm sitting, I can see the rafter poles where several coats and pieces of clothing are hung. The burned out Coleman and my new camera are hung from the bracing on the other side of the equipment box. Over the slightly cluttered equipment box are a couple strings of clothes pinned on binders twine. It's raining again and the doors to the equipment box are acting like windbreaks to keep the wind and rain under control. No rain fell this afternoon, saved it until tonight. I don't remember how many days it has rained, but the group has about learned to live with it.

Today has been a fun day. For several days we have been planning a birthday party for Camp. (It's hard to realize Camp opened with seven girls one year ago today.) We had heard about a big cave in the rocks where pirates used to hide, and thought that might be a good place to party. However, the cave, beautiful and fascinating as it was, was too public for our purpose. Not to be discouraged, we floated onto this sandy beach and had a real party. We began with skits, had a peach cobbler, root beer, popcorn balls, played all sorts of new group games and ended with vespers and pow-wow. The group still seems contented, eager for adventure, and ready to solve problems. However, I'm not satisfied, and want to push them for pulling strings of personal responsibility up tighter.

3:25 PM, June 4, 1970 Mile 898

Sunshine! A few clouds, but plenty of warm, drying sunshine. We spent the morning getting bedrolls and clothes dry, and "THE REAL PEOPLE" cleaned up. We spend a lot of time keeping our tiny living space in order, but there's nothing wrong with that. Now all but a few clothes are dry, and the group is making a line of action for the afternoon, and plans for the rest of the week.

A Raft Trip Discovery
to Find Myself

I am searching
For what I do not know,
It's something I can take hold of
It's something that will grow.

It will help me pick up and
look around
And help me take my stand
In the greatest mountains
Or in the hottest sands.

I realize life is sweet but short
And never a minute to lose
Myself, myself, I need myself
In everything I choose.
-Karin

4:30 PM, June 5, 1970 Mile 923

Sunshine? Not now. The rain has slowed down for a little while, but I'll bet it will be back before long. Yesterday, after I wrote about the sunshine, the group went in swimming and came out in the rain. Before long, thunder and lightning filled the air, bringing plenty of hail. Again, just as we docked for the night, a storm hit. It became necessary for us to spend the night on the raft.

12:20 AM, June 6, 1970 Mile 930

Chief Ann and I have just finished evaluating the day and swapping Camp stories. Pow-wow was good tonight, pretty much of a model. I set framework around the subject of how we require a little more of ourselves each day. The group responded by pointing out several ways in which this was true. They stayed very close to the subject, and really did some good thinking. Then, to bring a brief summary, we looked at an experience common to us all:

"As we float down the river on the raft, we often watch our speed or progress by watching trees or other stationary objects come and go. Sometimes, we look up to discover they aren't moving. The raft has drifted into a still pool of water or hit a sandbar. When the raft is moving, even if it is slow, a certain good feeling of accomplishment or success is present. When movement is not evident, a hopeless and helpless feeling closes in. Likewise, when we require a little more effort every day, we can feel ourselves improving, and it is a good feeling."

(The group walked into town and found the Paducah Water Works.) A man said it was okay for us to have the water. We began to ask him questions on where the water comes from. He started to explain, when another gentleman suggested instead to show us...The man first showed us the storage tanks where water from the Tennessee River is pumped in. In these tanks chemicals are put to kill the germs and bacteria that are in the water. Then the water is run into 20 feet deep pools of water. This is where more chemicals are placed in the water to kill the ph factor, this is the acid in the water. The water is then run through filters to make sure it is purified. After all these tests the water is then ready to be used. At the Paducah Water Works 12 million gallons of water are pumped through every day.
- Edie

We have been noticing that one corner of the raft has been sagging, so we removed two barrels and discovered they have leaks. We spent about an hour drying them and putting them back under. We are still going to need to replace them but temporarily, they work fine.

10:00 PM, June 6, 1970 Mile 944

Thought I'd give the group a chance to function by themselves to get an idea how they will do next week. I'm sitting among the roots of a huge cottonwood tree. A creek joins the river at this point and a railroad is just beyond that. I can see the wide spans of black steel through the leaves of some willows. There isn't much of a breeze, and the mosquitoes are sure to get me. I can hear them humming, but I can also hear the more pleasant sounds of bird, frogs, waves, and a few group sounds. There are also some distant city sounds and dogs barking. It's almost dark. We watched the sun setting through the railroad trestle while we finished an apple cobbler. It's still a delight to be on the trip with the group. They are eager to learn, adventuresome, and yet have a few problems to work on.

> We came into Paducah, Kentucky, and saw a dry dock...We learned that the docks are used for repairs. A ship or a barge floats in on top of the dry dock which is completely filled with water and is sunk down deeply into the water. Then the water is pumped out of the dock which causes the dry dock to rise. When this happens whatever is on the dock, a barge or ship, is lifted completely out of the water so that the men can repair whatever needs to be done. - Becky

Another Real Friend by Karin

We rolled into Paducah in need of a fresh water supply. While trying to find a place to dock we watched the big tugs pull in and out. As we traveled the shore line we were soon approached by a Kentucky State Police boat. It pulled alongside of us and we were soon introducing ourselves. The man's name in the boat was Officer Adcox.

We asked him if he knew any place near the banks where we could get some water. He told us he would get some water, even if he had to get it himself. We finally convinced him that wouldn't be necessary, we could walk to get the water. We'd like to see the town anyway.

We sat on the raft and talked for some time about problems in his town and got into his life. It was very interesting. He was a man with direction. He knew exactly what he wanted out of life. Officer Adcox was a very patriotic person. He fought in the Korean War. He didn't believe in it, but he had to fight for his nation. It interested us because he was such a unique individual in so many ways. He was a man that knew happiness, contentment, and knew his own strength. He took pride in everything he said and did. Our visit with him was a very touching experience. We ended it with "Battle Hymn of the Republic", and "Do You Know". He made the remark "Do You Know" was one song that really told the story.

4:00 AM, June 7, 1970 Mile 944

Today has brought another set of experiences to a stockpiling of adventures, even if no rain did come. The group got off before 8:00 AM and had the wood out and deck scrubbed and the whole raft in order before we got to the Tennessee River and Paducah. The new river was a beautiful blue instead of the muddy brown of the Ohio. As we got into Paducah, Officer Adcox of the State Police pulled in beside us, and we spent an hour or two talking to him. He was quite sharp and really won all of our hearts. He was a patriot and a Christian among other qualities. When he had gone, we left "THE REAL PEOPLE" at the wharf and went through the flood wall to the Paducah Public Water Works to get water. There, we met quite an accommodating crew who gave us a full tour of the water plant. The group returned to the river while I went to pick up a few supplies. A few negative characters had gathered at the raft and began giving the girls a bad time. However, they didn't get very far because no group of girls in the world knows how to tell a guy to get lost as effectively as these ten. They had the situation fairly well under control by the time I got there.

7:20 PM, June 7, 1970   Mile 962

The Ohio River has been wide and deep, today. It has hardly turned at all and, at one point, near Joppa, we could still see last night's railroad bridge ten miles back. Even now, I can see the smoke from the electrical energy plant behind us.

6:40 AM, June 8, 1970   Mile 964

The birds are singing and the roosters crowing. Haze covers the river but I can see the Kentucky Shore nearly a mile away. The sun will soon have that burned off, for there isn't a cloud in the already blue sky. No breeze stirs the willows nor the cottonwood trees. A fisherman and his son just left with a big catch of catfish. We camped in a public park near Olmstead, Illinois, so I could call Camp. It will soon be food pickup time, and that means lots of excitement.

The First Tour on a Tug by Karin

On the eighth of June we came into Cairo, Illinois. Chief Everett went to town to see if he could locate Chief Helen and the red camper for our food pick-up. The group decided to see if we could go on board a tug that was moored downstream from us. Chief Lynda went on the tug to try and get permission for us to board the tug. Permission was granted so we hopped on the tug and introduced ourselves to the Captain. His name was Captain Williams, a very quiet man.

On the tug we went straight to the control room and I thought that was the best part. I could just imagine myself as a captain, gliding at least 60 barges through the water without any trouble at all. He went about the control room explaining everything to the best of his ability, which was most impressing. Mr. Williams told us about the radar systems and we spotted the raft on it.

We were just about to leave the control room when the cook, Nellie Gallaher, came in and invited us to have some sandwiches and milk. That really sounded great! We accepted and continued the tour. We took a quick glance at the engine room but the engineer wasn't there, so we went on to the galley.

We walked into the galley and to our surprise there weren't any sandwiches but there was potato salad, steak, pork chops, fresh tomatoes, radishes, lettuce, pickled cucumbers and onions, cottage cheese, fresh bread, pinto beans, cold milk, and fruit punch. The food was delicious, and the group thought the hospitality was even better. They seemed to be delighted to be able to do something like this for us.

After we had eaten we sang some of our favorite songs. Appreciation was expressed from both sides and the group felt good about our new friends. The engineer had come in and wanted to take us back down to the engine room so he could show us how they worked. We went down and it was really noisy with one engine on. He made the remark, "If you think it's noisy now, you ought to stick around till I turn on the other two engines.

It was getting late and we needed to push on, so we once again thanked Mr. Williams, Nellie, and Mr. Gallaher for their hospitality. It was a very rewarding experience for the Cliff Dwellers.

The Mississippi River by Cindy

On June 8th, we made it to the Mississippi River. It was right outside of Cairo, Illinois...The trip really felt like it had begun when we got to the river. It gave us a good feeling to know we had made it this far on the raft. From Louisville to Cairo, the group had learned ow to function in ways unique to a raft.

> We learned two ways to dust crops. The old way was by airplane, but this is...too expensive to be practical. The way that will now be used is by helicopter, which is a lot more economical. This way only costs Mr. Larkins a dollar an acre and the helicopter could cover one hundred acres in one hour.
>
> -Deborah

It had learned about the river's currents, people, and campsites. We felt like going down the Mississippi River will be a way to solidify what we had learned on the Ohio River. As soon as we were even with the Mississippi River bank we gave three "Hows". Then we went and ate watermelon to celebrate the arrival on the Mississippi River.

The water was rough and dirty. It was more than we expected. We realized it was a big challenge to get to New Orleans and that we had a lot to learn.

11:10 AM, June 9, 1970 Mile 940

Time is flying by, and so are the miles. We are on the might Mississippi and are moving at speeds two to three times greater than the Ohio. That means we are making five or six miles per hour. The excitement has been up to expectations for getting on the big river. First of all, the noticeably faster current, and also big swirls of water that can be seen and heard long before we get to them.

It was getting late yesterday when we finally got all the food loaded from the truck and started crossing the river. The sun was a huge ball of red seen through the steelwork of Cairo's Ohio River Bridge. We gave three "hows" when "THE REAL PEOPLE" hit the turbulent muddy waters of the Mississippi. There were several songs to sing and a real air of adventure and excitement. From the earliest talk of a raft, we have had many stowaway offers. We now have on board a stowaway (Chief Helen). She got on last night with the consent of all and is doing a lot of visiting with each camper.

4:34 PM, June 13, 1970 Mile 868

"THE REAL PEOPLE" left the mayor of Tiptonville, Tennessee, the newspaper editor, several citizens and members of their families on the old ferry landing about an hour ago. We had a red carpet tour and met some real southern hospitality. Mr. Michaelcheck, Mr. Jones, and Mr. Jones were our hosts, and we saw Reelfoot Lake, a museum, and some of the countryside. We ate family style at a restaurant and the Jones Brothers showed us in great detail about the newspaper printing business. After we had finished our tours, they came down to the river and we communicated to them in song.

Sharing Feelings by Cathi

A feeling is very special to a person! Sometimes we find it hard to express a feeling but it's easy to find a way if we look for one. I'm glad that I can have a group to be able to share feelings. I've found that Cliff Dwellers are willing to listen to each one of its group members, or people we meet. Our raft trip is something that doesn't come easy. We've got to make it easy, to learn the things we are learning.

A Helpful Hand

When you get so frustrated you could pull out all your hair,
Just reach out, and someone will be there.
When you want to give up and say,
Life wasn't worth living anyway,
Just reach out, and someone will be there.
When all seems lost and you're in grief and despair,
Just reach out and someone will be there.
But, when your days are brighter and life isn't so bare,
Make sure when someone else reaches out that you're always there.
- Mary

11:10 PM, June 13, 1970

Pow-wow and Chief's pow-wow is over and it's time to go to sleep. I've been trying all afternoon to catch up a few experiences and incidents of the past few days. However, help was needed on articles, a few personal problems had to be talked out, a beautiful sunset had to be photographed, and I had to get readjusted to the excitement of floating down the Mississippi River on a raft.

Catching up on even a few of the highlights since Tuesday isn't going to be easy. First, the very special stowaway (Chief Helen) made herself useful and welcome by bringing news from Camp and by making each of us feel very special, too. She floated with us all day Tuesday, sharing and making our first full day on the big river even more exciting. By supper, we were near Dorena, Missouri, and thought it best that we stop for the evening. Since she had delivered the food supply in the Camp truck, I took her back to Cairo, Illinois, to pick it up and get a few supplies.

On Wednesday morning, we looked all over Cairo for barrels to replace the leaky ones, but didn't find what we wanted. On the way back to "THE REAL PEOPLE," we spotted some pretty blue barrels and stopped to inquire. It turned out to be a big farming operation owned by Mr. Choat and Mr. Larkins. Before too long, our stowaway and I had barrels but, more important, we had some real friends. It was Mr. Larkin who wanted to see the raft and the program, so he came with us to the river. The group fell in love with him and soon plans were made to visit the farms and surrounding countryside. The group saw grain elevators, cabbage fields, helicopters spraying corn crops, and a lot of friendly people. To be sure, they felt they knew more about the farming industry.

When evening came, the Larkins accepted an invitation to stay for supper and vespers. Other relatives and friends of the Larkins and we have vespers and a party. Believe it or not, it all turned out very positive.

Thursday morning, we got the barrels in place and pushed off by noon. Plans were for the group to arrive in Tiptonville by noon Friday and for me to stowaway with the stowaway. It all worked according to plans, except that Cliff Dwellers had a little too much excitement to arrive on schedule. It seems they lost the anchor, ran out of gas, met a friendly policeman, had a few problem sessions, rammed six barges, and generally kept pretty busy. It was getting dark when the stowaway and I spotted them.

Now the stowaway is on her way back to camp to be Chief Helen.

Lost and Found by Edie

My story is about the day we lost our anchor when we were one day north of Tiptonville, Tennessee. It all started when we had to stop on the river to discuss a few things. At first we tried to tie to a tree on shore; but it was impossible, because we were going too fast. We hadn't thrown the anchor out yet so we decided to. The anchor was working; it stopped us. But, when the time came to go on down river, our anchor wouldn't come up. We tried for quite some time, but it just wouldn't come loose.

Someone thought of a possible solution. We would cut the anchor rope and tie a ring buoy to it. Then we would try to turn around and go upstream with the motor. We tried for about ten minutes and nothing happened. So, we decided before we went down river too far we would pull over to the bank and tie up...(and) try something else...The group would walk a ways ahead of the ring buoy, then let Chief Lynda swim out to the anchor with a rope tied around her and a life jacket on. She would pull the ring buoy and anchor rope to shore. The group would then pull the anchor up. This had to work; but it didn't work. We would have to get as much of the rope as we could and leave the anchor there.

The day we were going into Memphis Tennessee, we found out our anchor had followed us. Sure enough, we saw a big one on a revetment. It was now one foot thick, three foot wide, and four feet long. One person said it was lost and found. Things like this happen every day with the Cliff Dwellers on our Ohio River and Mississippi River Trip.

8:50 AM, June 14, 1970 Mile 853

7:20 AM, June 15, 1970 Mile 812

The wind is blowing and I have a few chill bumps. The group is loading the last few tents and putting bedrolls over the rafter poles. The sky is grey and clouded, but I can't distinguish where the sun is hiding. I'm sitting on a giant tree that floated onto this sandbar a few weeks ago. The sand is pretty and white but plenty wet so that the wind doesn't shift any of it. I can still see last night's raindrop marks on it. Before the rain, great flashes of lightning and rolls of thunder made quite a spectacle of the river and our sandbar. Before that, a host of mosquitoes sang a symphony right outside the tent. Time was when the cool air of evening kept them down at night, but no more – except when it rains. The group has done an excellent job of accepting them.

10:05 PM, June 15, 1970 Mile 786

The tents are almost completed and some of the team jobs have begun. We floated almost thirty miles today, not quite like the forty of yesterday. Two things held us up today. One was a strong headwind and the other was a problem session. For the past few days the group has been sliding, and the time came for me to tune them up. I held a pretty tight line regarding lack of initiative and general attitude. That was this morning, and the response has been fair, although not overwhelming.

11:30 PM, June 15, 1970 Mile 786

Pow-wow was a good bounce back to some of the familiar good spirit of Cliff Dwellers. I am giving Chiefs more responsibilities and they are doing some self-investigation as well as responding fairly well. Tonight, we talked long and straight about supporting Camp's stand on issues.

I hadn't taken the time to mention it yet, but I do want to remember how excited and impressed the group was yesterday. The Larkins and another couple came all the way downriver to see us again. We sang and visited a long time before they had to get back in their boat and head back for Dorena, Missouri. Before that a patrolman for the Missouri River Patrol checked our papers and became very interested in our group. He floated quite a ways with us and we enjoyed his visit. When he got to us, an old riverman, Pat Patterson, had come out to meet us. He was in a small lake boat that looked like a motorized canoe. He told us a few river tales and that he had been on the river 47 years and had traveled it from one end to the other, many times. This series of visits took place just past Caruthersville, Missouri.

10:45 PM, June 16, 1970 Mile 761

More headwind and fewer miles. We pushed on pretty steady today, but did take time for morning baths and to "help" a goat get off the side of a cliff. At least we had a good excuse to get off and ramble a few minutes. I would suggest that we stop at least a few minutes every day for some type of off-raft activity. We are camped on a very large island with sandy beaches and a high bank. Many turtles had walked the beaches and, while the group put up tents, I located a nest of turtle eggs. We dug them up and had a lengthy discussion on how an egg becomes a turtle. Later, we had popcorn and songs and a fairly good pow-wow. The sunset was beautiful and the whole atmosphere here was the type that makes a person feel glad to be alive and in America.

Today, while most of the group was taking siesta, I began remembering some past thoughts on the art of giving attention therapeutically. A person can train himself to be constantly giving attention to the group. There are two kinds of attention, positive and negative. It is far better to provide the former before the latter becomes required. The ways and techniques are unlimited, especially on a 14' x 30' raft floating down a river. I like to help with articles or in writing objectives. Full attention can be devoted to each one individually for several minutes to an hour at a time. It is easy to forget to greet them several times a day when they are with me day after day. However, I believe it is good to find ways to call each one by name in special ways, especially the quieter ones who don't usually get much attention. Sometimes I pronounce a name all scrambled up like "Dane Joe" for "Jane Doe." When a child is particularly annoying by requiring more than her share of attention, this is a cue to jump the gun on her and flood her with attention before she can require it. A balance of serious positive attention and joking is desirable. It is fun to make all sorts of facial expressions at them and give them attention through eye contact. They like to know I'm concerned about their welfare. I show concern by making them wear life jackets, write first class articles, wear shoes at all times, solve problems thoroughly, and just generally hold tight lines. I believe that a quite valuable device for giving attention is, naturally, my clicking camera. Not to ever by forgotten is the attention given a child by showing her in great detail how to cook, build, or do something. People are about to starve to death for attention; find ways to feed them.

9:25 AM, June 17, 1970 Mile 752

11:45 PM, June 19, 1980 Mile 731

An almost full moon came up right over Memphis tonight. We are set up on a tiny sand beach just within sight of a few of the city's lights. I can hear the trucks and cars even above the crashing waves and spewing gas lantern. The group left the streets with a bit of a deflated feeling. Our other stops had produced many new found friends along with exciting adventures. However, this stop turned up no personal contacts and no real interesting side trips. We did walk a few blocks in the downtown section. It was hot and dry. Even the newspaper reporter and photographer did not make a satisfying impression. We took on our water supply and slipped quietly out of the harbor. Then, as we were left to ourselves, spirits began to pick up and disappointment quickly faded away. As Chief Lynda put it, "The group had to turn to itself for a lift in feelings."

12:45 PM, June 18, 1980 Mile 719

As a typical scene here on "THE REAL PEOPLE" let me describe what is happening. The cooks, Cathi and Cindy, with Chief Ann, are preparing lunch. Chief Lynda is running the motor to get us out of the way of some dikes. She is also talking to Karin who is working on an article. Teresa is rewriting her raft trip goals. Debbie and Edie are also working on articles.

9:05 AM, June 19, 1970 Mile 697.9

At last we have a morning with little or no wind, and are making four miles an hour. Once again, the group is deeply absorbed in studies. Some are writing articles, some are working out problems with Chiefs. The sun is shining and we are definitely in the South.

3:25 PM, June 19, 1970 Mile 670

We are still speeding along at better than four miles per hour! No wind is slowing us, and no one shows signs of needing a jacket. We are about fifty feet off the banks, which are about four feet high. The current has eaten away at them until many of the willows and cottonwood saplings have fallen away. Deer have held our interest for an hour or so as they come down for a long cool drink from the river. We stopped for a few minutes to dig and "grunt" for worms and found hundreds of them, about as many as the mosquito bites we also found. However, we all dug with excitement and are not putting them to use. No luck thus far, but hope is running high.

10:40 PM, June 19, 1970 Mile 667

This has been a beautiful day, one that Mark Twain would have popped his buttons over. Certainly, his best work would never come close to matching the story book we are in now. The wandering river makes a great bend just before it gets to Helena, Arkansas. It must be almost two miles wide across with an island sandbar stretching a fourth of a mile in the middle. On the down river side of the sandy island is a cove of almost still water. The highest point is about four feet above water level. We have our tents set up in a neat circle not far from "THE REAL PEOPLE."

12:00 AM, June 20, 1970 Mile 667

We spotted this little resort at 5:30 and decided to take advantage of it. We plan to pick up supplies in Helena, only two miles further, and needed to get there during business hours. First we explored, then a line of action. We finished supper and all the team jobs and then began to play some group games. We had great fun and even experienced a beautiful sunset at the same time. The quiet waters of the cove made for good bathing, so we feel much better. During pow-wow a red golden moon rose across the river and held us spellbound. We are hardly even bothered by mosquitoes since the nearest bush is at least a mile away, and only the bravest have come this far from vegetation. It's a beautiful camping spot for the night, but I don't think a full day would be a good idea.

Chiefs' pow-wow tonight included general evaluations, some small talk, and a challenge. The challenge is one we always have to involve ourselves with, "What are we willing to do to help a girl get on top of her problems?"

7:30 AM, June 20, 1970

A group needs several things in order to be a healthy and satisfied group: Variety, challenge, physical work, and self-improvement.

When there's a Willow, There's a Way by Edie

Cliff Dwellers found excitement and a challenge awaiting them on the morning of June 20, 1970. We took off from our campsite and traveled three miles downstream. We passed a boat marina in Helena just as we ran out of gas. The only problem was we couldn't get to the edge of the river because of the strong current. We floated down the river for about a half of a mile until the raft drifted into the willows. There we sat, hanging on to the willows. The group decided that the only way we could get back upstream was to pull ourselves along the side. We developed a system.

The group lined up along the side of the raft. Someone in the front used a push pole with a nail on the end to grab the willows to the raft. The next person handed the willows to the person behind them. With the help of the sweep oars, we managed our way up the edge of the river remaining parallel with the shoreline. We came within three hundred feet of the boat marina. We were able to stop pulling the willows and float with the current using only the sweep oars.

We pulled into the marina with drops of sweat pouring off of us. The group was really hot and tired. From this experience we learned two very important things: first, when a group is working together, it can get things done; and secondly, "when there's a willow, there's a way!"

10:10 PM, June 20, 1970 Mile 650

In climbing mountains one climbs higher and higher to the lofty peak for which the climb was planned. Then, after a given amount of time, he must return to lower elevations. A group is, in some ways, just like that. It builds and builds until it reaches a certain height before it declines to rebuild again. Today has seen another set of climaxes which makes this raft trip climb higher still. Since the first week, I've been wondering how we could continue climbing in spirit and attitude, but our experiences keep topping themselves. Getting up this morning on the clean white beach and sailing out of the little natural harbor was a beautiful experience bound to overshadow the rest of the day. Not so! We ran out of gas just before we got to Helena and missed the boat dock for gas. We had to use the sweep oars to get into a shore which happened to be fenced off with willow trees. For a good half mile, we had to pull on willow trees to make our way upstream to the gas dock. After about half way, a kind fisherman gave me a ride to pick up five gallons of gas. However, we were destined to make it on our own because the motor wouldn't start and the battery went down. Finally, we worked our sweaty way back to the boat dock and made repairs. After that experience someone said, "Where there's a willow, there's a way." To be sure, the experience was worth a whole day's experiences in itself. When we got to the dock, and Helena, we found the attendant and owner, Mr. Fridell, a real example of Southern hospitality. He sent his son and his wife to take me into town to do a bit of shopping. They graciously made several stops and were most helpful. When I returned with the supplies, I found that Mr. Young, the newspaper owner and city welcoming committee, had met the group and had made arrangements for a tour. He had been expecting us for several days and was clearly a fine gentleman. It was decided that his wife and daughter would take us on a tour of historical Helena.

Just as we were driving up to get into the cars, we heard an explosion and saw flames and parts of a very large luxury houseboat shooting up in the air. We had already heard of a fire there the year before wherein several boats had been burned up. I could imagine seeing "THE REAL PEOPLE" burning right where it was tied at the gas dock. I saw that the group was safe, and I set out to get our rig away from the danger. That was soon accomplished, but excitement was in control for a while. After it was all over, we continued our tour and enjoyed it thoroughly. We discovered that Helena, with its Southern hospitality, is enchanted with colorful history, culture, and variety. It was after 4:00 when we left the little city and didn't find an ideal camping spot. But, the edge of a soy bean field isn't really bad.

12:30 AM, June 22, 1970 Mile 607

Today was a suitable day after a day like yesterday. We started out early and floated until 6:00. The river has been beautiful and the group, still busy. We met one group of visitors but did set a record 43 miles. Now, we are on a sandbar island again, this time with trees. A cool breeze is keeping mosquitoes where they belong. We did take a fruitful ramble and discovered several dove nests, and a wild duck nest with hatching eggs. We watched two ducklings come out of their shells.

10:40 PM, June 22, 1970 Mile 568

Darkness is setting in and the last tow boat is almost out of hearing range. The current is swift enough here so that a constant gurgle can be heard. The group is making peaceful sounds as they set up tents in a freshly plowed field. The wind is strong enough, so far, to keep mosquitoes in hiding. The Mississippi banks, at this section, is solid asphalt, and is comfortable enough to sit on and write.

The day has been usual, except that we made about ten miles without being on the Mississippi River. We got detoured through a part of the Old White River and didn't make as good a mileage as on the big river. Also, we ran low on water and stopped at a River Grain Terminal for a fresh supply. Oops! The wind let down and here come the mosquitoes.

13:30 PM, June 23, 1970 Mile 537 Greenville

Our visitors have gone and the happy Cliff Dwellers are in their tents. Our Chamber of Commerce contact was Charles Deaton. Even though suppertime had passed, he assured me that he wanted to meet us as soon as I called. By the time we met, darkness was setting in. He had with him a reporter, a photographer, an insurance man, and another insurance executive who was also an electrical contractor. They showed us a sandy beach across the lake from the city, and we began our visit. The reporter and the photographer were quite young and, before long, we had them all involved in deep conversation. I suppose we must have been talking a couple of hours in small groups when someone suggested that we sing. And sing we did! I honestly feel that I can say, without bragging, that our visitors really enjoyed the event as much as we did. I was particularly impressed at the way our own girls conversed and held their own with a group of businessmen. They were dignified and intelligent, yet they were teenagers, excited and expressive. Mary could later boast that she had discovered that she could talk boldly and confidently with strange adults. Also, in pow-wow, Karin began telling how much accomplishment she felt in her efforts to get Teresa to express herself. But, to top everything, Teresa cut in and assured Karin and the group that she, Karin, had done a great job. Teresa, withdrawn Teresa, almost dominated pow-wow!

Earlier in the day, we began to gather that Greenville was a city with a great deal of self-pride and spirit. We read the literature sent by the Chamber of Commerce and grew excited about seeing and experiencing it for ourselves. From the initial reception, I don't feel that we will be disappointed. We have an appointment with Mr. Deaton in the morning at 10:00.

9:15 AM, June 24, 1970 Greenville, Mississippi

We're on our way across Lake Ferguson to Greenville and a new experience. "THE REAL PEOPLE" is in good shape and is getting better shape. The group is making all the last minute repairs and improvements that brush and mirror can assist them in making.

9:50 PM, June 24, 1970 Greenville, Mississippi

I feel terrible! I feel wonderful! I feel guilty! I feel deeply happy! Well, I guess I have mixed emotions. Today has been the fruits of much labor. For more than a year, Chief Mac, Chief Helen, Mom Carol, Chief Hubert, Mom Mildred, Mom Becky, and a number of counselors and I have been giving blood, sweat, and tears to produce an E-Nini-Hassee Girls's Camp. Although today has not been the first sign of success, certainly today has been a big payoff. Girls, broken girls...have had enough good feelings and just plain old zest for life today to justify all that has gone into Camp. I feel guilty that all these beautiful results are going by without Mr. and Mrs. Eckerd, Mr Glisson, Mr. Rehm, Chief Paul, and Camp staff being able to experience them. I feel ashamed to write about today because it has been far too glorious to communicate with words. Yet, it would be a worse shame to not even try. I'm really talking generally about the excellent performance of the girls.

2:00 AM, June 25, 1970

We just finished a final showdown with a girl regarding "Bill." She fought frantically until the very end to maintain her belief that she "loves" him. In the end, she admitted that she knew that he was a murderer and a gangster and all the charges the group brought against him. She knew all this for three years, but was afraid of him, not only because of his threat of physical harm, but because of the mental anguish she would have to go through. She cried much, and I believe she means it, although she will need a great deal of protection, both physical and mental. It was a dramatic session. As for the day, it will have to wait until morning; I'm too sleepy now.

Communicating Without Words by Mary

When the group returned from the library in Greenville, Mississippi, there was a man standing by the raft with a look of admiration. We went up to talk to him and discovered he could neither speak nor hear.

At first we felt awkward and didn't know how to talk to him, but he started making simple hand motions that we could understand. He moved his hands to symbolize waves and then he held his stomach to indicate sea sickness. He had a great sense of humor. He waved his arms and slapped his neck to ask if mosquitoes were a problem. We caught on quickly and were soon able to convey our messages without any trouble.

Mr. Wall had a bigger problem than most of us have to face during our life, but he has overcome it and his warm and interesting personality is the result of patience and faith.

Letter from the Cliff Dwellers to the Greenville Chamber of Commerce

Dear Charles Deaton,

We, the Cliff Dwellers, would like to say how much we appreciated the interest that was shown to us. We very much enjoyed seeing the Delta Democrat Times, the Indian Mounds, the Library, and the Chamber of Commerce. We especially enjoyed your telling us about the Chamber of Commerce and how it works. I believe we learned very much. Some of us are even considering trying to work in the Chamber of Commerce! We believe as you do about trying to solve problems by helping the people do it and not do it yourself.

We thank you for introducing us to the town of Greenville. You helped us to go out, meet the people, and begin to feel the spirit of the town. Seeing the attitude of Greenville has helped our group to face a little more realty. Just knowing there are other problem solvers who want to help other people who have problems impressed me deeply.

Once again we would like to say "thank you" for showing us your city. We feel that the people of Greenville are very real.

8:50 AM, June 25, 1970 Greenville, Mississippi

A bright sun warms a cool and peaceful breeze this morning. We are headed out of the long clear waters of Ferguson Lake. Two hours will have been used in making our exit, and the first is already gone. Again, it is with mixed feelings that we leave a city of new friends and delightful experiences.

At 10:30 AM, we met Mr. Deaton at the Marina to get a line of action. We finally decided to make two stops for the morning and two for the afternoon. First, we walked to the Chamber of Commerce office where Mr. Deaton worked. He explained in quite some detail the operations of a Chamber of Commerce. Soon, eyes began popping as campers began seeing the analogy between a Chamber of Commerce and Camp. They could see they were both problem solving organizations and that both worked on the basis of involvement. The whole experience was one of those experiences that make a day worthwhile.

Next, we found the W.A. Percy Memorial Library. Interest in the Civil War has been growing, and the whole group wanted to go to the library to find out more in preparation for today's planned discussion on the subject. We had been so involved at the Chamber of Commerce that we only had an hour left for the library, but we went right in, found the Civil War section, and soon were wordlessly absorbed. The library was a beautiful piece of architecture with a matching atmosphere. The Cliff Dwellers blended in quite well, and the sight of them studying so intently was enough to blur my vision. Back at the "REAL PEOPLE" for lunch, we met an elderly deaf mute who really touched our hearts. At 2:00, we boarded a Delta Coach line Bus and met Barry Farr, our reporter at the Delta Democrat Times office. He gave us a full escorted tour through the newspaper plant. At the end of the tour, we got copies of the paper with our picture and a long article about ourselves. We met Mr. Hodding Carter III, editor of the paper. He also provided our afternoon's transportation which took on from the newspaper office to the Winterville Indian Mounds and Museum. As with other museums, we took in all in with plenty of enthusiasm. From the museum, we felt compelled to return to the library. This time, however, the group wasn't to go empty handed. Armed with pen, paper, and goals, we descended upon the library with the eagerness of the Mississippi going downstream. Every girl was excited in a way that would have thrilled any educator. A full two hours passed with no signs of restlessness or boredom.

Back in Memphis, we had gotten a yearning for fresh donuts and had walked and walked looking for a shop. Failing to find one, we still had a taste for donuts. We drew ourselves away from the library to see what we could "discover." We walked through the downtown area and did a little window shopping. Before long, we passed a tiny sandwich shop and were called back by a retired Army Engineer. He and the store owner had recognized us from the newspaper article and wanted us to feel at home in Greenville. They insisted that we have a coke on the house, and made the warm spirit of Greenville and the South come alive.

We chatted and visited a while, and the girls took it all in with dignity and excitement, spiced with enthusiasm. Later on, we reached a donut shop and got four dozen donuts. By then, darkness was at hand, and it was past time to get a camping spot. While crossing Lake Ferguson for the last time, a certain atmosphere of excitement buzzed throughout the group. It wasn't the least bit noisy, just a deep happiness. Teresa sided up to me with a sparkle in her eyes. "I'm just so happy. I never thought I'd have a chance to be an important person," she said. She talked about how she had once felt so low that she thought she would never be able to come up. Every girl seemed to glow with feeling.

A Discovery of Love by Becky

I used to sit and wonder what I was put on earth for, and I didn't find out until camp opened the door.
The door to reality, confidence and goals,
I no longer had to play any false roles.
I had dreams I thought could never come true,
But then camp came brightly shining through.
It means so much to me, it gets quite hard to say,
But I want you to know, camp gets greater every day.
They're always ready to help and won't ever stop caring,
No matter what we have, we're taught to keep on sharing.
Of course I didn't think this when I first arrived,
I couldn't see all the beauty through the many tears I cried.
But when I took a second look at the situation,
I realized, being on my goals in like a graduation,
A promotion greater than my mind could ever conceive.
But I couldn't have done it without all the love I receive.

8:30 PM, June 25, 1970 Greenville, Mississippi

The group is finishing the tents and getting on team jobs. The mosquitoes are out pretty good, but seldom really bring complaints. We are learning how to dodge them by camping on open sandbars or where we can take best advantage of breezes. Weeds or trees in close are a sure hideaway for little pests and will make an uncomfortable campsite. Today has been more or less uneventful. We made about thirty miles with a little headwind most of the way.

10:10 AM, June 26, 1970 Mile 498

Cliff Dwellers are making plans for campsite improvements. We've talked about a craft tent and an entrance gate. As plans are progressing, the idea of a museum is drawing excitement. At first, it was just a group museum, but now it has become a camp museum. It isn't hard to get onto such a subject because of the real enthusiasm the group has developed for the museums we have seen. In our museum, we can see a section containing the things we have found on camp

> "The river is like a mirror reflecting the sky, and the group is like a mirror reflecting the beauty of an individual."
>
> -Unknown Camper

property. The most exciting section would be the one containing articles representing trips and group activities. It would preserve knowledge gained by the experiences of groups and would inspire future groups. Visitors would have a special point of interest to visit. Campers would make carvings and crafts to go in it. They would also write letters of advice to future campers.

11:20 AM, June 27, 1970 Mile 458

8:30 AM, June 28, 1970 Mile 447

We stopped here yesterday about 6:00 with a need to regroup and repair a few fences. Our plan is to spend the day and become mentally and emotionally prepared to go into Vicksburg. We have literature from the Chamber of Commerce to study, and have written letters informing them of our arrival. More than ever before, I have seen how important it is to have a visit like that well planned. The group needs to know what to expect in order to be able to see and take advantage of what is there. When we have personal contacts in a city, our visit becomes much more exciting, meaningful, and rewarding. These contacts can be made in several ways, such as letters to Chambers of Commerce and industrial organizations. After the contact is made, and in making new ones, the forwardness and aggressiveness of the counselor is key in importance. Also, the condition of the group is a major factor in determining how much advantage can be taken of a situation. The whole idea of making contacts and knowing what to look for in a visit is extremely important and is open to much exploration.

Before I go to breakfast, I want to picture what is here. A cool breeze is coming directly off the river, up the sloping sand bank, and into my tent. A towboat is steadily making its way upstream, pushing 24 barges. A comfortable warm patch of sunlight is coming inside the tent flaps. I can hear the frequent call of redwing blackbirds and the humming of several news bees that dig in the sand and are flying around outside the tent. The group is singing a grace song and, if I don't get down there, I'll miss breakfast.

2:00 PM, June 28, 1970 Mile 447

I didn't think I would ever be doing this again, but I am having a quiet time like we did in the mountains. Somehow, the idea of spending time alone came up and the Cliff Dwellers felt strongly in favor of taking it on as a challenge. Generally, I wouldn't go along with such an idea, but because of the advanced condition of the group, we decided to try it. Just at first, we talked about the limitations and waited a couple of days to get a feel for the reaction. This turned out favorably, so we began preparing them. We talked about the self-discovery and beauty of it and also about the difficulties and loneliness. Each person would take only pen and paper and would stay in a small area by the river from 11:00 AM until late sunset. Each would have a paper with four questions to think about. These included: 1) How is my participation on this raft trip helping me to become a better person? 2) What do I like about myself? 2a) What would I like changed about myself? 3) What are my realistic dreams for the future? 4) What are the things that mean most to me?

In addition, each had a copy of four passages from the Bible, including Philippians 3:13, 4:13, 1 Cor 10:30, and Isa 41:10. Other than clothing, nothing else was taken, and they planned to omit lunch and supper. A serious and quiet atmosphere was maintained this morning from the time of its first mention until each was placed in her own defined space. Each was assured that she did not have to try the experience but that to try to be determined to go all the way through with it.

6:10 AM, June 29, 1970 Mile 447

The sunrise is beautiful. A slight breeze is coming across the river from the direction of the red orange sun. Just above the sun is a cover of grey clouds. Ole Man River is fully a mile wide here, making a mile long golden path to the thick row of trees just under the center of attraction. The path is broken by little choppy waves and a giant black Gulf bound snag. Fresh morning quietness is broken only by the song of the redwing blackbird, the constant waves, the creaking of the raft, and the flutter of the flags. Soon the group will be up and busy making ready for the siege of Vicksburg.

7:15 AM, June 29 1970 Mile 447

Almost ready to push off

8:15 AM, June 29, 1970 Mile 444

The "Quiet Time" was a success. Every girl had good feelings about the time spent and felt she had discovered some worthwhile things about herself. One girl said she had found a new friend, and another realized that she hadn't gotten the least bit bored.

11:00 PM, June 29, 1970 Mile 437 Vicksburg

Vicksburg started out a little slow. We ran out of gas in the harbor just as we did in Greenville. By the time we got to the public docks, it was 4:00. Through the Chamber of Commerce, we got a guided tour of the Military Park. That was impressive! Plenty of references describe it adequately, so I'll only sum it up by giving this one impression: To me, it was hard to decide which was more important – the historical value or the beauty.

We made arrangements to set up tents on a wooden barge near the Sprague. However, when we started setting them up, the night watchman made arrangements for us to stay in the dining room of the largest towboat ever to push barges on the Mississippi. It is docked here permanently and is a museum piece. It, too, can be found in the history books. Now, the group is stretched out on sleeping bags under air-conditioning. They are a happy group that just seems to break out with a song spontaneously.

A Short Time of Peace by Mary

As we were going through the National Military Park in Vicksburg, Mississippi, we would look over the rolling hills and see the zig-zag trenches that the Union soldiers had dug during the Civil War. They dug these long, winding trenches in order to get close to the Confederate line, it appeared that the Union got quite close at times.

Our guide told us, during the truces, when no fighting was done, the soldiers from both sides would meet at the trenches and talk, exchange things, and sometimes they discovered they were fighting against some of their relatives or best friends. Then, when the truce was ended, they would pick up their guns and start fighting again. It was a weird thing to imagine but I'm sure they were thankful for even those short times of peace.

The Unusual Soldier by Becky

As we...were being toured around Vicksburg, we went to the National Military Park. While we were at the Illinois monument, our guide, Mrs. Hackett, told us a story of a woman who wanted to fight in the Civil War. The woman was very young, and her name was Ginni Hodges.

Ginni went to the army to enlist, but the army wouldn't accept her. She went to a different town, changed her name to Albert Cashier and had her hair cut. She tried again and was accepted. In the army she fought for the North. After the war, she was sent to a Veterans Hospital where they discovered she was a woman. Because she was a woman, she couldn't stay at the hospital and was sent to a mental institution. They knew she was perfectly sane; they just didn't have any other place to send her.

I thought about this story being very unusual and exciting. Ginni cared so much that she was willing to fight in the war. In studying the Civil War, we've found many unusual experiences.

7:30 AM, June 30, 1970 Mile 437 Vicksburg

Right now, I feel that the group's greatest need is to catch onto the idea of moving around and getting things going. Always, this is an art that Chiefs need to know how to work. Get a line of action with each other, then with the group, and keep them reminded of the time. Look ahead and see what needs to be done and lead out in doing it. Get some enthusiasm about what is ahead and move with determination, direction, and enthusiasm. Frequently, campers are immobile when it comes to starting. Start them by doing the first step or two before turning it over to them. Keep them reminded that "We need to be through in 'X' minutes." Keep them reminded what they are doing.

1:00 AM, July 1, 1970 Mile 437 Vicksburg

Although it's late, late, and my thoughts may come out muddles, I want to try to spill out a token of my feeling about today. Vicksburg has been an experience that has topped most previous experiences. In fact, I cannot think of any it does not top. Many people survive a lifetime on fewer rewarding events that we had just today.

Before we even left the breakfast table, we met Mrs. Marion Bragg from the newspaper. Now she is not ordinary person, but rather a person with great depths of feeling and interest. In no time at all, she had fallen in love with the group, and the group felt the same about her. She took pictures and interviewed for a story. We sang to her and, before it was time for her to leave, her interest in Camp had grown too great for her to drop.

The wonderful captain of the Sprague had informed her of our arrival, and she had gotten wheels rolling for our transportation to the Waterways Experimentation Station. When our bus arrived, she agreed to follow us for the day. At the Experimentation Station, we got a special tour with special treatment. The Experimentation Station is really something to see. Scale models of harbors, rivers, and dams have been constructed. We studied a working model of the Lower Mississippi River where we had floated. Every bend was there. We learned how studies are made of wave action on a California harbor. We saw a model of a dam that is to be constructed where we floated on the Wabash section of the Ohio River, and a model of Niagara Falls thrilled us. Our guide made arrangements for us to see a movie covering much of the operations of the Waterways Experimentation Station. A great deal of self-discovery was made there today, along with physical discovery.

Back at "THE REAL PEOPLE" for lunch, we had only a brief chance to evaluate and prepare a meal. By the time it was over, Mrs. Bragg was there with Mr. Needl, owner of the excursion boat, "Jefferson Davis." He invited us for a tour of the harbor and a run on the Mississippi. We mingled freely with the distinguished group of fare-paying passengers, and enjoyed the interesting change of pace. I wish I could related all of the individual experiences, but that would get too involved. In general, everyone on the boat had a more interesting and unusual tour as a result of Cliff Dwellers being on it. The girls didn't show off; they just moved around meeting people and acting like young ladies. I couldn't even keep track of the compliments I received from the "fine group of girls." Most of the two dozen passengers expressed envy of the girls' opportunity to make such an adventure.

After the boat ride, we were ready to take our official tour of the mighty Sprague. This great sternwheel towboat is on record for pushing 62 barges of coal from Louisville to New Orleans. It has been retired and is now an impressive museum. The gracious captain wouldn't let us pay for the tour, but did invite us to spend another night in the dining room. We accepted. The group really did enjoy the tour, and I went with Mrs. Bragg to buy a few supplies.

We had two guests for supper, Mrs. Bragg and an old riverman named Buck Chapman. We continued a delightful visit, singing and sharing experiences. When it was time for her to go, we sang, "No Man Is an Island" and "Each Campfire," and gave her three "Hows." It was a difficult farewell for both sides, to say the least.

How does a group have pow-wow after a day like this? So many feelings were bubbling over that, for two hours, we exploded with joyful feelings. I can think of scores of different campers' and Chiefs' emotional victories to relate, but it is already three o'clock in the morning and I wouldn't know where to start. Besides, I don't know how to write about such things. And, there are so many of greatest importance that I would run out of paper to write on. Some pretty big things are happening in these girls. One says, "It's too bad we can't wait to grow up until we want to." Another reminds me of a tulip opening up, or a chicken just hatching out of an egg and seeing life for the first time. A third says that she has discovered the beauty of expressing her own feelings. A poignant moment occurred when Melody told Becky that we love her. Mary glowed like a new camera. I am having a good time and feel that I am doing some growing like I haven't ever before.

Sleeping on the Sprague by Cindy

While the group was in Vicksburg, Mississippi, we met the captain of the Sprague. He talked with Chief Everett and later asked if we would like to sleep on the Sprague. The group was excited and willing to go. We got our sleeping bags and went up to the Sprague. The captain had turned on the air conditioner so it was nice and cold when we arrived, and there were no mosquitoes. The walls were painted with a mural of the race between the steamboats, the Robert E. Lee, and the Natchez. It covered the whole side of one wall.

We slept in the dining room. The tables were slid up against the walls to make room for dancing and there was a piano in there. There were sliding glass doors in the back of the dining room from which you could see the paddle wheel.

The group enjoyed the opportunity to sleep on the steamboat. We appreciated meeting the captain and realized that the raft trip has brought quite a few miracles.

7:30 AM, July 2, 1970 Mile 422

About noon yesterday, we finished the Old Court House Museum and slipped, almost unnoticed, out of Afazoo River Harbor.

7:30 PM, July 2, 1970 Mile 385

The sun is getting a little more tolerable and I'm standing in the middle of a several acre meadow. About 25 yards in front of me are several deer. One is snorting and stamping his foot. They are all watching me and swishing their tails. The young buck is leading them slowly toward me. I suppose they are just being curious. An armadillo is just a few yards away and doesn't even know I'm here. Birds of all kinds are singing and screeching. I can identify mourning doves, jays, mocking birds, owls, sparrows, redbirds, and red wing blackbirds, but most of them are unknown to me. The deer had run back into the thicker trees, but are coming back. The leaves of the trees are quite still and all is peaceful. I think I will go find the group and see if they can come enjoy this with me.

8:00 PM, July 2, 9170 Mile 385

Well, the group is getting a plentiful supply of wood so they could go swimming. And, since they have a firm line of action, I'll just sit here on this great section of driftwood and watch that ball of orange fire turn red and hide behind that dark row of trees. A bright orange path leads across the river that is turning pink, orange, and lavender. While all of this is taking place, I'll describe what happened in Vicksburg.

After that beautiful day of high spirits and feelings came another morning of the same. We walked to the Old Court House Museum and, right away, were enveloped in the emotions of the Civil War and that period of history. The Old Museum is crammed packed with more artifacts than I could remember. It really was a museum with a different and more personal touch. It had an air of nonsophistication about it that was a real pleasure. Perhaps this quality was achieved partly by the displays themselves. Many included personal photos and stories about individuals. One display case contained the following informal message, "This spot is dedicated to the THIEF who stole the derringer gun that was here." The museum attendants themselves were an example of personable Southern friendliness. They became personally interested in our group and wanted to be helpful in any way they could. One lady, Mrs. Terry Blanche, talked a long while with me about Camp and the work her son was doing. When we left, she presented us with a special gift that as clearly over and above her line of duty. The museum itself was a personal achievement of Mrs. Eva Davis, and still remained her personal project. Even the elderly janitor took a special interest in us and wanted to be sure we enjoyed ourselves. We spent at least two hours there, without a single camper getting bored. We all were struck over and over with the breathtaking interest of the Old Court House

Museum.

After leaving the museum, we took a circular walk back to the River and the Sprague and "THE REAL PEOPLE." We left many new friends and valuable experiences in Vicksburg and, like other stops, left with the fullest intentions of someday returning. The rest of the day and today was quiet and slow back on the old river routine. That means a hum of article writing, reading, planning, and clothing repairs. Now, the sun has completed its final act of the day, and it is time to get back to the "here and now."

11:40 AM, July 3, 1970 Mile 373

Our Mississippi River, at this point, is in one of its many moods. It seems hardly to be moving and is smooth from lack of air movement. The sandy and wooded banks are a full mile apart. At each end of our section of river is a hazy horizon.

1:30 PM, July 3, 1970 Mile 372

Problems are to be solved! During the time of this raft trip, we have been fortunate enough to have a number of very real problems to solve. I have described the rain and stormy week and how we coped with it. Then the mosquitoes had to be out-smarted. We faced the problem of boredom and have solved it before it could take a toll. From time to time, strong winds have been a real nuisance and have called for little creations of ingenuity. Now, the Cliff Dwellers are being called upon to solve a problem of heat. The sun is coming on strong, and no breeze is offsetting the effects. However, a solution has been found. First, we stopped and cut willow poles suitable for holding up the side tarps. Next, we wet the tarps and deck with river water. The result is an almost comfortable raft.

The People from Natchez by Teresa

The Cliff Dwellers were going into Natchez on July 3, 1970. We were reading Huckleberry Finn and combing our hair. Then we heard some kids on the side of the river swimming. We couldn't see where they were so we got the binoculars out and looked for them

We got close to where they were, and the kids called us over. We decided to go and see them. When we got over to the bank there were two families with kids who came to the raft knee deep in mud and tied us up. They told us they were from Natchez. We started to talk to them and found they were congenial. One woman asked if we wanted to swim in their pool. Then we had to go and get to Natchez. They told us where there was a place to moor.

We left and found our way into Natchez. Our friends were behind us. After we docked we got water and some men helped us to get it on the raft. We talked a good two hours when the people said they had to go. We went to Natchez.

Antebellum Homes by Karin

During the last three weeks of the raft trip, we went through a few towns with antebellum homes. We studied about them and were very interested in their history, but it wasn't until we visited one when we really saw the value of it. Everything was unbelievable. Inside the bedrooms were huge beds that sat way up off the floor and there were crocheted bedspreads. Over the beds were velvet canopies. Underneath one bed was a space for a sliding bed called a trundle bed. Each bedpost was made from the heart of a walnut tree. The handwork involved in the bedposts, and in all the woodwork was just so detailed that it's hard to describe.

The group noticed the structure of some other houses along the street. The bricks were placed so some walls were rounded. (I've heard bricklayers today cannot duplicate this design.) In one of the homes there was a cannon ball stuck in the wall between the twin parlors. It was left there after the Civil War. The stories these antiques could tell would be amazing, if only they could talk. It's really surprising that some things could last this long without being lost, thrown away, or just being worn out.

Thanks to these antiques, we've been able to learn even more about our forefathers' ways of life. Isn't it interesting?

7:55 AM, July 4, 1970 Mile 359

Everyone is pretty busy this morning: cleaning lanterns, cooking, cleaning the equipment box, writing, cleaning the raft, getting clothing in order and writing articles. I'm thinking about an unusual yesterday. Our big objective was to see Natchez and that we did. Before we got to the city, we saw some children swimming and went in for a visit. It was two or three families from Natchez. After we got to Natchez, we walked a preplanned route to see some of the old homes. We went into one and saw a good many pieces of old furniture and things. We met an elderly lady at the museum and continued our walk through antebellum homes and the downtown section. We stopped at a grocery store for ice cream, salt, and strawberries, and went on to the ice house for ice. The old southern sun was doing all it could, and we were glad when we got back to the river.

In spite of the time we spent, and the people we met, we did not discover the same warmth and friendliness that we experienced in Greenville and Vicksburg. A strange atmosphere prevailed even though everyone was friendly. The Cliff Dwellers sensed the people didn't have a group spirit. Instead, each one seemed to be more interested in making her own antebellum home a little better than the others. Not that anything is wrong with that, but we just didn't find a strong community feeling. One girl evaluated some of its citizens by saying, "I'm glad I'm me."

We were glad to get back to the river for several reasons. One was the anticipation of a special treat. In spite of some slight shades of skepticism, we built ourselves some homemade strawberry ice cream and without even an ice cream churn. When the eggs, dried milk, vanilla, sugar, and a touch of flour were properly and well mixed, we filled two aluminum pitchers. We packed ice and salt in the two foot tubs and churned the pitchers until we had hardened ice cream. I got to thinking how much simpler it would have been to have bought a gallon of ice cream, and the thrill we would have missed.

Holiday Ride by Edie

While floating very calmly down the river...July 4, we had a ride on a tugboat. We were about one and a half days out of Natchez. We had just finished our July 4 party when a large tugboat came up beside us. The men on it told us while we were tying on hat they would need to take us through some swift water. They said we would need to come aboard the tug. We agreed. We boarded the tug being very surprised. After we got on we were talking to one man who said he had twenty-three years of experience altogether on a tug like that one. He said we could go up to the pilot house if we wanted.

The pilot was interesting. He told us a little about the tug he was driving and a few other things about the barges he had driven before. He also told us a few things about the river. We were told we could see the engine room and the sleeping quarters if we wanted. We did want to see any part of the tug we could. The man that showed us around showed us the captains quarters, the galley, and the crew's quarters.

We enjoyed being on the tug. It isn't often we get a chance like that. The men aboard were very polite and considerate.

9:30 P.M., July 5, 1970 Mile 287

Our Nation's birthday was celebrated in fine style with skits, lots of conversation on early American history, games, and refreshments. To make it even better, a welcome north wind kept us cooled while it pushed us along a little faster. About the time the party was coming to a close, the Joachim, a Coast Guard tug, approached us. We soon learned that its crew of three were assigned to escort us past the dangerous opening for the flood control structure. We made the lines fast and boarded their boat for the tow. That was a new experience, and no one complains about new experiences.

Because of trouble in finding a campsite, we didn't get off the river until after dark. This was another first for us, but it ended with no mishaps.

People by Mary

People can be funny and hard to understand.
But show them that you care and lend a helping hand.
People are a mystery and have very confusing ways
Some don't try to fill every minute of the day.
People can be real and fun to be around,
So find a friend that's real and your relationship will be sound.

12:00 AM, July 6, 1970 Mile 287

"THE REAL PEOPLE" has traveled more than a thousand miles and doesn't have far to go. Next Sunday should find us in New Orleans. That's a frightful thought, bringing plenty of mixed feelings. But, I save the evaluations for later. Right now, I can only mention one of the most important events of the day and let it go at that. Before noon, we arrived at the Old River Lock where we had planned to stop for a phone call and water. The phone was out of order, but we got the water.

However, the stop would have been quite worthwhile, even if we had missed the water. Two brothers were in charge of the Lock and gave us a tour and a visit. They were fine examples of one more sectional society of our country. Their constant joking and good humor kept us laughing. Their helpfulness made us feel good all over, and their happiness made us happy. Their accents were quite interesting, and they really had a style much different from any we had experienced. I don't think the Cliff Dwellers will soon forget the brothers at the Lock, but we are looking forward to meeting other people of Louisiana.

Our church service tonight was built around "sharing," and we shared the Camp translation of Romans 8:8-13. I think we all got some spiritual food for thought.

8:00 PM, July 7, 1970 Mile 235 Baton Rouge

"Chief" is a group's greatest limitation. I know this is such an obvious fact that is seems foolish to mention it, but I'd like to mention a specific area of limitations. Organizational ability is an area of real limitation. It runs into time loss for one thing, and that means less time for giving attention to the campers. If the counselor has trouble believing things can be done, this, like all other counselor attitudes, is transmitted to the campers. If the counselor has imagination, she can lead the group to great heights. If she has a low self-image, she keeps the campers' self-images low. If she can accept new ideas from the campers, she can stretch limitations even more.

11:30 PM, July 7, 1970 Mile 235

The past two days have been fair enough. Everyone stays plenty busy on the raft, but I have the feeling some of it is just busy work. The miles keep slipping by and the end of the trip is coming on fast. We've been trying to hide from it, so it wouldn't seem to come too slowly. Yesterday, we met a new friend, a kid named Don. He was from Michigan and was plenty decent. We also picked up a dog and I believe that Chiefs can see why dogs don't mix with Camp. We also stopped for supper at St. Francisville, but all the stores were closed. Today was even less interrupted by outside events. The river has changed some. It is more constant and not so wide. The wind has continued to cool us from the north, and again no complaints. Last night there weren't even any mosquitoes.

Tonight, we are camped at the bend just before the big river gets to Baton Rouge. I can see all the lights, even car lights going across the bridge. Smoke is coming from several stacks as the industrial section makes their steady humming. We plan to spend only one day in the city, although we would likely have spent two days if it had been earlier in the trip.

The Louisiana State Legislature by Edie

The legislature of Louisiana consisted of the House of Representative and the Senate. While the Cliff Dwellers were visiting Baton Rouge, the capitol of Louisiana, we had the privilege of listening to the discussions of the legislature.

In the House of Representatives we saw the people who bring various issues to be discussed. Then the representatives make laws and amendments from these issues. If the House passes the issue, it is brought before the Senate. The Senate makes the final decision on the issue.

For sixty days the legislature is in session. The man have to work very hard and be very serious during this time to get laws passed and other problems discussed. Before the legislature goes into session they have already discussed the bills and amendments that are to be brought up in the sessions. The purpose for the sixty days of open session is to see both sides of an issue and to discuss it. Also, the sessions make a public record of all its events during the sixty days.

Our first impression of these meetings was that it was hard to realize how each person could take all the responsibility that they have to take to represent the people in their state. The men of the House of Representatives and the Senate are really remarkable men and play a large part in our government. These men are the backbone of America.

Jim Bullington by Ann

While we were visiting the Capitol Building, Chief Everett brought a young boy over to the group and introduced him to us as Jim Bullington. He was going to show us the capital. He was fifteen years old, lives in New Orleans, he comes to Baton Rouge every year to work as a page boy during the legislative session. Cliff Dwellers didn't know what a page boy was. Jim told us a page boy runs errands for Senators during their sixty day session. The way you get to be a page boy is to be recommended by a Senator. Jim was personal friends with a Senator, plus he was interested in being a page boy. Jim really impressed Cliff Dwellers. He had a very good future planned and he had respect for his parents. He made us feel like young ladies because of the way he treated us. He showed us around then he walked back to the raft with us. We talked for a while then he had to leave. After he left we discussed our feelings.

Just as we were pushing off, Jim came back. He had wanted us to know he did really like us. He got our address and told us he would try to see us in New Orleans.

9:10 PM, July 9, 1970 Mile 199

This could be the most beautiful night of the raft trip. The lightning is flashing with distant rumbles of thunder. A good breeze is blowing and the waves are small and steady. A large ship is stealing downstream, silhouetted by the lightning in the background. The group is quiet after a good day and a moving pow-wow.

10:10 PM, July 9, 1970 Mile 199

It looks like a storm is blowing in at last. First the gentle breeze changed direction and became a wind. Campers flew out and made tents a little tighter just in time for a light rain. I retreated to the equipment box, and can see through the cracks enough to see the effects of the storm.

Last night's problem session has proved a certain measure of success today. The girls have clearly been pushing harder, and we all have felt a closer group feeling. After pow-wow, Chief Ann commented, "I don't know what's happening, but I like it." My push was to make another round of individual conferences. The first girl was slow to talk, but finally opened up with some pretty good feelings about what this trip meant to her. She still needs to get more verbal. The second girl really gave me fit, but after she saw I wasn't going to solve her problem, she came around really well. She still seems mentally lazy, but that may be only a result of mental energy being sapped in other directions. She responded best to setting a firm direction for the remainder of the raft trip. A third girl came through best of all, verbalizing with depth and level-headedness much better than she would have a few weeks ago.

Our First Sight of a Ship by Cathi

We saw our first sight of our new challenge. We looked up and saw a big ship being loaded at a dock. Also, there were some ships out in the channel anchored waiting to be checked or loaded. One of the ships was loaded out in the channel by a barge that had come out to it.

We saw some ships from different countries. The people couldn't speak English. They waved to us and said something in Greek. Chief Everett said good day to them in Greek. It was different seeing a ship with people who spoke a different language from us. It's kind of hard to understand them if you can't speak their language.

Cliff Dwellers felt when we were on the Ohio River that is was going to be a big challenge to face the barges. Now that we're past Baton Rouge, we've got a new challenge to face with the big ships.

12:45 PM, July 11, 1970

This is the day before the last day on the river, and we are all busy with little details. Chief Ann is talking with a camper and running the motor. We have had to run the motor for the last sixty miles because the current has slowed to about a half mile per hour. The group is at work. Two girls are carving a plaque commemorating the raft trip. Mary is writing an article on "Excitement that Never Ceases." Four other girls are washing clothes. We have all become a little tense and excited, although not so much in negative ways. No one seems to really be uncontrollably anxious to get to the end, but rather everyone has a bad case of mixed emotions.

We have just finished bathing and have had a steady morning. The food and equipment boxes have been completely overhauled in preparation for New Orleans. Yesterday was usual, except that we couldn't find a suitable campsite. By 9:00, we still hadn't been able to even get to solid ground, so we had to tie up and wade ashore. The mud came up to our knees but it succeeded only in becoming another problem to solve. The group took it as a challenge and moved on.

Excitement Never Ceases by Mary

One night, after the Cliff Dwellers had all snuggled down in our bedrolls for a good night's sleep, a big ship came by. All of a sudden there were ten little heads sticking out of the pup tents. Everyone was really excited. It was a grand sight to see. The ship was all lit up and looked very proud and majestic against the dark sky.

No one went back into their tent until the last wave had crashed against the bank. After we were settled down, I wondered how many people can lay and look out of their pup tent and see a ship from a different country sailing down the Mississippi River. Having had the experience myself, I wish everyone could.

3:10 PM, July 12, 1970 Mile 108

Another hour and we will be at Nine Mile Point. Excitement is rising and campers are finishing articles on "What the Raft Trip Has Meant to Me."

8:30 AM, July 13, 1970 Mile 103

"THE REAL PEOPLE" is now making its final day with Cliff Dwellers. We left Nine Mile Point Power Plant and some new friends a few minutes ago and are enroute to Gov. W. Nicholls St. Wharf. There, we will meet several people before going on to Lake Ponchatrain. The Coast Guard will escort us and we will present "THE REAL PEOPLE" as a gift to the Kingsley House. The group has just finished washing down the deck and making everything ready for our big appearance.

Last evening, just before we got to the Huey P. Long Bridge, we saw some people on the bank, waving their arms. We motored over and found Mother and Dad, Aunt Polly and Uncle Bailey, and Chief Hubert. The group was quite excited to see them, and it was a good reunion.

Later, when we got to Nine Mile Point, we all had a big steak supper, together. We had a really good time, and the group performed beautifully. The Louisiana Light and Power Company extended to us some real hospitality. We showered, and then took a tour of the plant.

The Power Plant by Cathi

Sunday, July 12, 1970, Cliff Dwellers were on the outskirts of New Orleans, Louisiana. It was Cliff Dwellers last day on our raft, and we planned to stay at the Louisiana Power and Light Plant that night. Chief Everett had called the Power Plant previously and had made plans for us to take showers when we arrived Sunday evening.

We took showers for the first time in two months at the Power Plant and felt fresh and good! When we came out from showers the men of the Power Plant asked us if we would like a coke. We sat and drank cokes and talked to them. They then asked us if we would like to go on a tour of the building.

We went up fourteen stories high on top of a boiler to an observation point. We could see the raft, the Mississippi River and New Orleans. In the Power Plant we saw the materials they ran the plant with. We also saw where the gas was burned to heat water. We learned a number of things such as, the people who worked at the plant had to put their whole selves into their work. It helped my group see where and how our power came from. After the tour, the men took us to a room and told us we were welcome to sleep there. The room was usually held for meetings.

9:45 PM, July 15, 1970 Dauphin Island, Alabama

The Cliff Dwellers are spending this night in pup tents on a military base. They are putting them up now, and I'm a little bugged that they are taking so long to do it. I helped them get started, but expect them to pick up the ball and go with it.

We really picked up the ball and went with it the past few days. We could see the Gov. Nicholls St. Wharf from the bridge. Before long, we began recognizing people on it, and our excitement ran high. The big moment was a little thwarted by the shallow water preventing our immediate landing, but we finally did get tied up. Mr. Baker and several other officials and workers were there from the Kingsley House to receive "THE REAL PEOPLE." Capt. D.J. Thompson, MSMM Officer, had made arrangements for us to dock in the area and met us there. Mr. Larry Hill, in charge of Sea Scouts, was there to make arrangements to take "THE REAL PEOPLE" from Lake Ponchatrain to Bay St. Louis, Camp Onward. Mr. Keith Herrell, of the US Coast Guard, was there to arrange for taking "THE REAL PEOPLE" from the Mississippi River to Camp Onward. Several newspaper and TV reporters covered the occasion. Several tourists from the French Market came over the levee to see what was going on. The group got off the raft to meet people and finally to present "THE REAL PEOPLE" to Kingsley House. We told them what all had happened to it and how much it meant to us. I made the final words and shook hands with Mr. Baker and the others. Then we excused ourselves and retreated to the raft to vent a buildup of feelings. We are trading this day for a day of our lives. That's a high price to pay, and we need to make it a good trade.

Good-bye, Real People by Edie

Our final destination was reached as we pulled into Governor Nichol's Wharf in New Orleans. That was the day we gave away the "REAL PEOPLE" to Kingsley House. We pulled in the harbor and there were many people expecting us. The newspaper and television reporters were there. The Coast Guard greeted us. Mama and Papa Lindstrom, Aunt Polley, and Uncle Bailey, and Chief Hubert were waving at us. We climbed up the rocky bank and met them.

We were interviewed by the reporters and got to share our experiences with them. We then got everyone's attention, and Chief Lynda began the ceremony by telling what the raft has meant to us. The Group shared some experiences they had with the "Real People". The raft was officially handed over to the Kingsley House. Mr. Baker, the owner of the Kingsley House, showed his appreciation for the raft and he knew how we felt about the raft. He assured us that the "Real People" would be well taken care of.

The ceremony was concluded, and the Cliff Dwellers made their way back down to the "Real People" for the last time, to give a tear-soaked farewell. We had given the "Real People" life and a beginning, but her life is not over – it has just begun.

12:00 PM, July 16, 1970 Bellingrath Gardens

We are having lunch here at the Garden Shop. The group can sit down and order what they want with the greatest of ease. The garden itself was a wonderland for us. We talked to Jonnie Dickinson, the attendant, and sang for him. He added a great deal to our visit and communicated a bit of cordiality and friendliness of Bellingrath Gardens.

8:30 PM, July 16, 1970 Falling Water State Park

Falling Water State Park is a beautiful and ideal place to camp. The group is getting tents up fast so they can take showers. The blue jays are screaming and I'm intending to catch up on a lot of notes and thoughts I've missed.

After we left the lunch at the Gardens, the waitress told Chief Hubert, "That was the best behaved group I have ever seen." He also heard another visitor make the comment, "They are the best behaved teenagers I've ever seen." We were also invited back.

7:35 AM, July 17, 1970 Falling Water State Park

We are all taking showers this morning and anticipating Camp arrival. While some are showering, others are finishing up on article writing.

Meanwhile, back to expressing our building up of feelings at the presentation of "THE REAL PEOPLE." The group really made it obvious how strongly they felt. They cried for an appropriate amount of time and then we went to eat lunch. After lunch, we unloaded and dismantled the raft. We had a round of prayers and gave it "Three Hows" and departed. At the YWCA we showered and prepared to go out to eat. We saw part of our TV broadcast, took a girl to the doctor, and bought clothes for two campers and Chief Ann.

We had a beautiful supper at a hundred year old restaurant called "Tujaques."

Dining in Luxury by Mary and Debbie

We had planned to go out to eat when we got to New Orleans and we hoped to find a restaurant that had history and good French cooking. Many people recommended Tujacques so we decided to try it. The group changed clothes at the YWCA (in 10 minutes) and loaded on the bus. We drove down a small, narrow busy street and found Tujacques. It looked old and we later found out that it is 100 years old. When we arrived a doorman met all of us at the bus. We were again greeted at the door by a waiter dressed in a red coat. We were escorted into a beautiful porch. In the center of the room was a big long table, set with ruby red water glasses and candles. A white napkin and decorated silver and flowers delicately accented the room. We were given hand-written menus and told to choose a main dish and two appetizers. I ordered shrimp gumbo and oyster cocktail. The main dishes included duck to steak. I ordered duck in a glaze sauce. We were served our first appetizer and four loaves of bread. The head waiter, who had on a black coat said, "Don't use your spoons, but use bread and sop up the oysters with it." After our second appetizer, we began wondering where we'd put it because we were getting full.

I didn't have time to worry long because when I looked up, in came two big trays of platters! Some of us had ordered steak, crab mean and mushrooms, shrimp, crab tchoupitulas, and trout amandine. Also, a few of us experimented with duck in glaze sauce. The vegetables that came with it were plantains in sauce and spiced green beans. My duck and vegetables really looked almost too pretty to eat! For dessert we had strawberry parfait. It was really different.

From this experience at Tchoupitulas I learned what manners are and what it takes to be a lady. I know I never would have learned these things if I had not come to camp. It feels good to say I am becoming a lady.

Camp Onward by Cindy

The day Cliff Dwellers left New Orleans, we were invited to have lunch at Camp Onward...When we got there we went and ate lunch. We had beef stew over rice, cornbread and iced tea. For dessert we had cake. After lunch we sang some songs and told about some of the challenges we had on the raft. After talking for a while we went outside and played games. Some of the games we played were tetherball and football. We also talked to the boys and got to know them. The boys were 6-14 and all of them had problems. The camp was much like our camp but they were only there a week. The group had a chance to see a camp with an objective of helping problem boys as much as possible.

There's No Place Like Home by Becky

July 17, 1970 was a glorious day for Cliff Dwellers. It was homecoming. We had been on a two month raft trip. We reached the gate of camp and to our surprise we found the gate shut and a sign saying "Gone for the summer". Well, we opened that gate faster than any gate in our lives. We went back to the bus and started on through the gate. As we traveled on we found another sign saying, "We said gone for the summer". Well, by this time, we were so excited we didn't even stop to read the next sign, we just drove through it!

We finally arrived at the dining hall and there to meet us were Chief Mac, Chief Helen, Chief Lois, Mrs. Thomason, Mrs. Foster, Mom Becky and Mom Mildred. It was an exciting moment for us all. We talked a few minutes and then Chief Mac said for us to go on down to campsite and be back by 6:30.

We started off for campsite with Chief Helen and Chief Everett. As we reached campsite, to our amazement, campsite had been re-cleaned, our beds made, and cards under our pillows. It was just wonderful to be back and see such a great camp spirit. Then over the hill at full speed camp Kalapakans and Achenas and we ran to their arms. We then went over the hill with the groups and there they had cookies and lemonade. We exchanged happy feeling for a while and then said our goodbyes until supper.

We then went to unload the bus. We took everything that belonged at campsite and put it away. Then the group headed for the dining hall. We reached our ready logs and all the groups sang a song. Then we all went in for supper. As we walked in the dining hall we saw it at its very best. It was all decorated; a raft in the middle of the room. Then our table was a small raft and cards with each of our names at each setting.

It really felt good to be home again. The groups were at their best and the camp spirit was high. We all knew there was no place like home.

Excerpts from articles about What the Raft Trip has mean to me:

- The raft trip to me has been a self-discovering adventure. I've learned how important I am as a person. In order to be important I've had to be in contact with myself. The group has helped me to see I do have positive qualities and to bring these things out so I can help myself and others as well.
- Being on the river, close to nature, I have discovered some of the beauty of America. Sleeping on her soil, floating on her rivers, walking through her cities and towns and realizing the freedom of being an American, I've gained a deep respect for this great nation and what it stands for.
- The most important thing on the raft trip for me, was becoming a Christian, believing in God, and accepting the plans He has set for me. Life has taken on a new meaning. I no longer live to please others around me, but to do the right think in God's eyes.
- I've learned I was self-centered and didn't care about other people or their things, but I'm almost over that now. I am learning what love really is and what it can do to people, and how it can be real or just put on.
- I've become more willing to learn and read. In Greenville, I discovered I could read a book and know what I was reading. I can go to a library and know how to use it and appreciate what it has to offer.
- I'm learning to become real

- I started to express myself and I started to see the beauty around me. I can recognize the beauty in people, in the land, the sky and stars, in the river and in the sunset.
- I have learned to be a self-starter...my parents...won't always have to be telling me things to do because I will already have them done...I feel more responsible when Chiefs don't have to tell me what needs to be done.
- I have learned to appreciate things. Before I came on the trip I had fresh foods, showers and all the clothes I wanted. But I couldn't appreciate them until I came on the trip and have done without them. It's a great feeling to know who I am and how I can help others.
- I no longer have a wall between my parents and me. Being on the raft trip has made me realize how much I love them and how much I need them. I haove decided to make things easier for myself by sticking to the good things in life. Each person has their choice. I know that my choice will build me up, not bring me down.
- I have learned more on the raft trip than I would have six months in camp. I am really proud of myself that I have come this far.
- I want my name to be something good, not something people frown on. I will work for my name and make it good again. I want to change the things I've done into things that I am doing. I am able to accept that I have done wrong and I want to do right.
- I've realized some of what life really means. I can now see beauty in an old dead tree and flowers. God is an important part of life. Following His plan I have learned to see the meaning of living each day to the fullest. God is reality. Reality becomes easier to face when God is on your side. He has helped me to see my problems and face them and realize all people make mistakes.
- I have learned I can survive without all the modern conveniences of the city. Life is becoming more simple to me.
- I've gained a lot of knowledge during this raft trip, but most of all it has helped me to build a solid foundation on which to build the rest of my life.
- I've gained self-confidence and have learned that to be somebody, a person has to express herself. I'm able to require more of myself and be able to do my work and be proud of it.
- I'm able to take responsibility – to become a better person you have to take. I have a better understanding of myself, and I know what I

want out of life.

- The raft trip as a whole means a lot to me; it is something most girls don't get a chance to do. It is an opportunity, and a chance to do fast learning. At camp we learn fast but on a trip like a raft trip we learn faster.
- Nothing good comes easy.
- In two months, I've learned things I couldn't have learned in five years without coming on the raft trip.
- I've discovered that learning can be both rewarding and fun.
- Two sayings that I heard on the raft trip that I will always remember and follow are "Life is what you make it", and "Nothing good comes easy".
- One of the most important things I have gained is self-confidence. I'm able to feel satisfied with myself. For the first time I see good in myself and feel proud that I'm me. I don't have to play a fake or unreal role in life anymore. I've found myself and it sure was a great discovery.

"Treat people as if they were what they ought to be and you help them become what they are capable of being."

-Gothe

REFERENCES

1968 Roster of the Salesmanship Club of Dallas. December 1, 1967.

A Boy's World, Video Published by Camp Woodland Springs, 1954. *A Report on the Present Operation and Future Needs of Camp Woodland Springs by a Special Committee*, Salesmanship Club of Dallas: September 11. 1950.

Adventures in Camping. New York, NY: Johanna M. Lindlof Camp Committee for Public School Children, 1943.

Breining, Wilber Clarence Jr., *A Follow Up Study of Seventy-nine Maladjusted Boys Who Received Treatement at Camp Woodland Springs, Dallas, Texas* (Denton: North Texas State College, 1956).

Camp and Club News: Salesmanship Club Boys Camp 40 No. 1 (September 29, 1966).

Camp Woodland Springs Chief Orientation Manual, 1950.

Campership Manual for Participating Agencies, *Metropolitan Council for Community Service, Inc*, Denver, CO: April 1962.

Carlson, Julie. *Never Finished...Just Begun A Narrative History of L.B. Sharp and Outdoor Education,* Edina: Beavers Pond Press, 2009.

Chamberlain, Martha. "In Memoriam Jack Eckerd Founder of Eckerd Youth Alternatives," *Journal of Therapeutic Wilderness Camping,* no. 2 (2004).

Charity and Children, *Buford McKenzie Retires from Cameron*. 102, no. 1 (Jan 1989) 7.

Chronological Highlights of Development of Girls' Adventure Trails Program printed near August 1971.

"Church Branch of Division St. Y Opened Again." *Chicago Daily Tribune*, July 21, 1946, NW2.

Club and Camp News, Newsletter Published by the Salesmanship Club Boys Camp, Sept 29, 1966, Vol 40, No.1

Cobler, Sharon. "Camp for Girls Planned" *Dallas Morning News*, March 13, 1975.

Collins, Bill. "Tribute to Chief Mac and Lois". WRTCA Conference, August 30, 2014.

"Concentration Camps Exist in Dallas, but Toothbrushing, Butterfly Chasing Are Routine." Dallas Morning News*, June 1, 1939, (clipping).*

Conrad, Lawrence H. Sr. "Lloyd B. Sharp's Philosophy of Education", in *Perspectives on Outdoor Education...Readings* Eds: George W. Donaldson and Oswald Goering (Dubuque: Wm C Brown Company Publishers, 1972).

Dimock, H.S and Hendry, C.E., *Camping and Character*, New York: Association Press, 1929.

Eckerd, Jack. *Finding the Right Prescription,* Clearwater, FL: JME Inc, 1987.

Edgar, Ken. *Starting Eckerd Camps,* Unpublished Document.

_________. *Starting Wilderness Camps*, Unpublished Document.

_________. *Vermont,* Unpublished Document

Edgar, Ken and Flora with Amber Bateman. *Reflections Along the Trail,* Amazon, 2016.

Elliott, Harrison Sackett. *The Why and How of Group Discussion,* Association Press: New York, 1927.

"Escaping the Cities Heat." *New York Times*, June 8, 1925, 14.

Evaluation of the Adventure School – Report from Summer of 1965 on the Adventure Trails Program at Camp Woodland Springs.

Extending Education through Camping, New York, NY: Life Camps, Inc, 1948.

Frontier Boys Camp Newsletter 1 No. 2 (May 1962).

__________________________, 1 No. 4 (July 1962).

Fresh Air Charities, New York Times, August 10, 1925, 12.

"Girl is Killed After Ditch Caves In." *News-Press* (Fort Myers, FL), Aug 3 1978, 19.

Glission, Floyd. *Letter to Buford McKenzie* dated August 13, 1968.

Haile, Bartee. "Doak Walker's Last Football Season." *The Cameron Herald*, July 29, 2010 Online

Harrover, Tom. Unpublished Memoir.

Heald, R. Clare. "Good Song Leadership A YMCA Asset," Conference Handout for YMCA Midwest Conference Held at Lake Geneva Wisconsin, July 7-12, 1941.

Horner, Kim. "Tough Call for Youth Refuge: Camp program ends as laws change, kids problems grow more complex." *The Dallas Morning News,* May 13, 2004.

Hood, William. *1950's Camp Experience* (Unpublished Memoir).

"How We Came to Be: The History of Therapeutic Wilderness Camping as Practiced by Jack and Ruth Eckerd Foundation." (Unpublished Document).

Hubbard, Julie. *Eckerd Camp to Close*. Wilkes Journal-Patriot: North Wilkesboro, NC. June 15, 2011.

Jack and Ruth Eckerd Foundation Program and Policy Manual Vol 1. 10/16/1976.

James, Adrienne Brant. "Roots: The Life Space Pioneers." *Reclaiming Children and Youth* 17 no. 2 (2008): 4-10.

Jordan, Donna. *Camp E-Toh-Annee Is Set to Close Next Month.* The Colebrook Chronicle: Colebrook, CT. October 21, 2011.

Knapp, Clifford, "Learning From an Outdoor Education Hero." *Taproot* (Summer 2000): 7-11.

Lindstrom, Everett N. Report on E-Ma-Chamee Boys' Camp. April, 1973.

_________________. Report on E-Ma-Chamee Boys' Camp. May, 1973.

_________________. Report on E-Ma-Chamee Boys' Camp. June, 1973.

_________________. Report on E-Ma-Chamee Boys' Camp. July, 1973.

_________________. Report on E-Ma-Chamee Boys' Camp. Oct, 1973.

_________________. *Log for First Cliff Dweller Raft Trip*. (Unpublished Document) July 1970.

Loughmiller, Campbell. Conference Held in Southern Pines NC, June 1988.

___________________. *Kids in Trouble*, TX: Wildwood Books, 1989.

___________________. *These Fish Had Wings Vol 1* (Unpublished Autobiography, 1980).

___________________. *Wilderness Road,* Austin, TX: Hogg Foundation, 1965.

___________________. Letter to L.B. Sharp dated May 16, 1947.

___________________. Letter to L.B. Sharp dated July 29, 1947.

___________________. Letter to L.B. Sharp dated Oct/Nov 1948.

___________________. Speech at Dedication of Loughmiller Monument, Salesmanship Club Youth Camp, September 10, 1994.

Loughmiller, Grover. Origins and Directions of Therapeutic Camping, Copy of Keynote address delivered 4/15/1996 at the annual Conference of the National Association of Therapeutic Wilderness Camps.

_________________. Talk at Funeral, December 8, 1993.

Loughmiller, Lynn. *Camp Life* (Unpublished Memoir).

Lynch, Dudley. "Investing in Children of Despair." *Dallas*, November 19, 1975, 26.

McKenzie, Buford. *Autobiography.* (Unpublished Document) September 1962.

_______________, *Experience Curriculum in Camping and Outdoor Education at Camp Woodland Springs, Dallas Texas* (Paper Developed at National Camp August 17, 1950).

_______________, Letter written to Barnabus Club Board mid 1962.

_______________, Letter to Rev. Marcus Bishop dated March 22, 1962.

_______________, Resignation Letter submitted to Salesmanship Club Boys Camp dated August 31, 1968.

Manual of Policies and Procedures of Camp Woodland Springs.

O'Neil, Laura. "I Remember Chief Mac." *Independent Press,* September 20, 1978, 3A.

Partridge, E. DeAlton. "National Camp," *Nature Magazine* 36 no. 6 (1943): 322.

"Raft Carrying 11 Capsizes; 2 Are Missing." *Chicago Tribune*, November 26, 1964.

"Salesmanship Club Boys Camp Loses McKenzies." *Reporter-Journal and Tri-Area News*, September 12, 1968, 4.

"Salesmanship Club Children Enjoying Week at Camp." *Dallas Morning News*, June 9, 1933, (Clipping).

Sharp, L.B. "Camping and Democracy." *1939 Year Book*. Washington, DC: National Park Service, United States Department of the Interior.

_________, "Catch Up! Catch Up! Covered Wagon Camping," *The Camping Magazine* (June 1935).

_________, *Education and the Summer Camp – An Experiment* (New York: Teachers College, Columbia University, 1930).

_________, "Report of Childrens Camp Project Salesmanship Club of Dallas made by L.B. Sharp, National Life Camps, Inc. Feb 2-6, 1946." Copy of report obtained from Salesmanship Club of Dallas.

_________, "The Role of Camping and Our American Heritage." *The Camping Magazine* 14 (February 1942): 33-36ff.

_________, "Why Outdoor and Camping Education." *Journal of Educational Sociology* 21 (1948): 313-318.

Sharp, L.B. and E. DeAlton Partridge, "Some Historical Backgrounds of Camping." *The Bulletin of the National Association of Secondary School Principals* 31 (May 1947): 15-20.

Skipper, Kent. E-mail correspondence dated 10/13/2010.

Smith, Bert Kruger. *The Worth of a Boy* (Austin: The Hogg Foundation, 1958).

_________________. *The Worth of a Boy* (Austin: The Hogg Foundation, 1970).

State of Texas: Criminal Justice Highlights Vol 3, no. 9 September 1971. *Failure Cycle Broken by Wilderness Adventure*.

Swindoll, Chuck. Email to Stephen Ashton regarding Everett Lindstrom dated April 5, 2017.

The Whispering Pine. The Camp Newspaper of E-Nini-Hassee Girls Camp, Special Raft Trip Edition.

The Whispering Pine. The Camp Newspaper of E-Nini-Hassee Girls Camp, Vol 1 – July 4, 1969.

Trail Call: Rocky Mountain Mennonite Camp 8 no. 1 (Feb 1962)

Tribute to Buford McKenzie Adopted by the Board of Directors and the Camp Board June 1, 1961. (Unpublished Document)

Underprivleged Kids, 207 of 'Em, Go to Camp. Dallas Morning News, June 3, 1941, (clipping)

"War Chest – Agency No. 11 – Children's Recreation Camp." *Dallas Morning News*, August 14, 1942, (clipping)

"Week of Fun for Hundred Mexican Kids in Camp." *Dallas Morning News*, September 7, 1932, (clipping)

Young Citizens Camps Brochure, 1962 (Sponsored by Rocky Mountain Mennonite Camp, Divide, Colorado).

ABOUT THE AUTHOR

Stephen Ashton experienced firsthand the transformational power of the Wilderness Road Therapeutic Camping Model. While living in the woods for three years as a Chief, he witnessed incredible courage and transformation in the lives of the young men he served. Learning from men like Buford McKenzie, Ken Edgar, and Paul Daley kept him involved for over 15 years. During that time he helped to pioneer Camp Duncan for Girls, led Cameron Boys Camp, and served as the Vice-President of the Wilderness Road Therapeutic Camping Association. He lives in Greenville, South Carolina with his wife Abigail and four boys.

Stephen can be reached at Ashton.Communications.Inc@gmail.com.

www.ingramcontent.com/pod-product-compliance
Lightning Source LLC
Chambersburg PA
CBHW061957280526
45787CB00005B/1907

* 9 7 8 1 5 2 0 8 6 4 7 1 6 *